Finding a Father

By the same author

THE ROAD TO GUNDAGAI
HUMPING MY BLUEY

Finding a Father

BY

GRAHAM McINNES

Illustrated

HAMISH HAMILTON
LONDON

First published in Great Britain 1967
by Hamish Hamilton Ltd
90 Great Russell Street London WC1

Copyright © 1967 by Graham McInnes

Printed in Great Britain by
Northumberland Press Limited
Gateshead

FOR
MIKE SUSAN SIMON
THREE YOUNG CANADIANS
WHOSE BIRTHRIGHT THEIR FATHER
DID NOT SHARE

CONTENTS

7

ILLUSTRATIONS

FOREWORD

IN CONTRAST to its earlier companions which dealt with an Australian boyhood, this third volume deals largely with my discovery of Canada, which accepted me in early manhood and which I have served for twenty-five years. The quarter century happily coincides with Canada's own Centennial (1867-1967) towards the celebration of which this book may, I hope, be regarded as a modest (though entirely unauthorized) personal contribution.

I have to thank the following for research undertaken on my behalf. Any errors of fact or interpretation remain mine. Dr. R. H. Hubbard, Chief Curator of The National Gallery of Canada; the Directors of Public Relations of the Canadian National Railways and the Canadian Pacific Railway Company; Mr. Ronald Thompson, J.P., F.C.I.S., City Clerk of the City of Vancouver; The Canadian Government Travel Bureau, London; Mr. Clarke Davey, Managing Editor of the *Globe and Mail*, Toronto, and Mr. David Rhydwen, that daily's librarian; Mr. Shane MacKay, Executive Editor of the *Winnipeg Free Press*; Mr. Louis Crerar of Toronto, and my cousin, Mrs. Mary Ryde.

I also make the following acknowledgements: to Nakash Studios of Montreal for permission to use their photograph of Bernard K. Sandwell, and to Longmans, Green and Co. for permission to quote from the late G. M. Trevelyan's *Grey of Fallodon*.

GRAHAM McINNES

9

As *readers of* The Road to Gundagai *and* Humping My Bluey *may remember, my mother divorced my father, James Campbell McInnes, in 1917. She later married Captain George Thirkell of the AIF, and took the children of the first marriage with her to Australia. There my brother and I grew up. My own father continued his career in Canada.*

My stepfather's business in car accessories was a victim of the Depression and in 1930 Mother, accompanied by my brothers, returned to England to begin her very successful career as Angela Thirkell, the novelist.

I stayed on in Australia with my stepfather to finish my university career. During the course of this I learned for the first time since childhood of the existence and whereabouts of my own father in Canada. After almost eighteen years I set out across the Pacific to find him. 'Now read on . . .'

Chapter One

SOUTH PACIFIC NORTH

ROYSTERING 'yachties' roaring out 'Abie my Boy' in beery harmony brought their vessels round about us as we drifted in to anchor below extinct volcanoes covered with trees and grass. Poured about the feet of these conical tip-tilted hills was a large city: less terra-cotta and brick and more weather-board and tin-roof than in Sydney; but essentially still a metropolitan caricature. Here was the last lost no-place of the Anglo-Saxon antipodes, with broad, empty streets, rackety tramcars, cantilever verandahs out over the sidewalks and a feeling of permanent Saturday afternoon with half the people absent at some mythical racetrack or bay. They were, you felt sure, about to repossess the city; but not just yet. Where were the third of a million people? Fissures, split in the contorted rock by past earthquakes, gaped at us; some spanned by bridges, others choked with tree-ferns. By the ship floated the dead marines dear to antipodean hearts; bobbing brown bottles of Waitemata beer sloshing gently on the incoming tide.

When federation among the antipodean colonies of Britain had first been mooted in the eighties of last century, the Governor of New Zealand, Sir George Grey, made a telling point. There were 1,282 good reasons why New Zealand could never be linked closely with Australia. That figure, he said, represented the distance in miles between them across the Tasman Sea. The British (and the Australians) got the point and the two countries continued in their separate if related development.

The crossing of the Tasman Sea then seemed to me as adventurous, and New Zealand as remote, as in Governor Grey's day. The iron floor of the old RMS *Aorangi* (18,500 tons) shifted creaking through the Tasman's troughs, and after four days without a sight of land,

11

Finding a Father

New Zealand came in a strange guise. Our last collective land memory from the *Aorangi* had been of severe, brutish basalt cliffs rising sharp from the rolling combers and topped by the olive drab bush, leathery leaves hanging listlessly down in the heat. Tasman's islands came into view as steep contorted mountains, greenish-shiny with the small-leaved 'native bush' running like hair all over the steep slopes and narrow gullies of a land which looked like a rumpled unmade bed. Pines and a few deciduous trees waved unexpected banners from the empty coast; but the land, though silent, was not 'aware' in the cryptic Australian sense.

* * *

An incongruous trio went ashore to taste the delights of a strange and empty town. Flanking me—a gangling youngster of twenty-one with a barely visible moustache fed nightly with powerful unguents —were The Major and Engineer Ball. The Major was a stoop-shouldered and irascible slippered pantaloon with a scrofulous balding head and turkey-gobbler neck strings. He had endeared himself to us all at Table 4 of the Third Class Dining Saloon (actually, combined dining saloon and 'lounge') by producing a bottle of medicinal wine at our first dinner. In the best traditions of both the Canada and the Australia of those days, meals in the third-class dining room were very strictly dry. You could booze to your heart's content in the bar and come staggering down the companion way in the nautical version of the good old antipodean 'Six o'clock swill'; but once in the sacred precincts of the dining room the spirit of Carrie Nation reigned unopposed.

At our first dinner—the aroused Tasman starting to heave under our feet—we'd looked glumly at the water carafes and at the pitcher of milk (milk!) set out by Mr. and Mrs. Pott of Victoria B.C. for their only child. In vain we importuned the Head Waiter. 'Can't we have a drink?' He shook formidable jowls at us—suede blue from a wonderful conjunction of talcum powder on black stubble—and his small moist mouth mincingly harangued us from the midst of suety chins.

'The very idea! What do you think this is? A cruise ship?'

Crestfallen we retired, and then just at that precise moment the Major hauled out from beneath the long narrow table—as if he were gingerly playing in the day's catch on some northern lake—a half

12

empty bottle of dark red wine. He donned a pair of steel-rimmed spectacles, the bi-focal lenses greasy with innumerable thumb-marks, and surveyed the bottle with a critical eye. Satisfied, he gave a grunt and turned the bottle towards us. The label read:

VIN DE SANTÉ

TONIQUE ET RECONSTITUANT

(SELON LA FORMULE DU

DR VAUCRESSON)

We nodded, much impressed. The jowly Head Waiter moved ponderously towards us.

'Sorry,' he said majestically. 'No wine at table.'

The Major looked at him over the top of his bi-focals.

'You'll notice,' he observed dryly, 'that this is medicinal wine. I am required by my doctor to take it regularly and I carry a supply of it wherever I go.'

The Head Waiter wobbled his jowls while the Major continued to look at him benignly. He removed the cork with a pleasant twisting screech, and poured a generous dollop of liquid into the tumbler. Sediment swirled in it like scraps of burnt paper.

'Have some,' he said handing the tumbler to the Head Waiter who, however, was too old a hand to be caught that way and contented himself with observing ponderously, 'I may try it later.'

'Well,' said the Major, 'what about me?'

The Head Waiter brandished his jowls. 'I s'pose if the doctor says you're to have it you'd better have it,' he remarked ungraciously.

'Thank you indeed,' said the Major mildly, with a deft wink in our direction. 'I'll see that you get some after the meal. If you can call this a meal,' he added sotto voce as the Head Waiter waddled off.

I looked down the long refectory-type table with the sparse cotton table-cloth, the bent aluminium cutlery, the thick tumblers full of glass ulcers and hydroceles, the shepherd's pie on our heavy chipped plates, the soldierly little galaxy of sauce bottles, the cruet built like a marine engine. It might not look much to a seasoned old fellow like the Major but it looked pretty good to me. I said so. This was adventure; I was bound for parts unknown. The Major said acidly,

'Have it your own way. Personally, I think it's foul. But at least we can pep it up a bit with Dr. Vaucresson. Have a little.'

'Well, thanks very much.'

He passed it round the table: to Ball the engineer from Port Pirie

13

in South Australia, who was going to take a look at the smelting
works in Trail, British Columbia; to Mr. and Mrs. Pott from Victoria B.C., who, greatly disappointed with their stay in Victoria,
Aust., were now off back to the promised land; to the Canadian-
Irish deportee; to the American deportee nick-named Okole-Hau who
was on his way back, involuntarily, to his little grass shack in Keala-
kakua, Hawaii, and who'd greatly startled me when I first encountered him in the narrow ship's corridor by rasping out, 'Hey Mac,
where's the can?'; and finally to the steel-thatched elderly warbler
of evangelical hymns whom we were not to see again after Auckland. All refused the wine except Ball the engineer and myself.
Thereafter the Major addressed himself solely to us. He raised his
thick tumbler of Dr. Vaucresson's vin tonique et reconstituant.

'Chin-Chin,' he said. 'You know, I made these labels myself, up in
New Caledonia. Soon as I knew I was coming on this trip. My God
I thought, after ten years in a relaxed French atmosphere—I was on
a sugar estate looking after the ruddy machinery—to have to go all
British and what's worse, wowser British. I know these damned
colonial shipping lines!'

The Major smacked his lips and proffered the bottle. The Potts
looked faintly scandalized; Okole-Hau was asleep; the steel-thatched
evangelist rose heavily from the table and shuffled humming towards the companion way.

'I had some good claret laid down and I thought: why let it rot
in the tropics? So I had these labels made in the sugar estate prin-
tery and there you are. I think,' he grinned at us over the glass, 'I
think we'll have enough to last us—the three of us—until we get
to Vancouver.' He beamed at the engineer and at me. 'At which
point, of course, we'll have to deal with the Canadian authorities
who, I understand, are a good deal tougher still—more puritan anyway; though, of course, poor devils, they've got America right next
door to them with all this prohibition nonsense.'

Ball said, 'They tell me the Canucks' (it was the first time I'd ever
heard the word) 'are really tough. But haven't they repealed the
Volstead Act in America?'

'America!' The Head Waiter leaned on the end of our lean table
with his fat hands rucking up the thin tablecloth. 'Watch it when
you use that word. The Canucks are Americans, too, you know.
So are the Latinos. And they all object to the Yanks pre-empt-

ing the word.' His jowls nodded sagely. The Major harrumphed.

'They can call themselves what they ruddy well like. They'll never have the savoir faire to match us.'

'Us?' The engineer's eyebrows were cocked.

'Yes, us,' repeated the Major emphatically, pulling off his glasses with a brusque gesture and wiping the lenses with the ball of his thumb, 'I'm British and—'

'Oh, so am I,' said Ball, who was as Aussie as they come.

'I don't mean British in *that* sense,' said the Major with asperity. 'In that sense we're all British.'

'Amen to that,' said the Head Waiter, wobbling his jowls piously.

'All right,' cut in the Major, 'but I'm British within the sound of Bow Bells. The real stuff.'

'On the radio?' said the Head Waiter impudently. The Major sniffed.

'Anyway, the Yanks will never match us for quality,' he intoned, 'Asprey's, Locke's, Wilkinson's, Yardley's . . .'

'You mean Back-yardleys?' leered the Head Waiter. At this point Okole-Hau woke up.

'Whose back yard?' he said. 'Play in yo own back yard, honey. Remember that hit, eh?' He slapped the exiguous tablecloth with the flat of his hand. The Major looked disgusted. The engineer said, 'How's about getting up on deck?'

Okole-Hau gazed up at us with drink-sodden eyes and returned to his slumbers. We three—the Major, the engineer and I—pushed in our swivel chairs with extreme unction and not a little hauteur, and marched with dignity towards the companionway. Steel beams sprayed with Public Works pea-green grazed our heads as we marched erect to the door, beyond which lay the diminutive lounge and the cracked cottage upright (Collard & Collard 1898) at which the Canadian deportee was for ever playing 'Over the Waves'. The Head Waiter intercepted us at the door, jowls quivering with evasive good humour.

'That'll be all right about the tonic, Major,' he rasped. 'I've spoken to the Chief Steward.'

'Thank you,' said the Major, with a lofty nod. But as soon as we were up on deck and patrolling, three abreast, the miserable forepeak allotted to third-class passengers he said, 'Bugger wants some of my wine; can always tell. Just another brown-noser.'

Finding a Father

The South Pacific breeze stirred the brittle remnants of his once richly dowered tonsure, while the engineer clucked sympathetically. I followed nodding wisely in the background, and so it was the same odd trio—the septuagenarian Major, the engineer in his forties and the student barely in his twenties—who strode ashore at Auckland and, having pooled their meagre resources, discovered they could just afford to hire a taxi and go off together in pursuit of the pleasures of the New Zealand Babylon.

Unfortunately, it was an Anglo-Saxon antipodean Sunday. Not a drink to be had. We made a lugubrious tour of local beauty spots and returned to the ship just in time to be engulfed by a crowd of supporters of another Major—Douglas of Social Credit. He was about to leave the antipodes to preach the gospel in Canada with— as we now know—astounding results. The more famous Major delivered a brief harangue from the promenade deck to the faithful on the dock, but his style was severely cramped by the rival spectacle of an Australian race-horse being unloaded for the racing season at the Riccarton course near Christchurch.

As the horsebox containing him swung down, he neighed in terror thus distracting the crowd from Major Douglas' measured periods. At length the box reached the dock with a thud; the muttering and head-turning ceased and the Major squared his shoulders for the peroration. But at this point the poor horse, stricken with fright, fouled himself and began skidding wildly about on the dock. The Major's closing words were obliterated in mingled cries of laughter and dismay.

*   *   *

Three days later saw us in Fiji, and this time the incongruous trio was joined by the Canadian deportee. Okole-Hau had desperately wanted to come with us, for he was getting well and truly fed up with the cramped quarters; but the Authorities, in this case the Captain, took the view that they couldn't risk allowing an alien deportee to go ashore, even in the company of such solid citizens as the Major, the engineer and myself. So he remained sadly on board. 'Just bring me back a bit of frangipani, for sweet Jesus' sake !' he cried from the railing as we walked down the gangplank into the steaming streets of soupy Suva.

The Captain had no objection to the Canadian coming with us.

16

South Pacific North

He was a member of the Empire; and if he did escape—we three went surety for him—at best there wouldn't be an International Incident. The fellow was a street car conductor from Regina in normal life, and in addition to being a great bore with his interminable stories of how he'd Told the Inspector What, was to my ear barely comprehensible. I was being exposed for the first time in my life to the accent of the Irish-Canadian and I found it very hard to understand. No written dialect can hope to convey his guttural mangling of what in any case was, apart from the movies, still to me the strange tongue of North America. He seemed to drown his words in a sea of harsh 'r' sounds, and to perform the difficult feat of simultaneously speaking from the back of his throat and barely opening his lips. I thought him a drag, but being bound for Canada to discover my father, I felt some vague need to propitiate Canadian gods. Hence I was more pleasant to him than I really wished or he really deserved.

His name was Joe McGonigle and he'd come out from Canada to Australia—all the way from Regina to Redfern—to get a job as a street car conductor in warmer and, as he conceived it, more friendly climes. But he hadn't been honest with the Aussie authorities. It was the very bottom of the Depression, and he'd been palpably unable to convince the immigration officers that he was the globe-trotting gentleman of leisure he purported to be. They gave him a month's tourist visa and when he overstayed the limit they caught up with him. Ironically, it was his own alleged 'mates'—that is to say, the local Sydney union officials, to whom he'd naïvely applied for help —who turned him in.

'Listen, mate,' they'd said, 'we don't want any bloody Canucks coming out here and taking our jobs from us. Nuthin' against you personal y'understand, but we got wives and kids. Tell 'em to fix you up back in Canada.'

So McGonigle had been deported back to his native prairie, part of the unemployable flotsam and jetsam that was hurled from door to unwilling international door in those dreary days. He was very cheerful about it, and also, which much impressed me, entirely without malice. As he said for the umpteenth time, while we all trudged Suva's palm-fringed main drag, sweat pouring down our foreheads, cheeks, armpits and the base of our spines,

'Aw, ye can't really blame 'em. I guess they got their troubles too. I was on a street corner talkin' to a coupla guys only last week

17

an' they sez to me they sez. Sure, Mac and we got nuthin' agin' ye, but ye'll 'ave to hit the trail.' And much more in the same vein until the Major who, being older than the rest of us, suffered fools less gladly, said,

'Look, Mac-whatever-your-name-is, we asked you along for company and a monologue's not company.'

'A whut? Whut say?'

The engineer said, 'I suggest we have a drink.' A traffic cop in khaki and scarlet with his hair in an enormous fuzzy mass like a bearskin referred us to 'Honey Kate'. This turned out to be a sort of sidewalk bistro beyond which was a cool white-washed recess where you could drink either beer or Kaava, the local rotgut made from fermented coconut juice. We sat down in rattan chairs with unbleached linen slipcovers and tried this booze which was served in large oval logwood bowls and tasted faintly of soapy water. Its effect was nil until a bottle of New Zealand beer was poured down the gullet on top of it. Then indeed something sulphurous began to bubble somewhere deep down in the oesophagus, and we came out unsteadily into the sudden tropical sunset.

Oil lamps were stuttering to life along the main street; the darkness rushed down palpably on the tumbled woolly hills and only the curious twisted peak of Joske's thumb remained to catch a glint of gold as the sun tumbled into the Pacific. We staggered up the gangplank to the roar of the donkey engine, swinging bags of copra inboard and dropping them like stones into the hold. It was only when we finally sat down to Dr. Vaucresson that the mournful spaniel's face of Okole-Hau reminded us that we had forgotten to bring him his sprig of frangipani.

From Suva to Honolulu is 2,700 miles, about the distance across the North Atlantic. The rumbling old *Aorangi* took over a week to make the trip, and so vast and empty is the Pacific that during that interminable trek we were fortunate to see a single atoll and the smoke of a lonely hull-down steamer. These were the vast expanses across which the Polynesians had paddled their war canoes crammed with women and kids and cassava and yams. Our 17 knots seemed as interminable a crawl as theirs and over as trackless a waste of waters.

The island—it couldn't have been more than six feet or so above water—was Mary's Island or Mary Bulcott's Island, later to be much more famous as Canton, and the scene of a crucially important landing strip during the immediate pre-jet era. The Americans bull-dozed coral and sand into great mounds and poured cement on to it to make the necessary 5,000 foot runways. Viewed from the foredeck of the *Aorangi* at a distance of about five miles, it was quite simply the coral island of one's boyhood; a thin circlet of sand with a few coconut palms like tufts of grass on a vacant lot, the whole surrounding an immense lagoon of a daunting emptiness: flat, thin, lost and lonely.

Just as we thrummed abreast of Mary's Island there was a rush to the opposite side of the deck to see our sister ship *Niagara* chug-ging slowly southward crammed with homing antipodeans. We hung on to the rail watching her into the distance. About that time Mary's Island also vanished and for the next few days the endless Pacific claimed us: a speck in an ocean that became one with the sky, but a speck crammed with the inward-looking, intense and largely meaningless activity of a drop of pond water seen through a microscope. Then, one morning we woke to miss the beat of the screw. Water chuckled silkily past the hull, and across the circle of the porthole, grey in the first light, passed the purple serrated edge of an improbable mountain. I climbed up on the bunk. Lights, obviously left on all night by the rapacious squandering Americans, blazed at the foot of a mountain: Honolulu.

* * *

How can one now invest that mellifluous quadrisyllable with any magic? Paper leis, whining guitars with a movable metal fret, Diamond Head, Aloha-Oé, muu-muus, Queen Liluikilani, the Royal Hawaiian, The Surfrider: what's left? It has been denatured and diluted and, above all, rendered ordinary by democracy on the move in the jet age. Yet I must try and recapture the magic of my first foreign country, my first contact with America. Irreality was the keynote, but how was that best to be achieved? The deus ex machina was the Managing Director of the Bank of New South Wales.

One evening just before our desperately early tea (i.e. Aussie dinner, and the Chief Steward had warned us 'the proper time for yew to come down is half past foive') I was sitting playing a four-handed version of 'Over the Waves' with the Canadian deportee when a blonde vision exploded into our cramped stuffy little lounge.

19

Wrong notes burgeoned beneath my fingers and when the vision asked for me by name, I could hardly believe my ears. I accompanied her up on to the swaying deck to keep her to myself, away from the ravening glances of the fellow third-class passengers. I was a shade disappointed to note on closer inspection that she was 'a bit past it' (i.e. about 28) and also that she wore, as the then famous song *The Isle of Capri* had it, 'a plain golden ring on her finger'. But once I'd got over this, the purport of her message was electrifying.

'I'm Nancy Eves,' she said, 'and Mum and I are travelling with Sir Arthur Dobson.'

'Oh yes?' I said, noting the attractive blonde fur on her cheeks. The name meant nothing to me.

'Your cousin, Sir Hugh Poynter, gave him a letter about you. Said you were travelling alone. Well, he'd like you to come ashore with us at Honolulu as his guest.'

'That's jolly decent of him,' I said, thinking, well, you know there's really nothing quite like the Old Boy Net. For Hugh was my first cousin (twice removed) on my mother's side and I'd spent my last days in Australia at his house in Sydney before embarking across the Pacific to search out my father. Hugh was Chairman of Baldwin's (Australia) Ltd., and clearly on terms of intimacy with the great.

'I'd love to come,' I said, adding, 'will you be there?' She gave me a certain look, and nodded. We discussed the price of eggs while gulls—the first for days—dipped and wheeled, and flying fish skimmed over the silver sea. Then she turned and looked back at the great iron cliff housing the first-class snobs who stared down at us poor fellows in the forepeak well-deck. For the first time in years I felt shabby.

'Well,' she said, 'I must go. See you tomorrow. In the first-class lounge.' Was her look conspiratorial, or was it just that I was susceptible?

Dobson turned out to be a well-padded man with iron grey hair and rimless pince-nez. He gripped me absently by the hand but, after the manner of the well-heeled, seemed to be principally concerned that the arrangements should be very precisely *comme-il-faut*. I heard him fussing endlessly with the travel agent, and then we were at the bottom of the gangplank and climbing into a big chauffeur-driven limousine. As its tyres squelched richly down the cement dock, between rows of tourist-dressed Hawaiian maidens chucking paper leis at us, I caught a glimpse of the engineer and the Major legging it along the quay, and they of me sitting beside the chauffeur—for of course the three seats in the back were reserved for Dobson, the girl and her Mum. They pantomimed elaborate French bows as we sailed by—about half a block of 1930 Cadillac—as much as to say: Bloody tonks, think they're too grand for us. But with a very friendly smile. It's okay kiddo, we understand. Yer only young once. But where was the friendly trio of Suva? I grinned uncomfortably and tried to turn my attention to Honolulu.

It was all blare and blast and big limousines and jazzy hotels, terribly exciting because so sophisticated and brittle and brilliantine, but very disappointing to the homegrown Aussie. Diamond Head was bare and creased like the folds of a couchant lion, while I remembered Dromana. Waikiki Beach seemed small and mean beside the acres of sand at Maroubra and Coogee; and though the surf, we were assured, could on occasion be mountainous it happened to look flat as a plate of soup, and even Dobson didn't trouble to conceal his grave disappointment. He perked up, though, as did the girl's mother, when we entered the Royal Hawaiian Hotel. This was a garish confection in pink cement and stucco, with a vaguely Spanish Colonial cast. A Filipino flunkey bowed us to a screened verandah where we sipped sidecars and pink ladies—it was still the era of the jazzy cocktail—while a menu the size of a manhole cover was being handed round. The prices scared me absolutely stiff and, not realizing how well-heeled bankers are, I ordered a hamburger and fruit salad. This timid essay in gastronomy was at once countermanded by the banker.

'Got to enjoy yourself when you're out with me,' he barked in friendly fashion and fixed me up with avocado pear, tuna fish salad, a T-bone steak and pêche melba. I floated out of the Royal Hawaiian Hotel replete from ear to ear and, as the big car started to purr slowly up the long hill leading to the mountains, Honolulu began to take on the glaze and luxury of the traditional tropical paradise. Perhaps it really was more beautiful, for we were climbing up, with vivid aeroplane views of checkerboard sugar cane and pineapple, towards Pali where the Kona winds and rains from the North East trades came tearing through the spiny vertebrae of Oahu.

We stopped at a lay-by, prosaic enough in its tarmac blandness.

21

Finding a Father

Below it cliffs fell two thousand feet in a vertiginous plunge to a green stippling of tilled fields glowing livid in a spear of light as the sun struck through the hurrying shreds of Kona cloud. Behind us the contorted crags beetled into the shreds of mist and the soft blue sky. Beyond, the checkerboard of fields merged in a shoreline, visibly pounded even at this distance by white bubbling combers, and plumed by a haze of blown salt and spray. The guide was saying something about this having been a Tarpeian rock whence King Kamehameha had hurled captured enemies and treacherous courtiers. The scene did not need this adventitious gloss. It was dramatic and romantic and terrifying, and to complete the ecstasy I felt a hand involuntarily clasp mine. But when I turned in wonderment the girl's face was abruptly averted and I realized that the action had been instinctive and neutral. For a few seconds I boiled with hatred at being spurned, but then the magic of the scene recaptured us all and was only punctured finally by the flat nasal voice of the banker.

'I think that's about all Hay-way-eye has to offer us today. Better be getting back to the ship.'

So we slipped in silky ease down countless tarry bends back towards Honolulu. And there was the *Aorangi* dwarfed by the sleek slithery American ships the *Mariposa* and the *Monterrey*, and looking very squat and British and old-fashioned with her single rigidly vertical red funnel and the brown rust staining the plates of her worn old sides.

Ah yes, we thought, as we stood once again on the democratic third-class forepeak and saw the lights on Diamond Head and Koko Head slide by in the velvet dark, it's best to be British. Honolulu and all that tinselly stuff, basically corn you know; and the *Monterrey*'s smokestack may be sloped or streamlined, there may be a nile-green tiled bathroom to every cabin, but what about the seamanship, eh? Remember the *Vestris*. Wouldn't you rather travel British? And with that, Dobson and the Bank and the limousine and the spurned handclasp of the blonde furry-cheeked girl on the dramatic height of Pali, were all exorcised; and the Pacific re-gathered us to its swelling uncaring bosom.

Chapter Two

TRANS-CANADA EXPRESS

THE last 2,500 miles from the tropics to the temperate zone were streaked with storms. We encountered a force eight gale and the deadlights were battened down. After the storm it was cool and crisp; and one afternoon, distant headlands came into view to be crowned, as they drew nearer, with dense Christmassy conifers. The air was damp and raw, and remote crests were crowned with snow. Four hours later, brilliantly lit but open and empty streets swam by in the gloom, and a high thin air caught at the throat. This must be the arctic breath of North America. Night closed in on the Strait of Juan de Fuca and the trio drained the last of Dr. Vaucresson before facing customs and immigration in the morning. Next day the view from the tiny third-class cabin embraced our first skyscraper. The Marine Building in downtown Vancouver, though a junior of a bare 25 floors, seemed a giant after Melbourne's staid 132 foot ceiling.

Behind the skyscrapers heavily wooded hills clambered up steep mountains, the tops of which were streaked with snow and wreathed in scarves of mist. The sea that slopped gently at the ship's iron side was light green and odourless. On the docks one or two figures moved about slowly, wrapped in mackinaws, windbreakers and gum boots. A glimpse of a small canyon of office buildings seemed curiously empty. The time was 8.30 a.m. yet there was only a scattering of people, none of them walking very fast; a few automobiles and a cumbersome old-fashioned streetcar. The canyon was lined with gnarled and twisted cedar poles from which hung tangled festoons of wires so that the street seemed enclosed in a cage. One had the feeling that the forest had entered and overwhelmed the city. Over all rose a lean building with a flat roof, gaping semi-circular orifices two storeys high, spandrels of rectitudinous angularity like pursed lips: the whole a vague mixture of American skyscraper, Japanese torii and perhaps Frank Lloyd Wright. Beyond this building rose a very high mansard rooflet—a sort of cap—crowning a vast anonymous grey skyscraper with a vaguely châteauesque hood. From the hood steam billowed in white pennons into the frosty air. The temperature was 24, the coldest I had ever known.

It was the depths of the Depression. Roosevelt had been in office less than a year; the NRA was at last gripping the imagination and the biceps of the Americans, and Mr. Schechter and his chickens had not yet questioned the power exercised by the terrible-tempered General Johnson whose rugged, cross-patch features glared down from the posters. The Great Republic was on the move and perhaps a little of this was going to slop over into Canada which from the portholes of the *Aorangi*—dear familiarity soon to be lost again in the wastes of the Pacific—looked strangely quiet and empty and cold.

I was aggressively determined to like the place. I'd left behind sunny Australia and the girl I loved to seek out the myth—or the reality—of my own father, whom I hadn't seen since childhood. Because I'd been separated from him in Canada for seventeen years, and had grown up in Australia with a stepfather, his faraway figure coupled with my own dim memories, had produced a legendary bardic-King. For my father had been a singer to whose court in Toronto I was now making my pilgrimage. I had told no one of my plan and had clutched it to my bosom in a sort of private yearning. Not unnaturally, it had proliferated in a prodigious fashion in this hothouse forcing bed, and had assumed a strange and ferociously romantic shape which I was willing, in more sober moments, to concede might bear little relationship to any reality I might find.

Nevertheless, the aura I had constructed of my long-lost father had imparted a powerful radiance to Canada as a whole, and this, combined with the normal youthful zest and sense of adventure, helped to mist the grey Vancouver streets with magic. I imagined my father as the director of an opera company. I envisaged him holding thousands in thrall as he poured forth immortal sounds from beneath the great black moustache and the towering mass of wavy black hair that I fancied I remembered so well across the trough of years. I saw him conducting an orchestra; singing in white tie and tails in the mansions of Canadian millionaires; holding court after the recital among exquisitely gowned ladies—well corseted to be sure, but elegant nevertheless. I saw him in a vast studio with an enormous sky-light, teaching Bach to adoring pupils. I imagined him moving in the glitter of great social occasions. And in order not to mar in any way the image that I had so sedulously created, I didn't bother to find out where he lived nor to let him know I was coming.

I decided simply to cross the continent from West to East, establish myself in Toronto, look him up in the telephone book and give him a call. The thought of this delicious coup did much to reassure me after the rather depressing first view of Vancouver, and so when the Major suggested we travel together on the Canadian Pacific eastbound train and break our journey for a week-end in Banff in the heart of the Rockies, I was only too happy to agree. It was early March and the fact that Banff was a summer resort was mercifully hidden from me. I packed my exiguous bags light-heartedly; procured my first exciting Canadian dollars from the letter of credit at the local bank (and was amazed to be recognized by the cunning Canucks as an Aussie); made a brief reconnaissance of Stanley Park with the Major, marvelling at its enormous Douglas firs and the cathedral-like spaces which they enclosed; and then prepared to board my first Canadian train.

To anyone brought up on the romance of engineering, the very initials CPR evoked a thrilling and improbable atmosphere of wild west adventure and derring-do. The names along the line weaved a sensuous and exotic magic: Woman River, Fort William, Moose Jaw, Medicine Hat, Calgary, Banff, Kicking Horse Pass, Fraser Canyon. And who, having seen it, could ever forget the old sepia photograph of Donald Smith—later Lord Strathcona and Mount Royal—with his stovepipe hat and his snow-white spade beard, tapping the last spike into place at Craigellachie. 'Stand fast Craigellachie' had been the noble cypher disguising an anguished telegram from one financier to another as funds once again ran out and the prospect of a loan from Sir John A. Macdonald and his infant Canadian government loomed once more. Best touch of all, the last spike had been of iron, just like all the tens of millions of others before it, stretching right back to Montreal.

Remember the Americans? Why, when they completed the Union Pacific at Promontory Point, Utah, in 1869, they'd rammed home two gold spikes and two silver ones. What nonsense; what a display of childish braggadocio! How much more fitting was the British method. Tight-lipped self-satisfaction and an iron spike. And those Canadian peers: Strathcona and Mount Royal; Shaughnessy, Mountstephen; how rousingly Empire and Loyal and un-republican and undemocratic they had seemed. Economic royalists become almost true royalists of the purple, and a good old nose-thumbing to the wild disorderly democrats south of the border, even if it had to be admitted that the man who actually built the railroad was an American, William van Horne. But then, that was all right, wasn't it? Because he'd taken a title, become Sir William, been seduced by the velvet handshake. Ah, the Brits were pretty cunning; you had to hand it to them. And much more in the same vein.

The reality to my starry eyes was almost as wonderful. The train itself was enormous: larger, brighter and longer than anything in Australia, where we'd prided ourselves on the size of our own trains compared with those of Britain. It was a genuine iron monster, towering high above the platform and reached by clambering up half a dozen steps. The sleeping-car itself was the size of a station waiting room, its long aisles draped with reticent green curtain, and the friendly seats of green plush contracting to a vanishing point of brass handles a hundred feet away. Birch and maple panelling; crisp white napery and gleaming silver; big double windows against the cold; huge brass cuspidors; noble curved nickel faucets from which water positively gushed; floral, deep pile carpets for tired feet. Blasts of hot air, smelling of tin, cigar smoke and old fabrics, surged out from beneath one's feet. The whole consisted of a rake of eighteen cars, nearly a quarter of a mile long, at the head of which an enormous mastodon with eight driving wheels, each of them taller than the tallest man, stood rumbling and panting ready to drag us over mountain passes, across foaming muddy rivers, over mournful prairies and silent snow-choked forests three thousand miles from Pacific to Atlantic.

'Boarrrd! All aboarrrd! This train now leaving for Kamloops, Revelstoke, Banff, Calgary, Regina, Winnipeg, Fort William, Toronto, and Montreal! Boooarrrrd!'

We climbed high, the porter banged down the step cover, and bolted the door with an iron clang. With a tremendous shuddering jolt, the enormous train began to roll majestically eastward up the

Fraser Valley towards the mountains. I sat in the overheated car, my cheek against the fusty plush, my forehead against the cold window-pane watching the approaching peaks turn from purple to black as they closed in on the narrowing Fraser Valley, until my breath blurred the images and the negro porter began to fuss noisily with pillows as a not too subtle hint for me to get down to the smoking compartment while he made us up for the night.

*　*　*

We awoke next morning, the Major and I, to a dead world. We were in the heart of the Rockies and they were drenched with snow. The mountains were crowned with it and even their slab-sided precipitous faces were streaked with it in every cranny and hand-hold. It hung in great swags and rolls from the trees. It choked the brown undergrowth. It smothered the surface of congealed lakes. It yielded very reluctantly to the frenzied striving of untamed torrents which even in winter's depth tore great black holes in the ice and snow, gouged great tunnels over which snow and ice arched perilously while black water raged by beneath : the only living thing in that dead white land. Not a house, not a shack, not a man nor an animal; only the train trundling along on rails themselves almost buried by snow and seeming almost as if supported by snow, for the sleepers and ballast were totally obliterated by the white mantle.

The telegraph wires, dipping in endless arcs parallel to the track, were heavily freighted with soft wet mush which, as we passed, sometimes fell to the snowy ground with an unctuous plop. The thin chill lifelessness was in violent contrast to the warm rattling fug and stink of the immigrant 'colonist' car in which the Major and I were travelling to save money. Its seats were straw; the window-sills, a vehement shade of burnt-umber, were covered with a liberal sprinkling of smuts and snow crystals which had somehow managed to seep through the double windows and to survive the stupefying heat pouring in great gusts from the vents beneath our feet. We were too poor to afford the dining car and subsisted uncomfortably on thick sandwiches folded in bread like blotting paper, oranges, huge taste-less bananas and bottles of Coca-Cola. The ubiquitous 'newsie' brought these in with a yell every hour, encountering as he did so the hostile indifference of those who found themselves momentarily seated in the cold blast created as he banged in from the next car, trailing swatches of galosh-imprinted snow along the jazzy carpet. The heat and the food induced a powerful thirst which could be quenched only by frequent trips to the water-cooler at the end of the car. Here, from a stack of neat antiseptic paper cups, one could be pried loose and filled from a faucet trickling neat antiseptic ice-water.

About noon the enormous train snaked its dark sinuosities to a grinding stop amid wooden maroon buildings and outhouses, enormous piles of coal, a cement roundhouse and circular tanks high on stilts: the whole dwarfed to utter insignificance by immense mountains, 12,000 feet high, hanging valleys and great piles of rock. A signboard said: Field 4,072 ft. This was a divisional point.

Divisional points have vanished now, victims of the diesel. But in those days of steam the great locomotives required coal and water about every 150 miles and little hamlets sprang up all across Canada in response to the need. Sometimes they were buried deep in the mountains; sometimes out on the bald prairie; more often thrust down among a dense choking growth of conifers. They all looked exactly like Field, except that the shacks and sheds and tanks and roundhouses, while maroon for Canadian Pacific, were olive green for Canadian National. Now the trail pulled us slowly up the immense gulch of the Kicking Horse Pass from 4,072 to 5,353 feet via a couple of spiral tunnels, common enough in Europe but a wonder in North America. In an hour or so of wandering through a lifeless landscape of rock and snow and ice and conifer we reached Banff and bundled out of the warm fug into crisp cold air that cut through exiguous Australian flannels. The solid comforting wall of maroon iron steamed slowly away to the East, and left us naked in the heart of the Canadian Rockies at the fag-end of winter.

It apparently hadn't occurred to the Major—it certainly never had to me—that Banff as a resort was in those days limited entirely to the three months between June 15 and September 15. Though we knew we could never afford to stay at the Banff Springs Hotel, we thought we could at least have a look at this fabulous creation of the ad man's fancy and the hotelier's shrewdness, with its 'mile high golf course', mineral springs, châteauesque lineaments—something between Balmoral and Chenonceaux—known all over the world, even in far off Australia. But one doesn't play golf in the Rockies in March with the ground under four feet of snow; and the US vacationer didn't go anywhere in March except perhaps to Florida or the Caribbean. So although our own modest hotel, warm and snug for a few winter skiers, was doing a good trade, the town itself was dead. The great Banff Springs Hotel, when we eventually reached it after trudging a mile along a snow embanked gravel road, was only a mausoleum, though of monstrous proportions. Tramping round it in the snow—and in our totally unsuitable brogues, getting soaked to the skin and up to mid-calf—we peered through frosted windows at white shrouded shapes in the enormous public rooms; we gazed reflectively at the empty swimming pool littered with dirty snow and scrawny, blown branches. We craned our necks up into the grey sky—against which the falling snow looked unaccountably black, whereas against the conifers it was white—and saw the beetling crags and jutting tors of this wildly romantic steel-framed castle soaring eighteen storeys above the Bow Valley.

We thought, ah yes, how wonderful it must look in the summer, but then we trudged back gratefully to our own little warm hotel. The incomprehensible liquor laws of the province of Alberta (for it appeared that, contrary to Australian teaching, the mountains were in Alberta as well as British Columbia) forbade us a drink at a bar. There were no bars. Liquor was sold only by permit at a government store and we didn't have a permit and were too poor to buy one. We didn't want to drink cold beer in mid-winter in a 'Beverage Room', so we consoled ourselves in our bedroom with a Dr. Vaucresson which the Major had managed to avoid declaring and later that soft soundless wintery afternoon boarded the train again for the East.

It was our last stop before reaching Toronto. Though the train rolled majestically on for another three days and nights I never left its friendly fug again until Toronto's grey towers swam into view. Partly this was because—again contrary to what I'd been taught at school—the further east one went the colder it became. Calgary was jangling iron noises in the night. Regina was a bleak concrete and brick emptiness in the midst of the even vaster dun coloured emptiness of the naked prairie; as vacant as Australia but pitilessly cold. Winnipeg was fur booted women, and men with makinaws, fur hats and earmuffs, those ludicrous but oh-so-useful shields against the sub-arctic Prairie winter. The North shore of Lake Superior was an endless featureless tunnel of white in which Lake and rock, river and hill, conifer, road and railway were bludgeoned into faceless monotony by mile after mile of tumbled snow and ice. On the last night I said goodbye to the Major in the piercing cold of Sudbury, the great nick-mining centre where arcs pricked the boreal sky and all round us glared rock and ice, and not a single tree. He was going on to Montreal and we exchanged London addresses. As I clasped his papery old hand he slid a heel of Dr Vaucresson into my overcoat pocket.

'Against the law in this dam' puritan country,' he said, 'but it'll keep you warm in the night.'

I gripped his arm in real affection, and retired to the friendly fug of my upper berth and copious draughts of the Doctor. It was so effective that when the porter banged and tugged me awake next morning and I staggered down without benefit of the little step ladder, which somebody else was using, the blinds were already up. We were sailing past factories, the backsides of tip-tilted wooden houses, vacant lots and snow covered piles of bashed up cars and other debris.

I asked at the Union Station for a cheap but respectable hotel and was told: The Mott. I stood myself a taxi through empty grey Sunday morning streets lined with dirty crusted slush, and checked in. Once in the privacy of my little super-heated cubicle (with a view of enormous parking lots and the faceless rear ends of office blocks) I got out the telephone book. My goodness it was thick! Thicker than the Melbourne book, and Melbourne's population was almost twice that of Toronto's. As I looked under the Ms and then the Macs—separately listed, sensible fellows—a real surge of excitement gripped me for the first time. Yes, there it was. *McInnes. J. Campbell 91 Dupont Kingsdale 5691.*

It was my father all right; it must be. After seventeen years. Childhood memories came rushing back—including inevitably the lonely giant in the strange hat in the Kensington High Street in 1917—and I had a momentary frisson. Oughtn't I maybe to have written ahead? Supposing he was out? Was dead? Didn't, worst of all, want to see me? Oh well, too late now. And what was Dupont? A street, a place, a circle? I was ignorant of the North American habit of deleting all these unnecessary appendages in the interest of crisp efficiency. I asked the operator to get me the number and after a while the phone started ringing busily at his end.

Chapter Three

ENCOUNTER OF PRODIGALS

'HULLO.'

'May I speak to Mr. McInnes please?'

'This is he.' A deep, rich voice; grammatical too.

'Mr. *Campbell* McInnes?'

'Yes,' slight impatience. 'Who is that?'

'It's your son speaking.'

'My *who?*'

'Graham.' A long pause.

'Graham !'

'Yes. Look, I'm sorry to do this, but I've just come in from Australia, and I thought I'd look you up.'

'! ! !'

'Are you still there?'

'Yes.' More slowly. 'Yes. But Australia? Have you been there all this time?'

'Well, yes, ever since the divorce.'

Pause for ingestion at this unwelcome reminder at the other end of the line. I'm trying to place the voice. Can't quite figure out whether he's pleased or astonished or both. Certainly taken aback. Perhaps this isn't going to work out quite as I'd expected. But what *had* I expected? Finally,

'Where are you . . . Graham?'

'At the Mott Hotel.'

'Well, would you like to wait there?' An effort, 'Dear boy, and I'll come down and pick you up?'

'That would be wonderful.'

'Do you . . . do you think you'll know me?'

'I'm not sure, but I'm more likely to know you than you are to know me.'

'I suppose so. Well, wait for me, dear boy.'

'Okay,' I hung up.

I had a feeling that he was more excited than I was, but perhaps this was natural. I had been planning this rather theatrical, not to say self-indulgent but on the whole well motivated gesture, for months. But it had hit him out of the blue. I knew what I'd been doing for the past seventeen years; and I supposed he knew what he'd been doing too. But neither of us knew what the other had been up to. He was sixty-three and I was twenty-two. Seventeen years of my life was an aeon: almost my whole conscious recollection. To him it must seem like yesterday, and perhaps—now that I came to think about it—a not very attractive yesterday. One that he'd put behind him. One that he didn't want back again.

I looked out of the over-heated little cement box, which was my room, to the empty car-parks and the dirty snow, glinting now a livid intermittent powder-room pink as the neon signs started to twitch and flicker in the damp grey dusk. Rather an unadventurous place for a rendezvous. The city growled up at me through the gullies and ravines between the skyscrapers, a muted growl as if the ice and snow were suffocating it. Big wet flakes began to fall, steaming past my window and blotting out the twilight. I put on my unsuitable Australian top coat, went down to the lobby and took up a strategic position near the cigar counter between a public phone booth and a potted palm.

*   *   *

There was no mistaking him. In the instant before hesitant recognition dawned in his eyes, I saw an artist's wide floppy, black hat above a heavy square, grey face with grey-black eyebrows and a smudge of white moustache. The face was sunk deep in a spotted brown silk foulard scarf and a heavy navy blue overcoat with a velvet collar. He wore spats and funny half-galoshes and he carried a heavy silver-knobbed stick. He looked like someone out of the cast of *Trelawny of the Wells*. He looked not only as if he didn't know me from Adam, but as if he'd never been in the Mott Hotel in his life, and moreover was a bit fearful of being found there. I rose and went towards him and he managed a big smile, ever so slightly forced.

I said, 'Well, hullo.'

32

THE AUTHOR WITH HIS FATHER,
JAMES CAMPBELL McINNES, TORONTO, 1934

Encounter of Prodigals

'My dear boy,' and he embraced me right there in the lobby of the Mott Hotel before the incurious eyes of the cigar girl and a few drummers reading the *Evening Telegram* in scuffed leather arm-chairs, waiting for the beverage room to open. Being young and censorious, and a protestant Anglo-Saxon to boot, I stiffened at the embrace. Also, though I was myself a heavy smoker, there was mingled in his smoke a, to me, repellent perfume, which I vaguely thought of as Mediterranean, and a perceptible odour of mouthwash. Maybe I should have done something about that myself! I suddenly remembered that I hadn't been to the dentist for about a year and a half, and felt a twinge of conscience and of toothache. But he didn't notice my reticence, because it was submerged in the grandeur of my Great Gesture in coming across eight thousand miles and seventeen years to see him. Him rather than my mother! What balm to the man divorced for cruelty back in 1917. Besides he was a singer, a bard; and capable, as I later discovered, of being himself overwhelmed by great gusts of emotion.

He stepped back and gave me a fond scrutiny. What he saw, I don't know. What I saw, on closer inspection, was a leathery, large-pored almost olive grey face below a great mane of whiteish-grey hair, now that the hat was off and held with the cane and gloves in his left hand. A big knuckle of nose, brownish green eyes, a square chin and a big chest with a wonderfully erect carriage, suggesting the enormous reserves of lung and diaphragm required by a concert baritone.

'Do you still sing?' I blurted.

'Oh yes. But tell me,' and into the heavily pouched greeny-brown eyes came a remote pleading look, 'What is your last memory of me?'

'In Kensington High Street,' I said promptly. 'You were wearing a forage cap and had the uniform of the Royal Flying Corps.'

He heaved a deep sigh. 'I was hoping you'd say that,' he said. 'I tried to speak to you but your nurse wouldn't let me. I expect she was under orders,' he added hurriedly. In case I should take offence or in case I should mention my mother? No word of enquiry about her. I thought it best not to raise the subject. After all, it was almost four years since I'd seen her myself.

'Well,' I said briskly, 'what are we going to do?'

'You're coming home with me,' he said, 'back to the flat.'

B

33

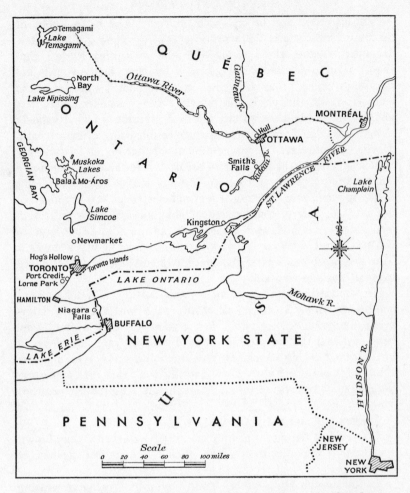

'Oh, now hold on,' I said, 'I've paid for a night in this hotel.'

'Of course, of course,' he said hastily, as if he'd got a fish nibbling on a line which might be easily scared away. 'But will you come out now and have some coffee and meet Tom and Betty?'

'Who are they?'

'Friends of mine. I told them you'd—that I hoped you'd be able to come. Then we could talk about your plans later.'

'I have to leave Toronto on Friday. I'm going on to New York.'

'Yes, of course, we mustn't interfere with your plans . . .'

34

'Well, okay, I'll come out now. How do we get there? In a taxi?'

'Oh no, we'll take the street car, it's no distance.'

Toronto at that time, I learned later, had no metered taxis. The city was divided into zones with a minimum fare for each zone and taxis were fiendishly expensive. But I was a bit let down to be travelling in a tram. It stopped right outside our hotel in the snowy darkness. It was a curiously old-fashioned, high wooden car, painted a dull red with the words *Toronto Transportation Commission* in dull gold on the side. Heavens, our trams in Melbourne were more up to date than this! Automatic doors opened with a bang and a clatter and we entered the warm fug of a one-man car. It seemed to me, as I watched him, monstrous that a single man should have to drive the car, open the doors, collect fares and make change. My father and I sat down side by side on a long empty slatted wooden seat curved to the proportions of a human backside yet to be invented. The car started with a jerk, throwing me against him. Neon signs swam by in the dark: SKF Ball Bearings; Involute Gear Co; Babloor Hotel; Imperial Oil; Sweet Caporal cigarettes. I wasn't very impressed and we kept up a desultory conversation through the empty barren streets until the car decanted us opposite a dark avenue, flanked with bare stunted maples and overlooked by a large factory on top of which blinked a red and blue sign: *Lake Simcoe Ice Co.*

The street was utterly deserted as we walked along, myself skidding violently from time to time on the icy sidewalks, because of course I was wearing my Aussie leather shoes, whereas what I needed were rubbers. On our right we passed a row of semi-detached houses of wood and dark red brick veneer with asphalt shingle roofs. They seemed to have been crammed and crowded on to the lots anyhow, tilting this way and that so that as we looked down the narrow slits between, the walls seemed rarely to be parallel. Piles of snow stood before each house, separated by a cindered front path. Before the last of the houses we stopped. I was beginning to get very cold and when my father said, 'This is the flat, but we live in a duplex,' I didn't ponder on this cryptic and meaningless statement, but followed him up a few wooden steps, along a piece of coir matting stretched across a desolate snow-filled verandah, and through a glass door into an airlock of welcome if suffocating warmth.

Here, backside to backside, we bent to shake the snow from the
cuffs of our pants and he to remove his rubbers. Before us were two
doors, one leading direct into the lower duplex and the other leading up steep narrow stairs to the upper duplex. As we mounted the
stairs I was aware of faces peering at us over the top floor balustrade.
I followed my father into the passage.

'Well,' he said, 'here are Tom and Betty. This is Graham.'

I grasped the hand of a sandy-haired nattily dressed fellow in his
early thirties who favoured me with a friendly smile. But it was the
girl who caught my attention: thirtyish, soberly gowned but breathing with suppressed excitement, she was the striking—deliberate so
it seemed to me—image of my mother, save that her hair, though
tied in a bun like Mother's and parted in the middle, was a flaming
red. Who were these people?

We talked of this and that, to many ohs and ahs from the two
strangers. The girl went to make coffee and I looked around the tiny
front room, suddenly feeling tired and let down. Two glass-curtained
windows looked across to the big sign: *Lake Simcoe Ice Co.* Musty
books in tall glass cases; an old-fashioned escritoire; a sofa without
springs; a small upright cottage piano. The rest of the flat was a
diminutive dining-room, a spare bedroom overlooking a garage, and
upstairs under the eaves, a dressing-room and another small bedroom.
The arrangements affronted me, and as the long lost son I took it
upon myself to regard these people as interlopers, forgetting that in
the intervening years my father must surely have had to seek solace
and support from someone.

But I nevertheless then and there made a secret resolve that I
would push on to Montreal and New York as soon as possible for a
real adventure. This was more easily said than done. Having at my
own wish enmeshed myself in the toils of my father's real or
imagined emotions and memories and sentiments, I was now caught
like a fly in a web and, unless I wished to be downright rude, I must
remain in Toronto at least for a few days. It was clear that my father
wanted to 'show me off'; and I conceded that this was a reasonable
wish on his part, though now that the contact had been made I
realized that an anticipatory glow had heightened my expectations
to the point where they were bound to be disappointed, even if I'd
found my father living in a mansion on Bayview Ridge rather than
in an upper duplex next to an ice factory. After some more desultory

chatter, I went back to the hotel, packed my bags, and the next morning moved in to 91 Dupont Street 'for a few days', and to meet my father's friends.

First came Tom Jackson. He was the youngest of five sons of a subsistence farmer who had worked a tract of land on the edge of the Canadian Shield, that adamantine wall of pre-Cambrian rock which dominates the Canadian north and before whose harsh granite reality farms soon falter and die. Father Jackson did his best in what was fine lumbering, fishing and vacation country, but heartbreaking for the farmer. He drove a team of horses across the lake, breaking a trail through deep snow after freeze up. He split maple and birch and red pine to build a farmstead. He broke the point of his plough on great sheets of striated rock lying a few inches beneath the penurious soil. He manhandled stumps and great boulders to clear his thin acid land. In a word, he exhibited all the pioneer virtues of Upper Canada; and in the end it was all done. Tom came down to the big city from the bush and got a job in a department store. He had a fine voice, and helped my father with his pupils.

Betty was the daughter of a capable, hardbitten country doctor, from the Ottawa Valley. She had broken the mould of low church rural conformism, for she too had a voice. This was initially regarded as flighty in the Valley, but when it was harnessed in the service of the church, that was all right; and when the parents made their journey to the big city, the girl's voice too caught my father's attention, to say nothing of her quite extraordinary resemblance to Mother. Dressed in velvet gowns and hats of a vaguely Tudor cast she and other young Canadian ladies were hammered, under my father's direction, into a group of Madrigal Singers who successfully toured the concert halls of Hamilton, London, Chatham and points west, with a Hey Nonny Nonny. Upon the depletion of their ranks by marriage what more natural than that Betty should become my father's musical secretary and amanuensis; a task which she discharged with deep and uncritical devotion.

Soon I met other members of the group as my father took me—sometimes by taxi, more often by streetcar—through the grey streets of Toronto where bare trees lifted their arms in late March over acres of wet snow, and grey skyscrapers rose into the raw humid gloom. In a mid-nineteenth-century flat-faced red brick house—an oasis of empty ground completely surrounded by automobile dealers and used car lots—lived 'Lady Mary'. Otherwise Mrs. L. A. Hamilton: tall, angular, kindly and eccentric, a passionate devotee of Bach and social justice, of the canon form and the rescue of the fallen. Her relationship with my father had, I gathered, been compounded of her interest in his music and in his welfare. She was a great helper of lame dogs over stiles, an indefatigable do-gooder, a picker-up of waifs and strays. I was later to be the beneficiary of her kindness; but for the present she was content to survey me with kindly quizzical eyes over a scuffed round table in a cavernous dining-room with the remains of a once opulent dado on its stained and smoke blackened ceiling, and to repeat over and over again to my father,

'But this is wonderful, Campbell. A real miracle.'

'Yes, indeed,' he would say, his handsome grey-white head nodding slightly, while he rolled and tamped yet another of the endless home-made cigarettes he was always smoking.

'Lady Mary. D'ye think' (the faint remnants of a north country accent), 'd'ye think ye could . . . ?'

'Another cuppa? Campbell, of course!'

And up she'd get to lumber, in her kindly awkward way, down six steps and across a little landing into a kitchen that was really no more than a lean-to, while I sat back and prepared to answer yet more questions about my boyhood.

'Did I ever tell you . . . ?' said my father. I was beginning to recognize this as a storm signal unwittingly hoisted by him to announce yet another extract of reminiscence. Some of these were interesting: tales of Bouhy, de Reszke, Santley and giants of the concert platform that he'd known in his youth. Others were pretty boring: about what he'd said to 'Me old friend Donald Tovey' or 'Me old friend Hugh Roberton'. I noticed, with the clear cruel eye of youth, that he repeated himself a great deal, though I had the grace to forebear from mentioning it. So this time when he said, 'Did I ever tell ye about the time . . . ?' and then paused with a roguish twinkle, I said, 'Oh no, do tell me.'

'I tried to write to you.'

'Did you!' I was genuinely pleased and surprised.

'Oh yes,' he went on, his big lower lip starting to roll out a bit in a moist shelf as he gathered speed for another reminiscence. 'Oh yes, I wrote to you often. It was—'

'I never got any letter.'

This abrupt interruption annoyed him slightly.

'Well, I don't know what became of it. I certainly wrote. I tried to make contact with you.'

'Was the letter returned?'

'No. It just went off into the blue—a message of fatherly love— and then . . .' he let his hands fall to his side, shrugged his shoulders and assumed a tragi-comic smile.

'Where did you address it?' I pressed.

'Oh, I don't remember now,' he said slowly and softly. 'Somewhere in Australia.'

'4 Grace Street, Malvern?' I said, not so ingenuously.

'Yes. Yes, that was it. That must have been it. Grace Street.' He started to roll another cigarette. 'But, as I say, I never had any reply, so I didn't know what had become of you.'

I nodded sagely. 'Perhaps Mother intercepted the letter,' I suggested.

He lit the home-made cigarette and it flared wastefully up one side. Shreds of smouldering tobacco fell on to his lap and he got up fussily and brushed them away.

'Perhaps,' he said. 'Who knows? But as I say . . .' his voice trailed off and he looked beyond me and out of the big double glazed window across the dirty swathes of snow, and the used car lot with its melancholy freight of half buried automobiles. Clearly the owner wasn't doing much business, for some of the cars had great layers of snow on them almost two feet high, on the side of which successive falls showed like the layers in a cake.

Old boy, I thought irreverently, I think you're fibbing. I don't think you ever wrote to me. Now why do you have to pretend you did?

'Here's your tea, Campbell.' Lady Mary came striding in, grey eyes gleaming good-naturedly behind her silver-rimmed bi-focals, wisps of grey hair falling into her face.

'Thank you, dear,' said my father.

'Isn't it wonderful, Campbell?'

'A miracle, dear,' and he began to sip his tea.

This business of 'Campbell' bothered me a bit. It seemed to me that my mother, in the dim and far-off days when she had ever spoken of him, had called him 'Jim'. Certainly in the scrapbooks and family albums during his brief tenure as master of the household, he had been enshrined, in Mother's pretty rounded Greek handwriting, as 'Jim'. Perhaps though, in his view, life after the divorce. . . ? And all these cups of tea? Why was he continually drinking them, and using saccharine tablets from a little silver snuff box, or vinai-grette—I wasn't sure which—that he kept in his fob pocket? I didn't think I perhaps had the right to ask him; but I made a mental note that one day I would.

At the moment, though, I didn't have much time, for he wanted to show me to other friends and the process, though tedious, was also balm to the soul of a self-conscious, insecure young man.

First, the University. It appeared that my father, over the years, in addition to singing the Christus in the Bach Passions, had also conducted a very successful group of undergraduate singers. He took me along to see this scene of his former activity and we lunched 'in hall', built in the best style of Oxbridge girder-gothic. The stale bread and draughty corridors of Melbourne seemed curiously displaced by rolls, fruit cocktail and central heating, but one thing at any rate Ormond College and the hall had in common : both were teetotal.

Next, my father took me to see Fred Ince, who ran the Handel Society and was about as Canadian as steak and kidney pudding. Lithe, under-slung jawed, cockney through and through, Fred had an unslaked passion for plainsong which had sent him my father's way. He'd come out to Canada after the First World War to avoid the demon rum, which had caught up with him in the Euston Road while being demobbed; and he tied himself like a dog with a tin can on its tail to the head of a large firm of building engineers. He was bodyguard, confidential agent and johnny-on-the-spot to this powerful tycoon, and his unswerving devotion was rewarded by tips on the market, which enabled him, even in the depths of the depression, to run a Lancia convertible. Fred Ince took me for a ride in his royal blue convertible along the drear pre-spring banks of the Etobicoke Creek which flowed into Lake Ontario at the west end of Toronto. We parked the car in a snow-streaked lay-by while he explained to my at first incredulous ears that he and my father used often to go 'on a bender' together in the old days.

'Just a couple of homesick cockneys on the loose.'

'But my father's a Scot.'

'Same fella different hat,' said Ince jauntily. 'He's not himself now. Never will be. Any more than I am. Once you decide you can't touch the stuff, you have to quit cold. No half measures. So he's surrounded himself with a bunch of blue-ribboners. The Holy Camp I call 'em. But he's safe.'

'What about you?' I asked.

'Me? Never touch the stuff. Can't afford to. Your Dad's a wonderful man—a great singer too, once.'

'Once?'

'Well, he's past his prime now, ain't he?'

'I don't know,' I said, 'I've never heard him sing.'

Ince banged yellow-gloved hands on the wheel.

'That's right, neither you have. Sorry; I'd forgotten. Well, I tell you. He's still a wonderful teacher, and he can still do more on his technique and on what's left of his voice—and believe me he had a great voice—than most of us could do in an evening's bellowing. But as a concert artist he's past it.'

'You mean he doesn't sing any more?'

'Oh, he sings all right, but only in certain registers—certain parts —like Christus in the Matthew. He's got to be careful of his voice you know—what's left of it.'

'Then why does he smoke so much?'

'Oh well, cigarettes never did any harm. Anyway, that's just the larynx. With a really great singer it comes from the diaphragm. Nothing wrong with yer Dad's diaphragm. Besides, when a man's had to get off the hard stuff, he's got to have cigarettes, or cuppas or something to keep him going, hasn't he?'

'Well, yes, I suppose so.'

'Good. Just wanted to fill in the picture. Those aren't things that you'd learn from him,' he grinned, 'or from the Holy Camp.'

We drove slowly back to 91 Dupont Street through the grey soggy afternoon and, though I was to see Fred Ince many times in the ensuing years at the Bach Society, he never again made as vivid an impression on me, except when one afternoon in Trafalgar Square he showed me, with a true cockney's knowledge of London's peculiarities and prides, just how one could manoeuvre so as to get Nelson and the hilt of his sword in a certain position.

By the end of the week I was thoroughly disgruntled with my role, unreasonably fed up with my father's sentimental possessiveness and dying to get out of Toronto from which I had yet to see the sun. I took the plunge and told my father that I really would have to be

B*

getting on, you know; Montreal and New York couldn't wait, I'd come 8,000 miles, etc., I promised that I'd come back again for a brief visit after three weeks. He finally let me go after a last clinging reminiscential breakfast at the Diet Kitchen on Bloor Street and I blithely boarded a Gray Coach bus for Niagara Falls and Buffalo.

Chapter Four

BORDER TROUBLE

L AKE ONTARIO, fringed with honeycombed ice and as limitless as
a sea, drifted by on our left while we whizzed through a continuous clutter of wooden houses with asphalt shingle roofs,
looking curiously poverty-stricken and barren among the bare-
armed trees, the dank sombre conifers, the great swathes and
swatches of deep-piled dirty snow. The road however was both busy
and bare; well salted and sanded against the remnants of the Canadian winter, and crammed with cars and trucks and buses. It was
wider and smoother than its Australian equivalent, and in a land
where the railways were state owned and country trucking prohibited
you would never have seen such a dense press of vehicles: enormous
tractor-trailers and double-headed trucks hung with blinking lights
like a Christmas tree and careering down the highway—The King's
Highway, I noticed from the signs—at fearsome speed.

Presently dusk came creeping in, and into the grey damp night
came thousands of arc lamps and lights. Even the meanest house, it
seemed, in Southern Ontario, could afford two or three standard
lamps in the living-room. What a change from the single bulb suspended from the ceilings of many Australian homes. I began to feel
adventurous again. The bus was thoroughly warmed; I had a seat
up by the driver; and as our lights cut lemon beams through the
night Toronto slid back into limbo.

At Niagara Falls we roared through a little town and suddenly
came abreast of the great Falls themselves. Not quite so spectacular
as one had hoped, because they were half frozen in winter's grip
with great gouts and gobbets of ice smothering the water. Also, as
the road ran along the edge of the cliff, the Falls were below us and
we missed the awe of looking up at them. But they were raked

43

with purple and pink and green from great batteries of coloured lights on the New York and Ontario shores. Vulgar but vivid; gaudy but grand. Half an hour later we were grumbling up a high bridge over the Niagara River towards the United States. Great chunks of ice sailed by on the black water beneath us, and in the distance revolving beacons on the skyscrapers of Buffalo pierced the night. A spasm of excitement ran through me. The bus pulled up in a brightly lit bay marked *US Customs and Immigration. All Vehicles come to a Dead Stop.*

Our door clanged open admitting into the bus a chill blast of air and two crisp-looking immigration officers. As they approached me I reached blithely for my Australian passport.

'Where you from?'

'Toronto.'

'Where you going?'

'New York.'

'Where you born?'

'England.'

'Let's see your passport. Australian eh? Thought you said you was from Toronto?'

'Well, yes. That's where I came from. I've been there for a week. I boarded the bus there.' My Aussie accent fell awkwardly on the frigid Yankee ear.

'Driver!'

'Yup.'

'Get this guy's grips off the bus. He won't be goin' on.'

I scrambled to my feet.

'But, officer . . .' I began.

'Just follow me, bud,' he said. Pierced by the curious eyes of my fellow passengers I shouldered my way out of the bus into the raw night. A moment later my Revelation suitcase, yanked unkindly from the rear trunk by the driver, hit the concrete with a smack. Poor fellow, he was probably annoyed at having to be delayed.

'Want me?' he said to the immigration officer who shook his head.

'Get going.'

He sketched a salute and the warm friendly bus growled off into the night, New York and Ontario licence plates glowing below its rear lights. It gathered speed down the great ramp of the Bridge and on into Buffalo, leaving me shivering on the naked cement at the

US end of the International Peace Bridge over the Niagara River.

'In here, buddy,' the officer gestured not unkindly. Annoyed, mystified, a little apprehensive and minus my passport, I followed him into a bleak lino-floored hall whose essential disinfected anonymity was softened by the glow of warmth from enormous radiators. I parked my suitcase. The officer gestured with his thumb towards a counter behind which was a grey worn man with rimless glasses and an eye that missed nothing. He brandished my passport offhandedly.

'This is no good,' he said.

'No good!'

'Cool off,' said the official, not unsympathetically. 'What I mean is it's no good to you—here—now.'

'But it's valid.'

'Sure it's valid; but you ain't got a visa.'

'But I'm a British subject.'

'Don't make no difference.'

'But Canadians don't need visas.'

'That's right.'

'But they're British subjects too.'

'Can't help that, son; they're Canadians and you're not.'

'You mean you won't let me in?'

'Let's not say we won't; let's just say we can't.'

'You mean I have to go back?'

'That's just about it.'

My face must have fallen about a yard because the official wrinkled his tired grey eyes below his peaked cap and smiled toothily above his grey shirt and rubber snap-on bow tie.

'Look son,' he said. 'All you gotta do is get a visa. Cost you ten bucks maybe, but once it's on we'll let you in for a visit. That's all you want, ain't it? Not immigrating are you?' he added with a sudden thin surge of suspicion.

'No,' I said. 'No, I'm just planning to pass through the States on my way to Britain.'

'That so? Well then, the best thing for you to do is hop a train to Ottawa, see our Embassy there and get a visa. It's a bit further than Tronna, but they've only got a consul there and you'd maybe find it easier in Ottawa.'

'Gee, thanks,' I said with the ludicrous and touching gratitude of

youth, which always thinks that someone who's merely pleasant
has done something positive. 'Thanks. I'll do that; but, well it's ten
o'clock now. I'll have to wait till morning.'

'That's just about it,' said the official again.

'Can I stay here? Sleep in the building?'

That really got him, though I meant it in all seriousness. He
laughed long and loud and rubbed his knuckles in his tired grey
eyes. I waited, a bit affronted, for him to cool off. Finally, 'Sorry, son,
we can't let you do that.'

He handed me my Greyhound Bus ticket. 'Sure hope ya get a re-
fund on this, buddy. That's the tough part of it. No offence, you
understand? But I just can't let you stay here; you gotta go back to
Canada.'

'How? Do I walk?'

'No, no. There'll be a bus along in half an hour bound for Fort
Erie. They'll take you over the bridge and I guess you can find a
rooming house there for the night and take the bus back to Tronna
in the morning!'

I nodded glumly. There didn't seem to be much else to do. He
handed me back my passport and cleared some goo from his throat.

'Don't worry,' he said. 'Happens to lots o' people—you shoulda
bin here in the bottom of the Depression before Roosevelt got in.
Hell, we were turning 'em back by the hundreds. Even the Canucks.
Well, gotta go now. You've kinda kept me late.'

'I'm sorry. I . . .'

'Joe'll look after you. You can sit here till the bus comes. It'll be
by in twenty minutes. You'll be warm anyway. So long.'

He heaved himself into a big mackinaw, jammed a pair of earmuffs
on his head and clomped over to the door.

'So long,' I said, 'and thanks.'

Snow swirled in and a chilly wind sent long fingers all across the
waiting-room floor groping at my ankles. A sour-faced fellow entered,
head down, driving against the cold; he gave me a laconic nod and
went into a small glassed-in office. I sat down on a leatherette settee
and began to wait. The ticking of the large hexagonal clock on the
pea-green wall sounded louder than ever. On the bottom half of the
dial was lettered in gilt the statement: 'US Time' and underneath in
small letters 'Pioneer Time Keeping Co Inc, Waterbury, Conn.' On
the soupy walls were signs saying no smoking and no spitting. They

were in English, German, Spanish, Polish, Ukrainian and Italian; but not in French.

My head started to nod. . . .

'Do you intend to subvert the Constitution of the United States of America. . . ?'

'Have you any shrubs, plants, bulbs or flowers likely to contain the Colorado Beetle or the spruce budworm. . . ?'

'Okay, buddy, here's the bus for Fort Erie.'

All at once I was awake and a couple of dim headlamps carved the swirling snow. I grabbed my grip and stalked across the brown lino and out through the door, into the cold and into the bus, and out of the USA. Five minutes later the bus stopped at Fort Erie, Ontario, Canada.

'End o' the line,' said the driver. Apart from a drunk snoring in the back seat I was the only passenger. I clambered down into the snow and stood peering for a moment while flakes, invisible in the dark, pelted down like plummeting birds in the brilliant cone of light cast by a lonely street lamp. I peered through the gloom and in the distance dimly descried a sign: 'Rooms'. I ploughed on towards it through the soft driving snow, mounted a few snow-sprayed wooden steps to a verandah and banged on a glass-curtained door. After a few moments a man in braces and shirtsleeves opened it.

'Come in outa the cold,' he said, adding, 'Kinda late ain't it?' I explained my predicament.

'That's okay,' he said. 'You can take the upstairs room on the left. A dollar fifty with breakfast. You can get the 8.30 bus back to Tronta in the morning.'

My little room was wonderfully snug; from a register in the floor great life-giving gusts of hot air came streaming up from below. Before getting into bed—pink chenille spread and two pillows—I turned out the light, crossed to the window and parted the net curtains. Almost at my feet ran the Niagara River, black and sleek as it flowed north out of Lake Erie towards the Falls. Icebergs—dim shapes against the blaze of light from the US shore—scudded by like the grey ghosts of rafts. On the far side the night sky was ablaze with concentrated might and romance, displayed in garish neon for all the world—the Canadians at any rate—to see: Consolidated Edison; Lehigh Valley; Erie RR; Wurlitzer; Socony Vacuum; Buffalo Evening News; WBEN; Reading Anthracite.

Finding a Father

So near and yet so far!
Ah, well . . .

*   *   *

Next morning things looked much brighter. Under friendly Canadian skies I glanced coolly across the silvery river at the industrial agglomeration of Buffalo. Well, I thought, I'm not a stranger here! No sir! Nevertheless I decided to keep my adventure to myself and though the combined bus and train schedule to Ottawa left me five hours in Toronto to kick my heels I sedulously avoided contacting my father. Instead I parked my bags in a locker at Union Station, lunched at a greasy spoon and took myself to a downtown movie house to see *The Gold Diggers of 1933* with dear old Joan Blondell. A behemoth as tall, as gargantuan and much faster than the CPR Transcontinental whirled me through the rich, though curiously empty heartland of Southern Ontario: Oshawa and automobiles; Belleville and cheese; Kingston and aluminium. As the sky darkened, the snow and ice returned and late evening found me in a tiny little overheated box behind another Union Station looking out on the snowy spires of Ottawa.

In the morning I went straight to the United States Embassy and, as the official at Buffalo had predicted, I was granted, after answering a few routine questions (and upon payment of ten dollars), a visitor's visa good for three months. The ten dollars, steep though it seemed, didn't really hurt much because this was one of the rare occasions when the US dollar was at a discount in relation to the pound.

Fresh in the possession of my brand new visa I stepped jauntily out into the snowy Ottawa streets. How soon could I get to the US? Well, it turned out there wasn't a train until that night and it went from Montreal. So I spent some hours in leisurely contemplation of the incredible congregation of feathery iron filigree work and tortured stone castellations which make of Ottawa's wildly fretted skyline so magnificent an exercise in High Victorian bravura. I ascended the Peace Tower at the centre of the Parliament Buildings, and from its cold windy balconies saw stretching north and west in desolate magnificence a vast land carved in the grand manner; an infinity of low ridged hills that filled me with a powerful sense of wonder and melancholy. Man seemed both to have shrunk and to have increased in stature in this bleak environment. Shrunk, because

48

the landscape crushed him into dwarfish anonymity; grown in grandeur because his very defiance in daring to tackle such a vast anonymity had in itself a nobility that set the blood racing. By the time I came down from the Peace Tower to a meal at Bowles Lunch (the table being the splayed out arm of the chair you sat in) I had decided to put off my visit to the United States and explore this unknown cousin-country more carefully.

The train to Montreal that afternoon was filled with smallish dark neat-handed men. Their faces lacked the Anglo Saxon beef-and-milk complexion; they were a light olive. Their chins were blue and their upper lips often garnished with a small black moustache. Some wore snap-brim fedoras, some caps; some fur hats and some earmuffs. The women had brown eyes and looked quick and neat. I listened carefully and after a while my schoolboy French ear became attuned to the cadences and intonations of another race. I had a distinct sense of 'foreign-ness' and then caught myself feeling ashamed of this for I knew, from book learning, that almost a third of all Canadians were of French origin.

The train roared over enormous endless steel bridges; rivers as wide as seas foamed underneath. Then it droned to a stop and I found myself out in the cold, with the raspy night air catching at my lungs and signs everywhere in two languages. Traffic roared and surged round the bases of skyscrapers with incongruous ionic pillars high up on the twentieth floor. An electrically outlined cross glittered high on a hill. Neon-lit North-American streets skidded end on across the taxi windows, but the man who dropped me at the YMCA was small and dapper, and the illuminated licence holder in the cab said his name was Jean-Baptiste Polydore Gagnon. This must be Montreal. If it in turn was so strange and exciting why hurry south to the USA? Why not go further and explore Quebec City itself?

Montreal intoxicated me. It was my first 'foreign' city. I wandered aimlessly, head in the air, mouth agape, through the bleak windswept March streets and saw romance in old scraps of Le Devoir eddying round a lamp-post; in the thick blue-jowled policemen with their white brassards and immensely tall beaver and sealskin hats; in skyscrapers thrusting twenty-five storeys out of the clutter of commercial building at their feet; in the lean querulous towers of Notre Dame de Montreal; in the noisy confusion of Bonsecours Market with its bulging stalls and a babel of French breath rising in spurts of mist into the raw morning air; in deep grey walls towering round the convent of the Grey Nuns, with street cars and trucks and automobiles roaring past on their way out of French-speaking Montreal into English-speaking Westmount. I found romance too in the towering Scottish-baronial pile of the CPR offices matching so well, and so unconsciously, the châteaux and castles—indeed the keeps and fortresses—built up the steep slope of Mount Royal by the Scottish captains of industry: a people sensing themselves beleaguered not only by the poor but by the alien; their homes a strange combination of palace and prison, of self-assurance and self-doubt, of bluster and reticence. The innocent lineaments of Notre Dame de Bonsecours, an eighteenth-century statement of enduring faith in an age of classical scepticism, were now almost buried by the warehouses and lofts and grain elevators of 'Les Anglais'. From a dozen little cafés and bistros along the rue St Denis and the rue St Roch oozed enticing odours of rich sauces and meats that I couldn't afford. The great bare-branched maples and elms setting off the grey stone of McGill campus seemed romantic to me; so did the rattling canyon of St. James Street and the crowded counters of Dupuis Frères.

Over the city rose Mount Royal like a beetle-browed lion clothed almost to the summit with feathery trees. No matter where you went in the city it was there at the end of each street, in the gaps between yawning buildings; and as you approached it the streets themselves grew ever steeper till they failed utterly against the precipice of its flank. Dominating everything was the great River, the St. Lawrence, binding the city together on its island, washing its feet with an inexhaustible outpouring of cold greenish-grey water that flowed inexorably out of the middle of the continent a thousand miles behind and poured on into the Atlantic Ocean a thousand miles ahead. From the lookout on the top of Mount Royal this great river spread in a tremendous arc round three quarters of the horizon; beyond it tiny long-extinct volcanoes poked up through its flat glacial peneplain. In the distance was a line of greeny-blue serrated mountains lying in the United States—which was only twenty-five miles south of Montreal. The St. Lawrence here was about a mile wide and the slender bridges flung across it seemed tenuous links indeed with the southern shore. The St. Lawrence: the River of Canada.

I took a night train two hundred miles down the River of Canada, dozing fitfully in the stuffy heat and inhaling millions of particles of dusty green plush. Strange names swam by in the night, lit by naked bulbs in the freezing blackness: Batiscan, La Perade, Trois Rivières, Yamachiche; and in the grey dawn I arrived at the Palais station in Quebec, and felt I'd come from North America to Europe. Not that I'd ever been on the Continent, ever seen a single one of its tight little cities. But Quebec was so different from anything that I'd ever seen in my life before, that I felt: this must be Europe.

To someone whose infant memories of England had been long erased by exposure to Australia where, at that time, there was scarcely a single building that had been in existence more than a century, the sight of houses and churches and fortifications two and three times as old made a very strong impression. The ancient city slid down from the immense grey height of the Citadel in a slither of steep-pitched *fer blanc* roofs, nightmarishly tilted gables, congested stone walls and tall narrow windows with that peculiar thin-chestedness which Anglo-Saxons at first sight find so odd. The city stuck an immense rocky prow into the St. Lawrence, almost as if it were cleaving the river in a last effort to strain every nerve to return to the Europe it had never seen and the France which had abandoned it. Below in the St. Lawrence which already here, nearly eight hundred miles from the sea, was tidal, great hunks of ice jostled and banged in the counter currents of river and ocean, while twin ferries made their crabwise passage from bank to bank, smashing ice and sprayed by the choppy waves. Up ahead a low island humped in mid-stream and tiny spires pointed frail fingers into the immense grey-blue dome of the sky.

The sky itself defied accurate description. It was so immense and mournful, so full of lost imaginings, and an overpowering sense of melancholy, which yet had in it traces both of ardour and of regret. Man, the land, the low purple mountains, even the great river itself flowing and battling far below, shrank before this remote and enormous statement of cold nothingness. It was more than the spirit of the North. It was the spirit of unutterable emptiness against which the work both of nature and of man, when one lowered one's eyes, appeared at once petty and heroic. Petty in size, heroic in daring to oppose itself to uncaring chaos. Here, if anywhere, was Ajax defying the thunders; here man's deeds were bound to be on a daunting scale.

I went down the steep side of the scarp into the tiny little church of Notre Dame des Victoires and there amidst guttering candles and ex-voto portraits dim and soot-blackened by the passing centuries found not only peace, but a sense of scale. Who were these extraordinary and heroic people? Outside the frigid wind cut round the corners; high up on the top of the rock someone's concept of Chenonceaux or Chinon beetled above, its structure well protected against boreal blasts by a skeleton of high tensile steel. This, I reflected, as I trundled back once again on the high iron towards Montreal and the Adirondacks, and ultimately the temptations of New York, is a land I must see again.

* * *

'You will come back, won't you?' my father had said, his pleading eyes gesturing an entreaty that in my youthful intolerance I found intolerable.

'Well, I don't know,' I'd said ungraciously. 'I have to go on to Europe and see Mother. Why don't you come to England, and we'll all have a jolly reunion?'

His mouth pursed in what I thought was a rather prim distaste but he added hurriedly in case I should notice it, 'Well, we'll see about it. I might come over with Tom.'

'Fine,' I said unthinkingly, except for a cunningly masked desire to get out of the clutches of one whose approbation I had up till now so ardently desired. 'Do that, and afterwards I might come out to Toronto.'

But I'd see England first, and America, and of course, Baghdad on the subway.

But in the end there were no spangled lights hanging from the sky, no breathtaking forest of steel and concrete up the East River, no spires of aluminium catching the sun's first rays above the clouds. No faery towers, no cliff-dwellings, no dramatic canyons, no yawning vertical vistas, no crisp clear New World sky. For I slunk into New York by the back entrance in a New England pea-souper that made of the skyscrapers felled forest trees ending in a vaporous swirl, and of bold vistas misty English equivocations.

Chapter Five

UNWISE MAN IN GOTHAM

THE Dorp Hotel at 36th Street and Seventh Avenue in the heart of the garment district was eighteen storeys of liverish-grey brick veneer with an enormous cement coping of steel-girdered consoles, built about 1910. I lived for about a month there in a small single room with a diminutive bathroom painted public works pea-green, in that singular state of lonely ecstasy only possible to a very young man by himself in a large and totally unknown city. To say that New York intoxicated me would be an understatement: it practically paralysed me.

It was to me all that Australia was not: jazzy, vertical, speedy, up to date, rectilinear, strange, free, tolerant, laconic and bold. I did not see, with a twenty-two-year-old eye, that it was also oppressive, uniform, aggressive, nerve-racked, and cold. To live among these acres of steel and cement and glass was my greatest ambition, and I even gloried not so much in the dizzy thrust of Radio City or the Chrysler Building, as in the endless twenty to twenty-five storey height glimpsed, as each street flashed by like the spokes of a wheel, from a cruising taxi cab or a Fifth Avenue bus.

These were the days of the wonderful green double-decker open-air Fifth Avenue buses, and there was no better way for the penniless to see New York. The buses ran from Washington Square, with its faint echoes of Parisian greenery and triumphal arches, all the way up the length of Manhattan to the heights above the grey windswept Hudson within shadow of the George Washington Bridge. On such rides what impressed me most was the immense scale of everything. Viewed up the Avenue's immensely long gully, the tall buildings at its intersecting ganglia—Union Square, Madison Square, Herald Square—seemed to crowd towards you. But they were so high that

53

they dwarfed the true distance. In Paris it comes as a shock to learn, as you look at the enormous bulk of the Arc de Triomphe from the Place de la Concorde, that it is close to two miles off. So it was with New York.

Strange how anonymous numbers and figures became charged with meaning as the bus progressed. Even the imposition of a numbered grid on this huge city couldn't prevent the busy hum of men from filling certain figures with intense or symbolic meaning. A week ago 1st, 8th, 14th, 23rd had been cyphers on a meaningless abacus. Now 8th meant Washington Square and Greenwich Village and Paris in New York; 14th meant Union Square, S Klein and harangues against the capitalists; 42nd meant Times Square (less a square than the nodal point of an immensely long pair of scissors) and theatres and cross-town traffic; 57th meant art galleries; 59th meant Central Park; the 80s meant lovely ladies ('from the eighdies' as the song said); and 110th St. meant the end of Central Park and the beginning of Harlem.

The bus skirted its south end and presently purred beneath the immensely high meccano rig of the 8th Avenue elevated railway. How these 'Els' fascinated me. They straddled whole streets, clattering north and south up what were to me avenues in name only; for they were drab, endless, cobbled streets unrelieved by a single tree, and lined with grimy tenement houses, their fronts festooned with great iron spider-webs of fire-escape ladders. Beneath the El one dwelt in penumbral gloom. On a level with it passing passengers stared in at the living room and the bedroom. Above it the din and clatter common to all mounted to a level that was barely tolerable : treeless corridors of a reverberating, ferocious gloom. And atop the El was the Express El, running in central tracks and leaping up a fearsome cant to roar over the top of intermediate stations on a rickety centipede of shuddering iron.

I got back to my hotel after a four hour bus-ride of acquaintance with Baghdad on the subway and fell asleep exhausted. I dreamed that I was a great jazz composer and when I awoke at dusk the tunes I had written were still so vivid in my memory that I took sheets of Dorp Hotel writing paper, ruled out a stave and began to set down the impromptu songs before they should fly forgotten as a dream. This was a most laborious process, as I had abandoned musical notation at the age of fourteen when Mother refused to go on paying for

music lessons because I was taking short cuts by ear. But eventually
it was all written down; at any rate the melody line and the 'chord-
ing'. I hummed it over to myself and it sounded pretty good. I went
into the bathroom and looked at myself in the little deckle-edged
mirror over the washbasin. I looked pretty good too. Okay. Now I
must start my great career as a jazz composer by selling my first
song. That was the way they all started in Tin Pan Alley, wasn't it?
Well, here was I right in New York. What better than to take the
song straight to George Gershwin and sell it to him? I looked up
his office and made an appointment to see him the following evening at the studio in Radio City where he was putting on a show
with his brother Ira the lyricist. Maybe Ira could help me too. Then
I went out into Seventh Avenue and found an automat where I ate
in solitary and excited contemplation among the clerks and drunks
and impecunious young couples and harassed Mums with whining
kids, in the marmoreal public-lavatory style solitude.

The contact hadn't been too hard to make for I had a secret
weapon. Some time before leaving Australia I'd been an occasional
contributor to the *Australian Music Maker and Dance Band News*:
jazz at the University and that sort of thing. When I told the editor
I was planning to visit the United States he gave me letters of introduction to his local New York stringer and visiting cards to present
to the great. Nothing excites people in show business so much as
the chance of free publicity. Though I kept from Mr. Gershwin's
office the fact that the circulation of the AMM&DBN was less than
2,000, and that I wasn't being paid for my articles, the office had
nonetheless made the appointment.

Sharp at seven I presented myself at the studio in Radio City,
headquarters of the National Broadcasting Corporation, and was
conducted by a young hostess with a steatopygous behind to an
honoured seat in the glassed-in control room. The show was in rehearsal and seemed to be generating a certain amount of heat which
we could hear coming in over the control room mike. I spotted
Gershwin at once. He was at the piano in a dinner jacket and his
eager profile with the thick hooked nose and the slightly underslung
jaw was directly in front of me. I knew it as well as my own for I'd
had a photograph of it ever since I first heard *Rhapsody in Blue*. So
here I was; actually within sight, if not yet of touch or sound, of
the Great Man. He was about 34 at the time but to my hero-

worshipping eyes he looked the very embodiment of glamorous middle-aged success. Perhaps the fact that he was partly bald helped. A soft voice in my ear,

'Mr. Gershwin will see you now.'

It was the steatopygite. I followed her out of the control room into the studio, surreptitiously stroking in my inner breast pocket, as I trod warily over cables and cords, the little piece of hotel paper with my tune on it. I was shaking with stage fright now and wondered how I could ever muster the nerve to show it to Gershwin. All around us was an impatient bustle. The show was being shot for the newsreels and in addition to radio engineers, electricians and carpenters there were a couple of cameramen, a big camera on a boom and a dolly, and three or four grips manhandling five kilowatt lamps. Clearly I was being taken on the wing. I approached the piano where Gershwin was animatedly jabbing at a piece of manuscript with a sharp pencil and arguing with an assistant. The girl smiled encouragingly. Suddenly he looked up.

'Yeah—yeah—yeah?' he said in a harassed voice.

'This is the representative of the *Australian Music Maker and Dance Band News*, Mr. Gershwin; you remember?'

His face creased in a smile full of toothy charm and he eased out a hand which I clasped almost as in a dream.

'Australian, eh? Sure a long ways from home. Certainly glad to meet you!'

The warmth of his welcome staggered me. I really believed that he was glad to meet me. Only much later did I learn that most Americans said this as a matter of course in the same way that they said 'You're welcome' after you said 'Thank you'. I responded with equal warmth.

'And I'm certainly delighted and honoured to meet you, Mr. Gershwin, I've been . . .'

He withdrew his hand smoothly from my fevered grasp.

'You gonna be here long?'

'Just a few days. This is my first visit to New York, and back in Australia . . .'

'First visit, eh? Well, you have a lot to see. We're mighty glad to have you in the studio with us tonight. Oh, Joe!!'

'It's a great honour for me to be here, Mr. Gershwin, especially as,' I took the plunge, 'I write music myself.'

'That so?' His face assumed a distant look as Joe hurried up with a sheet of manuscript paper. 'You got any of it here?' he asked in jocular fashion. Little did he know. 'Hey Joe, here's a fella from Australia writes music.'

'Nothing like *Lady Be Good*,' I blurted out. 'Nothing like *Embraceable You*.'

He patted my arm and turned to Joe.

'Nice fellow, eh? Joe, for pete's sake get the alto sax to come in after the rest in bar 35 and let's have a bit of bite from the guitar when he's soloing in bars 42 to 43. Tell him he's a new Eddie Lang. Get him working with you.'

'Uh, uh, but George—'

'I've got a piece of music here now,' I said loudly.

'Outa the way PUL-EEZE.' Two grips bumped me aside as they manhandled an enormous 5k into place. I brandished the music under Gershwin's nose.

'Eh, what's that? Fine! Tell you, I'm busy right now. Be on the air in three minutes. Show it to Joe, will you?' He put out his hand. 'Mighty glad to meet you, Mr. Um. Have a good time in New York. Now, Joe, what seems to be the trouble?'

'Mr. Gershwin's going on the air,' said the jiggly-bottomed girl in my ear. 'We better get going.'

'Sure thing,' I heard myself say and almost in the next minute it seemed I was back in the control room, and the sweep hand on the studio clock was coming up to the hour and the show was on the air. I watched it entranced. It was a pot-pourri of Gershwin songs. He played like a dream, in his own faintly regretful idiom, his own delicate, yearning, wailing-wall melodies. I was particularly attracted when he said: 'Words by my brother Ira and music by—Ira's brother George.' In the midpoint of the show two thickset fellows came to the mike and started to talk about indigestion and gas pains and upset stomach. I don't know why it should have shocked me so much to think of Gershwin in the pay of a stomach powder, but somehow the gilt was off the edge of the evening, so that when Joe came in to the control-room and slouched moodily in a chair, chewing gum and staring at vacancy while he listened for faults in the show, I wasn't very hopeful. I was right not to be.

'Excuse me,' I said. 'What about my music?'

'Huh?'

57

'The music Mr. Gershwin said you'd look at.'

'Oh yeah. You got it?'

'Here it is.' I handed it to him proudly. He gave my noble kunst-
werke a cursory glance, then handed it back.

'Not our type,' he said.

'You mean it's no good?'

'It's okay, but it's not our type of music. Not the type we could
use in a show.'

'You mean you don't like it?'

'Sure I like it. It's fine, but it's not our type. Now you take a
fellow more commercial. Rudy Vallee. Now he might use it.'

'You really think so?'

'You could try.'

'Could you give me an introduction to him?'

He fished in his pocket and brought out a card, which he scribbled
on and handed it to me. It said 'Joe Swayze. Arrangements. MUR
43567' and on it 'A guy from Australia with a song.'

'Gee, thanks,' I said, almost crushing the card in two in my
excitement.

'That's okay,' he said. His jaws worked morosely and he returned
to his glum contemplation of the show. Apparently nothing was
going just quite right. Clutching my treasure-trove I rose silently to
my feet and let myself softly out of the soundproofed double
doors.

I now tried the same procedure with Rudy Vallee. Though Bing
Crosby was coming rapidly up the ladder, Rudy Vallee was the idol
of the college crowd (*The Stein Song*) and the ladies (*Weary River,
Give me something to remember you by*) and I thought: well, why
not? He may take my songs and, if he doesn't, it'll at least be good
copy for the AMM&DBN. Again a rendezvous was arranged for
an NBC studio in Radio City and again, close too, the effect was at
once larger than life and simply not credible. Vallee was in his
shirtsleeves in the midst of another rehearsal with headphones over
his ears and conducting an orchestra. His wistful spaniel's face
looked tense, drawn and gravelly from close up and he was in a
thundering bad temper, beating the music stand impatiently with
his baton and saying in a tense sarcastic voice,

'All right! All right! Let's take it again from the letter J? The
letter J. Okay? and WATCH IT.'

When I was brought up to him by an understrapper he said,

'What's the name? Oh sure, Mr. Um, glad to meet you. Okay, take it again from the letter J.'

While I stood, highly conspicuous and useless amid a tangle of cables and music stands, with the orchestra blaring around my ears, he threw himself into the rehearsal with such vigour that sweat stains started to spread across the shoulders of his shirt. He looked nothing at all like the rather effeminate crooner beloved by the crowds. He looked like an extremely tough hard-working professional musician. When he stopped for a breather, I waited for him to notice me and, as he didn't, I said in a loud quavering voice,

'Mr. Vallee!'

'See y'ina minute.' And up they started again. I waited another few minutes in the blast and din of six saxes, three trumpets, two trombones and traps.

'Mr. Vallee!'

'Minute! Okay, fellows, take it from the letter J.'

The caterwauling started anew and at last I just couldn't take it. I slunk over to the wall of the studio and sat down on a folding metal chair next to a busy looking woman with tight blonde curls, who, however, glanced at me sympathetically. I made a wry face. She said,

'Mr. Vallee's kinda tied up right now.'

'I wanted to show him this,' I said, and I whipped the immortal composition out of my inside breast pocket and shoved it under her nose. She gave it a quick once over.

'Not the number for him,' she said. 'Whyn't you try it on Ethel Waters?'

'Who's she?' She gave me an astonished look.

'Where'd you say you were from?'

'Australia.'

She nodded sagely. 'If you ever get to see Ethel don't ask her that question. Right now she's in a show at the Music Box. *As Thousands Cheer.* Heard of it?'

I shook my head.

'Well, whyn't you go along and see her there?'

'Do you really think she'd see me?'

She gave me an appraising up-from-under glance.

'Sure, why not? Anyway, you can take in a good show.'

'Oh, thank you,' I said, in my latter day Candide role, and tiptoed gratefully out of the studio.

The woman turned out to be right. It was a very good show indeed, even as glimpsed from $2.50 seats in the upper circle, though as I wasn't very familiar with the US political scene a lot of the contemporary satirical skits went over my head. Music and lyrics were by that indefatigable giant Irving Berlin, and the stars in addition to Ethel Waters were Helen Broderick and Clifton Webb. This was long before Carson McCullers' *Member of the Wedding* and I hadn't realized that Ethel Waters was both coloured and an actress. She caught my fancy in two diametrically opposed numbers: *Heat Wave* where she did a frenzied Cuban rumba, and *Supper Time* where she was the widow of a freshly lynched cotton picker from the Deep South.

After the show I went round to the stage door and asked to see her. It seemed entirely natural to me that the request was immediately granted, by a surly fellow sitting in a metal chair with his hat on and a cigar in his teeth reading *Variety*. I found myself in Ethel Waters' dressing room. She looked a little startled, but not much.

'Miss Waters,' I said, 'I've greatly admired you tonight and I just had to come round to offer you my homage and congratulations; but as a matter of fact . . .' At this point I started to go into my spiel about the AMM&DBN, and suspicion began to climb into her face. When I paused for breath she said in a wonderful furry contralto,

'I appreciate your interest, Mr. Uh, but I'm not in the business of writing testimonials. You better see my agent.'

'Well,' I said, whipping the immortal song, by now somewhat crumpled and soiled, from my pocket, 'if you don't write testimonials, is it possible that you'd consider this song?' I thrust it under her nose.

She blinked a bit, then smiled and said, 'Thanks all the same but I don't need any material.'

'Well then,' I said as I took the battered composition back, 'can I at least have a photograph of you?'

'Sure you can,' she smiled and plucked one out of the edge of her dressing-table mirror.

'Will you write something on it?' I asked and had my pen out faster than the immortal piece of paper. She looked quizzical.

Unwise Man in Gotham

'What'll I write?'

'Oh, anything at all would be wonderful,' I breathed.

'You're a funny fella,' she said and wrote on the card and handed it to me. 'Yours sincerely Ethel Waters' scrawled over her in Cuban costume singing *Heat Wave*. I placed it next to my heart with the immortal music.

'Oh, thank you, Miss Waters, thank you.'

She took my outstretched hand and smiled. 'Have to ask you to leave now. I got company coming.'

'Of course,' I said moving swiftly backward and knocking over a metal chair. 'Thank you. Thank you very much indeed.'

'That's okay. Glad to met you. Good night.'

'Good night, Miss Waters.'

I walked through the whirling brilliant neon and electric gyrations of Times Square almost without noticing them. Almost without seeing or feeling the vast press of revellers and sightseers and plain rubbernecks who thronged the sidewalks of Broadway and Seventh Avenue and 42nd Street. As I entered the lobby of my dingy hotel, I was walking on air. I opened the door of my little bedroom and there on the faded dusty flowered carpet was a letter: Shell Oil Co. Duty, stern daughter of the voice of God! This must be my former benefactor from far-off Australia reaching out to see that I saw the proper people in New York; that I didn't spend all my time in frivolity. I came down to earth with a bang, but before reading the letter I propped Ethel Waters reverently up on the little dressing table. Then I went into the bathroom, tore the immortal composition into small pieces and flushed it down the toilet. I started to read the Shell letter with a lighter heart. Maybe I wasn't destined to be a jazz composer after all.

* * *

The Shell office turned out to be in Radio City and, of course, after my sessions with Gershwin and Vallee, I knew all about that. Late next afternoon, armed with my letter I waited on the Managing Director on the 47th floor. He turned out to be a crisp well-dressed Englishman, with a hectoring voice.

'You'd better have a look at our terminal facilities while you're here,' he said. 'We've a bunkering depot in Queens; that's over on—'

'The other side of the East River,' I said. He didn't relish the

61

interruption. Behind his tweedy back and his waistcoat with its daring collar rose the great fistful of skyscrapers down towards the Battery. I looked cool and pert, trying to disconcert him. But he was an old hand.

'Yerss,' he said. 'But our major operation is at Sewaren in New Jersey. You can take a train on the Pennsy—' how he relished the familiar diminutive, redolent of an Englishman who was really with it in up-to-date New York—'a train on the Pennsy to Rahway. Morse will accompany you.' He pressed a buzzer and an earnest, competent, zealous woman in her mid-thirties zoomed in. 'Please ask Mr. Morse to come in.'

In a moment or two—spent by the Managing Director and me in gazing over each other's shoulders at the towers of old Manhattan —in came a tall fresh-faced fellow of about thirty with curly blond hair and an unexpected pipe. The Manager confided me to his good offices and ushered us blandly out. I followed Mr. Morse down a corridor to his office which was very tiny and informal. When he'd shut the door he said,

'Say, you really *want* to go over to Sewaren?'

'Well . . .' I temporized.

'Not a goddam thing to see there,' he said. 'Waste of time.' He picked up a paper-weight in the shape of a shell and started to fiddle with it. 'What doing tonight? I'm having some folks in to cocktails. Care to help out?'

'You bet!' I said, falling into what I hoped was the correct idiom. He leaped into life.

'Okay, fine,' he said. 'Let's get some liquor, but fast. You couldn't help me out with a ten-spot, could you?'

My heart sank a bit. If only the gregarious Mr. Morse knew the true state of my Letter of Credit. But I didn't want to seem mean, and anyway the idea of cocktails in a New York apartment appealed to me.

'Sure,' I said, whipping it out.

'Thanks a million,' he said with engaging New World candour and exaggeration. 'I'll let you have it back Monday. Let's go.'

'Where?'

'Get the liquor.'

'Don't you have to go to a speakeasy?'

'No, sir. Not any more.'

We bustled down the grey lino corridor and into the elevator.

'Hello, beautiful,' he said to a very plain stenographer with rimless glasses. Then he turned confidentially to me.

'Hell no,' he repeated. 'That was true till just about yesterday. But now we got Repeal. I don't have to go into speakeasies any more and say "Hey, my name's Joe Zilch, how do I go about getting a bottle?" No sir. It's great what I do now. I just walk right into a grocery store and I say "Gimme two fifths of bourbon." Just like that.'

So indeed it proved; just like that. We bought the liquor at a grocery store and then took the 4th Avenue subway down to his flat on 22nd Street. It was a little boxy place; combined living and dining area, tiny hall, one bedroom, a kitchenette and a john. I helped Morse fix the ice and mix the drinks and, with several pre-party martinis under my belt, I was feeling no pain by the time the guests arrived. Pretty soon the tiny little apartment was crammed with people and I found myself talking animatedly to a girl with a pair of enormous cornflower blue eyes. I dived right in. When I finally surfaced we seemed to be talking about negro jazz.

'You can call me Pris,' she said. 'It's short for Priscilla and I kinda hate it, but for my friends—' and she flashed heavy eyelashes at me— 'it's special.'

'In that case,' I said, well lit on Morse's martinis, 'let me ask *you* a special question.' I paused. She looked enquiring.

'What are you doing tonight?'

The enormous cornflower eyes widened. 'Tonight?'

'That's it. I thought maybe you'd like to come up to Harlem with me.'

I saw a vein beat along her throat and the cornflower eyes were masked as she dipped her nose in the drink. When she too surfaced, 'I'd love it,' she said.

The trouble was I'd given the ten-spot to Morse. The party had reached the stage where you couldn't hear yourself speak unless you went into the bedroom, but when you went into the bedroom, other couples were already hard at work. So Pris and I went into the bathroom. She sat on the john and I sat on the edge of the bath. I found the situation piquant and it had the effect of projecting us straight towards each other and, when we came to, she agreed that it would be fun to go to the Savoy Ballroom on Lenox Avenue in Harlem and hear Duke Ellington—for whom we had discovered a common adoration. We lurched out of the party, giggled into the elevator, hit the sidewalk of 22nd Street with a bang and grabbed an idiotic sandwich at a Childs on 4th Avenue before grabbing a taxi up to Harlem.

The Savoy Ballroom turned out to be a really enormous dance hall like an underground cave. On its polished floor two or three hundred couples could perform with the greatest ease. It was loudly and garishly lit, and the decor, far from being that of a *boîte de nuit*, husky and subdued, was in bold, bright primary colours. Several score of small tables surrounded the big floor and shelved off gradually with banquettes and stalls in the far corners. The noise was deafening, even though we arrived at the pre-cabaret intermission and the band was resting. A negro pianist played slow dreamy blues music which just managed to trickle through the noise. Across billowing scarves of grey and blue cigarette and cigar smoke, heads and profiles of every conceivable hue and cast nodded and chatted and drank. Pris and I were squeezed into a table right on the edge of the floor, but were too euphoric to feel as conspicuous as we looked. I ordered bourbon and water as the cheapest thing on the menu and she didn't seem to mind. Black negroes with European features below their woolly hair talked to *café-au-lait* girls with straight hair but everted lips. Lithe boys as pink as me sported blond kinky hair and noses with wide septums. Some faces were black and shiny, some black and matt, some brown and beautiful, others brown and plain. An immense assortment of shades and colours, and over all a lithe grace and an electric tension that made us grip our hands together under the table.

A trombone flared red into the smoke-shrouded hall; the lights dimmed and an orange spot picked out a tall muscular negro in full evening clothes of glittering silver cloth with white lapels, a maroon shirt and a yellow bow tie. He lifted his baton and in an instant the crowd was stilled and a 32-piece jazz band erupted into a blazing inferno of sound. It was Jimmy Lunceford. At first I was terribly let down for I'd been expecting Duke Ellington, and the Lunceford pianist—it wasn't the leader himself—was a grievous disappointment. It was dreamy and hopeless enough—it was the period of *Star Dust*, *I'll Get By* and *Dancing in the Dark*—but none of the Maestro's incredibly agile arabesques. But when we got up to dance and melted into each other's arms the true magic of Lunceford came alive and we

PROFESSOR J. W. MACKAIL, O.M.

finally crept away from the Savoy Ballroom at three in the morning convinced that he was a very great jazz band leader indeed—or else that we were in love. The taxi cruised slowly through the deserted concrete avenues of Harlem. Couples argued in doorways; old newspapers swirled round the ankles of rubbies and bums in the vicious April wind; the airy knives of a Manhattan spring made the cop on patrol at Lenox and 110th pull his coat up further round his ears. Safe in our taxi (with the driver's name, licence number and photograph comfortingly illuminated in a special holder on the back of the front seat) we shuddered at the cold and the violence and the crudity. We expressed heartfelt gratitude that despite our poverty and joblessness and the bleak prospects of the Depression, we belonged to us and not to them. We might lack the integrity of dissent, but we were warm. We might be ignoble but we were safe.

There followed for Pris and me an idyllic week of economic royalism (though on a very modest scale), of parasitic dolce vita, of conspicuous waste fuelled by my insurance policy (taken out on my behalf by my godfather at my birth) and her father's pension and savings. She'd been born to the outer fringe of the Manhattan and Long Island purple: an apartment on the East Eighties, a summer home on The Sound; schooling at a private girls' socialite academy; finishing school in France; the cotillion Ball; young men with orchids and top hats and tails; a nodding acquaintance with Picasso and Poulenc and Le Corbusier; a Lincoln convertible and a Ford runabout. And then—1929. Father's business collapsed; disposal of Long Island home at fire-sale rates; move to cheaper apartment; mother getting a job with the Junior League; all of a sudden the Irving Berlin-Fred Astaire-Ginger Rogers dream world collapsed, later to be achingly mirrored for the nostalgic poor in a hundred first-run movie theatres: *Top Hat, Dancing Cheek to Cheek, Caught in the Rain.*

So there she was and there I was, and what more natural than that she should show me the scenes of her former glory, now that she was 'clerking' in Bloomingdales'? That weekend we got out the elderly but beautifully preserved Lincoln convertible and I paid for the gas, and off we went to Long Island. Early April is not of course the best season to taste the Island's joys. Trees were still bare and grass still brown as we threaded the tarmac intricacies of the great motorways and ended up eating clams in an out of season dine-and-dance joint by the mournful sedge and springy dunes fronting the grey Atlantic.

But coming back at dusk the starred towers of Manhattan beckoned with all their potent magic across the spider's web bridges. Serried yellow windows hung floating in the sky; neon hopped and twinkled in multi-coloured glory; beams revolved above barely apprehended slabs of darkened concrete, or cut mercury-white swathes through a night sky where it was never truly night. But on such nights, intoxicated with New York and new love, I'd creep into my sad little bed in the dingy old Dorp on 7th Avenue and before going to sleep compose some more immortal dream music to sell, if not to Gershwin or Vallee then—who knew?—to Ben Bernie or Irving Mills or Cab Calloway?

Suddenly I was running out of money. That meant I had to get on to England in a hurry. But what about Pris? And what about my half-promise to return to Toronto and say a fond farewell to my new-found father? Well, women and children first. In this case him. For I just couldn't bear the thought of returning to his Toronto after exciting Manhattan. I wrote him a cheerful, friendly and mendacious letter explaining how the Shell people had wanted me to do work in New York. Had to stay on. Ended with a rousing plea for him to visit me and my brother in Europe that summer. This adjuration, since he believed that I meant it, stored up a Homeric dose of trouble for the future, but of this for the moment I was unaware. Well, that's that. Now, how does one go about prolonging one's stay in good old NY? Obvious thing to do is change my sailing date.

I made a precarious but precise calculation as to my rate of expenditure and discovered that I could stay on in New York for three extra days if there was a ship sailing for Britain on the fourth day. I went to the office of the Cunard Company to explain and apologize. Bless you, that was all right, they said. Happened all the time. After all, a young fellow on the loose; bound to change his mind. No trouble at all. Glad to have the business. (It was of course the middle of the Depression.) The SS *President Roosevelt* was sailing from a North River Pier in four days' time. Bound for Le Havre, Rotterdam and Hamburg, but she'd be standing off Plymouth and a tender would take us ashore. Please pay the extra charges at the next counter. I did so and breezed brightly out on to Fifth Avenue looking forward to three more unadulterated days of New York and Pris. I had just enough presence of mind to write a letter to Mother in London telling of my change of plans. After all she might be thinking of throwing a party. Best to be considerate. The letter eventually reached London the same day that I did, but this too was hidden from me. On with the dance.

Into this carefully planned arcady of the concrete canyons odiously intruded the Shell Oil Co. It began when, feeling a bit straitened, I phoned Morse to ask for my ten dollars back.

'Oh say,' he said, 'glad you called. The Old Man would still like you to go out and visit the ocean terminal at Sewaren, New Jersey.'

'But I thought you said—'

'Oh, sure, sure I did. I still think it stinks. But that was last week. He'd like you to go. Anyway it'll give me a chance to slip you that ten-spot. Don't want to have to mail it to you.'

'Oh gee, do you have to go?' said Pris, clinging to each other in the hallway of Washington Square. 'Couldn't I come too?'

Alas no. So I called in at the Shell Offices in Rockefeller Centre at nine on a bleak grey morning, and one single whole precious day was wasted. Morse gave me the dough and handed me over—with a grimace implying he'd have loved to come but was called by Higher Duties—to a taciturn young-old man in a brown snap-brim fedora who, with an impatient cry of 'Okay, let's go!', in turn handed me into the express elevator and thence down the basement garage, into a Chrysler Airflow and out, headed for New Jersey.

The actual trip was in fact like Fritz Lang's *Metropolis* because though presumably of the earth we were rarely on it. We zoomed up out of the basement garage and quickly over to the West Side Elevated Speedway. This we followed to the Holland Tunnel which plunged us beneath the Hudson. We emerged in Jersey City and almost at once roared up on to the Pulaski Skyway. On its enormous steel stilts we sped high above the mournful brown marshes of the Passaic and the Hackensack until we arrived in Newark with its own knuckle of skyscrapers. An elevated freeway next whisked us to smoky Elizabeth and then to Rahway and a clutter of stores and service stations and rooming houses. Finally came the docks, tanks, towers and barges of Sewaren, all clustered together in the pile of debris that lay between the brown bare land and the cold ice-fringed oily sea.

At first I tried to make bright remarks about bulk loading but my tight-lipped companion, who drove with suppressed fury, finally shut me up with a series of 'Yup', 'Thatso?' 'Uh-uh', 'Yup'. So silently we arrived at Sewaren to be met by a guide so voluble, so knowledgeable, so brightly determined to Tell All that I wilted anew, this time from a surfeit of sound rather than its absence.

No guide to a Venetian palazzo, a Rhenish cathedral or a French château ever exceeded this fellow in the interminable, remorseless, enthusiastic chatter that poured in a cataract from his eager lips. Oil barges evoked in him an enthusiasm akin to that aroused in others by gondolas; his Bridge of Sighs was the electric hoist and transporter crane for the barrels; his flying buttresses were the catalytic cracking towers. He was himself inexhaustible but to me exhausting. To make it worse the side kick in the snap-brim fedora said absolutely nothing. I couldn't tell whether he was by nature taciturn and morose, or whether he'd seen it all a thousand times before, or whether he felt put upon at having to waste the best part of a day carting me around. Maybe it was a bit of all three.

At noon I decided to put us all out of our misery and suddenly remembered an urgent appointment in Manhattan. To my great relief the reaction was simply: how would I get to Manhattan on time? Fred here with the car had a date to go down to Perth Amboy to check on bunkering facilities. Consternation glared out at me from the visages of both the Shell men.

'Oh that's okay,' I said, 'I'll take the train.'

They relaxed visibly and while the guide pumped my hand in friendly frenzy, the fellow in the snap-brim fedora started to twiddle a chain with a key-tainer in a whizzing uncomfortable pattern, saying—

'C'mon, then, let's go. Let's go eh? C'mon let's go.'

He drove me hell-for-leather to Rahway station, bade me a curt goodbye and took off in a curving stream of slush into the brown mournful afternoon. I stood waiting by the quadruple electrified tracks of the Pennsylvania Railroad. The high iron gleamed pewter in the cold April noon; amber lights winked down the tracks. Pretty soon an enormous train thundered in, about a mile long, five hundred feet tall and drawn by coupled electric locomotives with high pantographs striking sparks off the catenary. I got in and in less than thirty minutes whisked smoothly and almost silently over the melancholy marshes, the grey cement cities, the ragged leaden estuaries and the roaring tunnels. I emerged in the Pennsy Station at 30th Street right opposite the Pennsy hotel with its thousand bedrooms and thousand bathrooms towering in sanitized immensity (complete with deodorized toilet seat covers) 500 feet into the crisp blue spring sky.

I boarded the *President Roosevelt* with an aching heart. England Home and Beauty, the prospect of a long-lost Mother, brothers, multitudinous cousins and uncles and aunts and grandparents all unglimpsed for close to twenty years, failed to equal in the balance the girl I left behind me. But leave her I did, and with her the magic aspiring megalopolis with its fairy spires and its midden heaps; its ethereal pinnacles and the iron clangour and the windblown debris of the Els; its dreams for the young and its unceasing clatter for the middle-aged.

An orchid in the cabin which I shared with four other single men in the Eastbound version of the immigrant ship was in the end all that remained. She shouldn't have done it, of course, but I was glad she had. That and the vague insistent uneasy nagging feeling that I ought to have returned to Canada to see my father, before finally shaking off North America. That and another feeling that I would return some day, and maybe soon. That and the vision of the fading towers of Manhattan, slipping astern like an ancient Babylonian citadel as we cleared the Verrezano Narrows; sliding finally into oblivion as we breasted Ambrose light in the chilly April afternoon and set our heading three thousand miles east for Plymouth Hoe.

Chapter Six

---

6 PEMBROKE GARDENS, W.8

ON the last night before we were due to land at Plymouth, there was a big beanfeast, with caps for the kids and booze for the adults; and the more daring or bumptious passengers put on an amateur cabaret. The leaflet for this memorable evening was entitled SOUVENIER PROGRAM which indelibly stamps the peculiar composition of the SS *President Roosevelt's* passenger list. It was American first, after that it was German, Slav and Italian in that order. French and English came absolutely nowhere. We were a thoroughly mixed lot: earnest German-Americans from the Middle-West on their way to see the Passion Play at Oberammergau; blue-chinned, lively Poles from Buffalo on their way to take a look at Marshal Pilsudski's New Poland; a couple of English war-brides from Texas on their first trip back home for fifteen years; an Italian guitarist who regaled us with *Tango della Rosa*; a Swiss from the Vaud on his way to see his aged grandmother; a bus driver from Avenue A, Brooklyn on a cheap excursion to Lourdes and the shrine of St. Jago de Compostella.

All Europeans; yet at the same time all Americans with a simple faith in bigness and efficiency and a curious mixture of affectionate envy and good-natured contempt for the Europe they'd none of them seen: the Europe of Hindenburg, Alfonso XII, Vittorio Emanuele, Benes, Dollfuss, Admiral Hörthy, Magda Lupescu and Stanley Baldwin. The disembarkation points were overwhelmingly Continental; it seemed that almost the only people bound for England were the war-brides from Dallas and me. In an early summer morning with the sea a flat silvery blue we were decanted off Plymouth Hoe into a land of miniature railways, rich red earth and verdure of a brilliance so incredible that it almost hurt the eyes. This was England, indeed this was the town from which we had embarked as children on the long voyage to Australia so many years ago. I craned my neck at the suddenly remembered Priest and Clerk tunnel near Dawlish; heard with awe a red-necked Colonial Office type exclaim 'By God, there's a real shoulder of Dartmoor'; and saw with awe the thickening arteries of peripheral London. Suddenly it was Paddington and there at the end of the platform was Mother. I gave her a great big hug and said,

'You know where I've been? I've been in Toronto and I've seen my father!'

Mother's reaction to this tactless first greeting after four years was manful.

'Did you indeed, darling. And how was New York?'

I launched into a lyrical description of the great city while she collected the bags, she tipped the porter, and she managed to commandeer a taxi. Her smooth efficiency after a while left me tongue-tied until I remembered that of her forty-four years all but ten had been spent in London. We chattered happily through the slanting evening summer sun as the taxi crawled through Bayswater and down Church Street—look, darling, that's where you were born—and then across the great ugly 'modernistic' face of Barker's and along Kensington High Street past the very spot where I'd said good-bye to my father in his RFC forage cap in 1917. It all came flooding back, though still in bits and pieces, like flotsam and jetsam on an incoming tide: Earl's Terrace in yellow-brown Georgian brick; the perfect pattern of Edwardes Square (was Henry Ford's studio still on the South side? Yes it was. Was he—er? No, he wasn't). Then the green painted 'Kensington Italianate' portico of 6 Pembroke Gardens, my grandparents' house which for so many years had meant letters from far-off England or those wonderful pink postal orders for ten bob or a quid. Mother paid off the taxi and I lugged the trunks up six well-scrubbed freestone steps and in through a heavy green painted front door.

My grandmother was standing on top of an oak chest beside the big grandfather clock, so that she would be able to reach to my shoulder. I seized her with a glad shout crying, 'I'm going to break every bone in your body.' Her fragile fairy face with the lean beautiful nose and charming twisted smile revealed teeth irregular and luminous as a necklace of real pearls. I had fallen in love with her when I was seven and she was fifty-three. Then I had had to stand on the oak chest. I was now twenty-two and she sixty-eight and I still thought she was the most beautiful woman I had ever met. Presently my grandfather came down. He had shrunk, I noticed, and with his decrease in stature had come an increase in benevolence and a lessening of the awe which his formidable mental equipment merited. He too embraced me in the French fashion and then almost at once it seemed to me that a well-built youngish fellow with wavy black hair and a noble bashed-in nose was standing beside Mother. My mouth fell open and Mother laughed.

'This is my publisher, Hamish Hamilton,' she said. 'Jamie, this is Graham. You see, darling,' she explained, 'your letter saying you were coming didn't arrive till this morning and I couldn't put Jamie off, could I?'

'Well, I hope you wouldn't want to,' said Jamie.

'Of course,' I said, 'of course.' Delighted and bemused and coltish and anxious to be of help.

'You'll have a homecoming dinner with us,' said Maany, my grandmother, putting her arm through mine. The door slammed behind Mother and her publisher, with all my unspoken welcoming questions swallowed up, and we went in to a frugal dinner at a long white scrubbed oak refectory table with a London vista into a small garden of brick walls and big chestnuts rising behind into the milky-golden twilight.

After dinner my grandfather walked slowly up the creaking stairs with their cold green linoleum and shut himself into his study. My grandmother lay down on the sofa in the big drawing-room and, closing her eyes, asked me to tell her about my voyage. Delighted at this show of interest I rushed up to my room at the top of the house and snatched from the suitcase the diary I'd laboriously been scribbling ever since I left Australia's faraway shores.

'What shall I read to you?' I said. 'Would you like to hear about New York?'

She nodded and I embarked on a hurriedly gabbled description of the salient features of the great city which was already beginning to take on at this distance something of the magic of the topless towers of Ilium. After a few minutes I suddenly caught the sound of my own voice and realized with annoyance that it was boring me with a catalogue of meaningless details. Without pausing, I raised my head and saw on my grandmother's face a look of long-suffering patience which filled me with remorse.

'Am I boring you, Maany?' I said. She smiled but did not answer. After a few moments, she said,

'Why don't you go to bed now? You must be tired coming all the way from America.'

*   *   *

Now began a period of three months' busy idleness and exciting discovery during which time I was fed and lodged free of charge by my grandparents at 6 Pembroke Gardens. Since my Mother had also been living with them for the past four years I suppose it seemed natural to them to put up with their grandson too. At any rate it never occurred to me to be astonished at their generosity. Though I was grateful for it, I rather took it all for granted. Perhaps at this distance one can look into the circumstances a bit and see what it was that made my grandparents extend over the years this continuous if sometimes resigned and anaemic hospitality.

My grandmother had been born Margaret Burne-Jones, the only daughter of the Pre-Raphaelite painter and his wife Georgiana. Georgiana had herself been one of the remarkably strong and tenacious daughters of an Ulster Methodist divine, Rev. George Browne Mac-Donald, notable in the family hagiography and to my generation—which was four removed from him—for the arresting locution : 'Offspring, spring off,' when one of his daughters sat too long on his lap.

My grandmother—the Margaret became Maany and she was so known to her friends and confidants, to her children and grandchildren—inherited the tenacity, not to say the stubbornness of her mother, combined with an exquisite faraway romantic streak from her father. She was very beautiful in a dreamy faerie queene sort of way and had a wonderful pure voice with a hint of throatiness in it that remained enormously attractive to me from the time I first remember her when I was four to the time I last saw her when she was well over eighty. I was in love with her all my life, and though I saw her for a total apprehended period of only five years, and at very long intervals, her memory remains vividly with me.

She was full of well-bred sparkle and wayward 'literary' mischief of a rather unconventional sort. She endeared herself to my brother and me as children by permitting occasional and so designated Bad

C*

Behaviour Days when we were allowed (usually in the safety of the servants' kitchen) to throw food at each other, pour mustard into the water, upset the soup, manufacture bread pellets and belch loudly. She kept in a drawer a list of all the misshapen variants of Mackail addressed to her by illiterate or careless correspondents. She also kept more startlingly—and this I didn't become aware of until the period of this book—another list of all the curious English names she had been able to find which implied the nether parts of the body, names such as Longbottom, Pricke, Codball and Glasscock. She was skittish and a bit of a tease but wonderfully humane and sensible in her judgements of people. Despite a highly literary-artistic upbringing and a pretty thick dose of William Morris socialism in her girlhood she had a strong sense of the orders and classes into which England was divided. No servant would ever use anything but the servants' entrance. On the other hand she always spoke with kindly politeness and charm. It was she who taught me that you should always praise when service of any kind was good and always complain when it was not. In the present age of jets and international travel I've still found it a good rule to follow.

Maany was—perhaps petite is not precisely the word—but delicately and neatly built, and of below medium height (her own mother was only five feet tall). She used only colourless lip salve and a faint dusting of pale pink powder; and she dressed in a way that was timeless because it had never been in or out of fashion. She carried her own air of artistic distinction and personal magnetism which depended neither on her dress, nor her furniture, nor her table.

Certainly not on dress. She wore pleated woollen or silk skirts that came to within six inches of the floor, long strings of glass and turquoise beads of the 1910 First Russian Ballet type, old rough pearls round her throat, and blouses which effectively concealed everything except her small neat waist of which she was very rightly proud. Her hats awed me. One was all of feathers in the shape of a great bird minus the head and beak, its wings stretching back and sideways, its tail at the nape of her neck. Another was like a flat soup tureen. Yet she didn't look old-fashioned or even recognizably of any particular era, unless it was the timeless eerie Arthurian land created by her father as he painted and re-painted the search for the Holy Grail: a land in which the women were apt to have smooth oval faces like my grandmother's, and be dressed in flowing robes of stuff heavy

74

enough to impart shape to the robe without imparting much to the women (or spirits) who inhabited them. Yet her style was highly original and she commanded attention whenever she entered a room.

Certainly not on furniture. To see how bizarre and eccentric, how very strange, without being ugly, was the furniture, it is necessary to take a brief tour of Number Six Pembroke Gardens. The house was built in the forties or fifties of last century in the wake of Cubitt and his merry men after they had drained the Belgravia marshes and begun the westward expansion of yellow stucco London. My grand-parents bought a fifty year lease of it in the mid 1890s and my grandfather died there in 1945, though my grandmother lived on another eight years in the care of her younger daughter in Surrey.

One opened the green front door with the red-painted knocker, straight into a small vestibule closed by glass doors of striated trans-lucency behind which vague nebulous shapes moved like fish in an aquarium. These doors in turn opened and straight ahead lay a corri-dor leading to the back of the house and into the garden; and also a pair of very steep stairs crawling up one wall and round the corner into mysterious upper quarters, yet lit dramatically at its first turn by a half landing, open to a view of the garden. This half landing, which contained two opposing wooden banquettes with straw-filled flowered linen bolsters, was surrounded on three sides by windows. My uncle when a boy had christened it 'The Semi-Turret', and the name stuck.

To the right as one stood at the front door was a large hall partly separated from the main corridor by a low revetment of bookcases. The main window of the hall looked out on to Pembroke Gardens. These, like many similarly named areas in London, were not gardens at all, but a street; the true garden being the Georgian Edwardes Square just beyond, and the private estate of Pembroke Lodge at the back with its huge chestnuts and oak trees. In the window-seat, in the period when I had lived at 6 Pembroke Gardens as a child between my mother's divorce and re-marriage, I used to sit playing marbles or dominoes with Maany and watching for my own mother to come down the street, or for Learie the lamplighter with his bicycle and long pole to tip the cocks of the lamp outside our house so that it surged into the pale chemically-yellow light of the famous—and now almost vanished—incandescent mantle. It was in this nook too that Maany told me of the cruel joke played on her by her brother, my Great Uncle Phil, when they had been waiting for their own mother to come home. 'Quick Margaret,' he'd say, 'Here she—ISN'T!' This, so Maany told us, reduced her to tears; but on her own admission she fell for the same trick time and again.

The rest of the hall was taken up by large glass-fronted bookcases containing many a wonderful treasure: The New English Dictionary in XIV volumes; collections of comic drawings by Caran D'Ache and H. M. Bateman; volumes of pioneer comic strip steel engravings from the pages of *Fun*, an early but now defunct rival to *Punch*, entitled *The British Workingman (By One Who does not believe in him)* and *The British Tradesman*.

And over in one corner, awkwardly perched on a small triangular shelf at elbow height and usable only by oneself perching on the edge of an oaken chest, was that indispensable but much mistrusted tool of the twentieth century: the telephone. Right up to the end it was of the antique two-piece variety and it was the only one in the house. If you lived on the top floor, you had to run down four flights of stairs to answer it, and your conversation was about as private as one held in a railway waiting-room.

Off the hall was the dining-room, a cheerful oblong giving on to the garden. This garden, in the curious way many London gardens have, no matter how small, gave the illusion of country because of the great trees which over-shadowed it from Pembroke Lodge. It was in fact no more than a square lawn surrounded by a gravel path and flowerbeds which seemed most of the time to contain golden rod and michaelmas daisies, or else the cook's ill-tended tomatoes.

The dining-room had Morris wallpaper, a chimney piece beneath which in winter burned a cheerful fire of anthracite flanked by brass andirons and backed by William de Morgan tiles. It also contained in one corner Maany's writing desk and just about the only comfortable armchair in the house.

But the principal piece of furniture was the long scrubbed-oak refectory table flanked by eight spindly black wooden rush-bottom chairs. When I was a little boy my grandfather used to up-end the table on two chairs and immediately it became a wondrous slide for children. My Great Uncle Phil used to amaze us all by passing coins right through the table, to our open-mouthed dumbfoundedness. Now of course it was more prosaic. Though the dining-room had occasionally been the site of well-remembered Bad Behaviour Days, what struck me about it now were the appalling and, as I fancied, appallingly primitive arrangements for serving the food and getting it up from the kitchen.

This particular chore was performed by Annie, a maid who had been with my great-grandmother up to the time of her death in 1920. Annie was gaunt and thin with wisps of sparse grey-brown hair, pebble lenses and ill-fitting store teeth the consistency of china eggs which shifted to and fro sideways—most alarming this—behind thin nervous lips. But Annie was a good sort, the nearest you could get to a family retainer, and three times a day each and every day she would struggle up a flight of narrow uneven wooden stairs from the basement kitchen with a tray loaded with hot dishes for the current meal. She arrived at the head of the stairs and leaned panting for a moment or two against the door-jamb before negotiating the final four feet to the dining-room table. My heart was torn between a gallant desire to help Annie and an ecstatic apprehension lest the tray beneath which she staggered might in the end prove too much for her and the whole kit and caboodle crash to the floor with a gratifying clatter. Unfortunately this never happened and Annie would creak unsteadily down the narrow wooden stairs with her dishes balanced precariously on the tray, held manfully against a jutting hip, into the penumbral gloom of the kitchen.

This was enormous and full of ancient bits of nineteenth-century kitchen machinery: a clumsy coffee grinder big as a ship's capstan, a circular knife sharpener; a great oval pan for boiling fish; green baize aprons for non-existent butlers and bootboys; silver dish covers hanging on hooks near the ceiling; a round earthenware filter upon stilts for purifying the chalky London water. The kitchen was a 'half basement' so that those washing up could just see over the red deckle-edged tiles and the scrawny lilies-of-the-valley on to the lawn, much as one might glimpse the surface of the surrounding sea from a submarine's periscope. To those in the garden the washers-up appeared as disembodied heads grinning up from the nether pit.

Off the enormous kitchen were a scullery, a pantry and a larder, all rather dark and mysterious. Forward into the front of the basement was the 'servants' sitting-room' with a view on to the 'area' and the iron railings along Pembroke Gardens. This was a comfy cosy little room with a fireplace and ornamental decorations of scalloped crepe-paper, oleographs of George V, Queen Mary, Edward

VII, Queen Alexandra and Albert Chevalier, for Annie had been a great admirer of his when he was 'on the halls'; a round table covered by a velveteen cloth with bobbles depending from it; a couple of old worn-down armchairs and of course always the *Daily Mirror* or the *News of the World* open at the 'Torso found in bath' story. These were kept fresh for me on the odd Saturday evening when, the grandparents and my mother being out, I would regale Annie with a bottle of surreptitious beer and she would take out her false teeth and tell me tales of my great-grandmother. On such nights we would cackle together like a couple of old crones and with catlike tread switch on the single bulb to examine my grandfather's modest wine cellar, or peer into the coal hole where the coke was kept.

Barbarously, or so it seemed to me though it was perfectly normal in all Victorian houses, Annie slept right at the very top of the house in a little slit of a room off the boxroom into which, neither as man nor boy, was I ever allowed to penetrate. But the rest of the top floor was open to all comers. Facing Pembroke Gardens was what had been in my boyhood the Day Nursery, notable for the scrubbed deal table in which was a large hole blown by Uncle Denis, when he was a boy, through injudicious blending of saltpetre in his chemistry set. This room had now become my mother's study where she wrote *Three Houses*, her girlhood reminiscences, her earliest 'Barsetshire' novels and her pseudonymous send-up of a voyage to Australia, *Trooper to the Southern Cross*. It had of course shrunk enormously in close to twenty years and was now a cheerful low-ceilinged room with the light from the Gardens filtering in through the tall sycamores. There was an easy chair, and a fireplace over which Mother had installed a paper-spiral snake on a spike, like the string of peel brandished by the smiling head waiter after he has successfully skinned an apple 'in one'. In the brightest corner of all was Mother's desk, an old-fashioned roll-top with innumerable pigeon holes stuffed with bundles of family letters tied in pink ribbon.

Opposite the Day Nursery and hence looking out on to the tall chestnuts and oaks of Pembroke Lodge—with a glimpse through the trees of St. Mary Abbot's Church and the modern roof of Derry and Toms' department store—was the Night Nursery. This was now my room, and even though it had shrunk so much, it still seemed strange to me to be sleeping now as a young man in the room where I had slept as a boy. No doubt to those whose homes are not disrupted by divorce, re-marriage and travel this is quite a normal experience; but to me it had two effects, one only odd and the other faintly disagreeable. It was odd to feel the years telescoped; to feel, as a palpable presence, the room surging forward to blot out my intervening years in Australia, to possess me as an 'Englishman', to forgive the fourteen years' antipodean hegira as an aberration, an irrelevance.

Less pleasant was the strong feeling of dependence induced by the room. It reminded me that I was not yet an earner; that I was wholly dependent on the bounty of my grandparents, as indeed was my mother who, during the whole seventy-one years of her life, lived over forty under their roof. I found this distasteful, and it was at this point that a small voice inside started nudging me back in the direction of Canada and of independence. But that was still a long way ahead, and if I wanted to shake off the domination of the 'night nursery' I could always go into 'Aunt Clare's room'.

My Aunt Clare was my mother's younger sister; gifted, warmhearted and amusing. I carried giggling memories of wonderful boyhood times with her, drawing pictures, playing the flute, reciting mildly naughty rhymes, interceding as peacemaker between my brother and me, and during the years in Australia the wonderful provider each birthday and Christmas of the pink Post Office money orders. I was therefore greatly disappointed now to learn that she was living in Germany and that I couldn't see her; but her room, the mirror-vision version of the night nursery, also looked out on to the big chestnuts and sideways across the parallel brown brick walls separating the back gardens, to the house where Mr. Bonar Law had spent his last years. I was allowed to use this room as my 'study' and in it I composed many unsaleable short stories and, of course, the immortal songs which were to earn me my future career with the jazz boys of Archer Street and Leicester Square—if I ever got to meet them.

The main disadvantage of the top rooms were that the lavatories were so inhumanly inaccessible. There was, it is true, a john in the sole bathroom of this large house, halfway down the stairs from the Night Nursery to the middle floor and the grandparents' room. It was, in fact, above the 'semi-turret' into which it not infrequently leaked and oozed if anyone—never me of course—stood too long dripping on the lino without putting down the cork bath mat. Never go to sleep in the bath, said Maany, with her horrendous tales of strong men who had come in from the hunt to steaming luxury and had been found hours later by the tweenie delirious with double pneumonia in a huge cube of ice. But it was considered 'unhealthy' to use the john in the bathroom—if you were male that is; the females were permitted its unrestricted use. The only alternative was to dash madly down four flights of stairs in a rush against time in the hope that when you finally reached the place of meditation— tucked incongruously beneath the stairs and just off the entry from the kitchen up into the dining-room—it would be 'vacant' and not 'engaged'. It was the old-fashioned type shaped like a desk with a large hole, and with a lever at the side which, when given a power-ful yank, produced an effluxion of water never quite powerful enough effectively to perform the function for which water closets are pre-sumably designed.

But on the way back, before creeping up the stairs decorated with my grandfather's plaster busts of Caesar and Vergil and the horse of Silene from the Parthenon, you could always peer into the Drawing Room and see if anyone were there. And if not, have it to yourself for a few strange minutes, for it was a really extraordinary room: a thin, fine-spun, pre-Raphaelite oasis in the heart of good grey bourgeois Kensington.

The room ran the length of the house from front to back with large windows at either end giving on to Pembroke Gardens and Pembroke Lodge. The first thing you noticed about the room was that, although it was cluttered, what it contained, being thin and spindly, somehow did not clutter it. Immediately opposite the door was a harpsichord above which hung a very large thinly painted study from Burne-Jones' briar rose series, *The Sleeping Beauty*; to the left was a clavichord painted red and lettered on the lid with the words *clavis cordi*, a gift to my grandparents on their marriage from Burne-Jones himself. Beneath the window was the Steinway grand bequeathed to his sister by my Great Uncle Phil when he died in 1926. Over the clavichord hung the study for Burne-Jones' *King Cophetua and the Beggarmaid*. Strawbottomed chairs with black precarious legs alternated with wooden chairs designed as studio props for the innumerable paintings Burne-Jones did of King Arthur and his Knights in their long progress from the sword in the stone to the Vale of Avilion. I think my great-grandfather's Welsh blood must have had something to do with his absolute obsession with the story of the San Graal. Arthur and Merlin; Galahad and Nimuë; Guinevere and Gawain: he just couldn't leave them alone.

Over beneath the back window was the sofa, the only comfortable piece of furniture in the room; for the rest—the rush-bottomed chairs and the King Arthur chairs—were not only very hard and uncurved to the appropriate human dimensions, but rickety as well. One sat on the very edge of one's seat, not only because to do anything else was uncomfortable, but because you felt that at any moment the seat itself might collapse. As an aid to easy and relaxed conversation these chairs were about as effective as a circular saw suspended over the head.

For the rest, the room contained my grandmother's second pigeon-holed leather-topped desk, convex mirrors in gilt frames, Dresden china, plates and tiles by William de Morgan, and, only partially hiding the wide dark stained and polished boards of which the floor was made, exiguous carpets and scatter rugs varying from Turkey through Axminster to Numdah. Not a room in which to feel comfortable, but on the other hand not one you'd be likely to forget. What my grandfather thought of it was difficult to tell, but to find the part of the house which reflected *his* atmosphere, as opposed to that of my grandmother, one had to mount the stairs to the middle floor—the only one which we have not so far visited—and open the door into his study.

My grandfather married my grandmother in 1888 when he was 29 and she 22—'the magic gap' as the Hindus call it. He was a son of the manse born in Ascog on the Island of Bute. He was sent to Ayr Academy and subsequently to Edinburgh University from which he graduated—urged on by helpful but minatory letters from his father in the best mid-Victorian-cum-Scottish evangelistic tradi-tion—at the incredible age of sixteen. It was all done on scholarships with that wonderful if slightly daunting combination of a piercing brain and a parsimonious frugality for which the Scots are famous. At Oxford where, appropriately enough, he was at Balliol, he secured a brilliant First in Classics and the Newdigate Prize. He also gained fame as the author of the immortal distich:

> My name is George Nathaniel Curzon
> I am a most superior person

Curzon, along with Canon H. C. Beeching of 'Going down hill on a bicycle' fame, was his contemporary. He continued as a don at Oxford, lacking some of the malicious asperities for which the breed is famous, and eventually gravitated into the Burne-Jones circle via William Morris whom he greatly admired and whose biographer he was to become.

His impact on my grandmother was such that *her* father assumed that the initials 'J.W.' must stand at the very least for Johann Wolfgang (in fact John William or 'Jack' as he soon became). Her impact on him has to be inferred. It might be said to have been deliberately played down in the bookplate which Burne-Jones designed for them: 'Ex libris Johannis et Margaretae Mackail'. Or perhaps this was regarded as the proper sequence of the sexes in Victorian times. But that there was an impact, that there had to be if my grandfather were flesh and blood (however much a younger generation might doubt this indisputable fact) is evident from my grandmother's looks at the time. She was a really shattering beauty. What the PRB called 'a stunner'.

So they were married and in 1890 my mother was born, and in 1892 my Uncle Denis; and we find them living in London, to be precise at 27 Young Street, Kensington—now utterly vanished, being simply a parking lot for John Barker & Co—and he working in the Board of Education. My grandfather had been offered the post of Master of Balliol, and, family rumour had it, other exalted Oxford positions. But he had preferred the humdrum life of a Whitehall civil servant and at the Board he served—home every weekday for 4 o'clock tea according to my mother's girlhood recollections—until his retirement in 1919 at the age of sixty. He had in the interim held the chair of Professor of Poetry at Oxford for the statutory five-year period; and he had also published and continued to publish an industrious and enormously distinguished corpus of biography, translation and essays.

But somehow his contemporaries believed that this brilliant and meticulous scholar had been denied—or had denied himself—the topmost academic achievements that were his for the plucking. He ended his life an honorary Doctor of Letters from both Oxford and Cambridge and from many other universities, and for the last ten years of that life he wore proudly the ribbon of the Order of Merit. Sufficient of an achievement, one would say, and certainly one of great distinction. Yet his contemporaries seemed to feel that he ought to have stayed at Oxford and for the fact that he did not they blamed his marriage: the tender trap; the silken embrace.

How true was it? His wife was certainly the apple of her father's eye, much as the son was a disappointment; not his fault, poor chap, he inherited the Burne-Jones melancholia and had the bad luck to try his skill in his father's own profession of painting. The family rumour had it that when my grandfather was offered an important post at Oxford—perhaps the Mastership of Balliol—he was willing, eager and able. It would seem almost incredible that he was not: his own old college; a life amid the dreaming spires where he had first known fame.

But, said the family, Maany threw a tantrum and said she couldn't bear to live so far away from London (distance London to Oxford by the GWR 63½ miles); couldn't bear to be separated from her father; from her mother. Whatever the truth, Ba gave in and though Burne-Jones died in 1898 one must suppose that in the preceding ten years the London habit had become too firmly ingrained to be further resisted.

To a young man all this seemed evident in the way Ba shut himself up and remained remote and fastidiously aloof from the family. Tallish, spare, slightly stooped with a head of thick and most distinguished white hair, he had a bristly white moustache over a firm chin, and blue eyes that crinkled with fun at the corners. With a most mellifluous Scottish voice he could nevertheless on occasion 'retire' into an impregnable citadel of gently smiling equivocation from which would occasionally emerge shattering dismissive monosyllables. Mother has drawn her own parents' portrait so well in her first novel, *Ankle Deep*, that it would be an impertinence for me to try to improve on the performance.

Certainly one didn't blame Ba, with this constant procession of children and grandchildren, for withdrawing into himself. Equally certainly the study, once one entered it, was a formidable, indeed a daunting place. It smelled partly of pipe tobacco, both fresh and old dottles; partly of Ribbon of Bruges which my grandmother was fond of burning on the middle floor, and some of which seeped and curled through the chinks of the closely guarded door. But the overwhelming smell was of books. Hundreds and hundreds of them, on three sides of the room; the fourth being a window looking out on to

Pembroke Gardens. They reached from floor to ceiling; and though the majority were the classics, Eng. Lit. and other learned or standard works, a very large proportion was his own output. These included the corrected galleys and—very donnish this—a first edition with meticulous notes of all printers' errors against the next edition. It was a memorable list: *The Life of William Morris* in two volumes; the translations of the *Iliad* and the *Odyssey*; of the *Georgics* and the *Aeneid*; his *Lectures on Shakespeare* and *Approach to Shakespeare; the Biblia Innocentium* (the bible simplified for children) and many many others. And yet the study was not a comfortable nor even a bookish place. It was not my idea of a don's study. There were no leather armchairs; no armchair at all in fact. The curtains were thin cotton Indian Tree-of-life pattern. My grandfather worked at a table, not at a desk. His seat was the similar spartan rush-bottomed spindly affair that was found downstairs. It was a room for standing erect while one thumbed books, sitting erect while one wrote them; but not for lounging or relaxing.

The top shelf of one bookcase was filled entirely with his diaries. He had kept one since he was a boy and he allowed me to read them. Though they interested me as family fodder I was in general much disappointed at the banality of the entries. If I'd known then that the thoughts which careful men (no matter how distinguished) commit to their diaries are so often colourless, I might have been less disappointed. For he was the most careful of men. Kindly but remote, with the lightsome malice and dry wit of the don. Somewhere fires must have burned; must once have burned. I was too young to be able to detect them. A vague family rumour referred to an infatuation with Mrs. Patrick Campbell. But of course that was not for the diaries. But one evening, browsing through the latest diary, this present year in fact, I came across an entry that electrified me. 'Graham brought an Australian friend to dinner. Afterwards they both went out *without saying good evening*!'

Suddenly I saw vividly not only my own unthinking conduct, but also how paper-thin was the welcome which had met me at 6 Pembroke Gardens when I first arrived. Here was my grandfather snarling. But not directly at me; only into his diary. It was time for me to leave this grandparental nest. I did, but not before I had averted by a hairsbreadth being evicted.

* * *

6 Pembroke Gardens, W.8

One weekend my grandparents announced that they were going to the country to stay with friends. Mother was going away to stay with other friends. Everyone concerned was very sorry no invitation had been extended to me. They hoped I wouldn't mind being left alone at 6 Pembroke Gardens. With visions of stately homes perhaps forever denied to me I nodded glumly and helped them all down with the baggage: my grandfather's leather gladstone bag from his sparse spare single room with its cold china ewer and basin standing forlornly in one corner; my mother's carpet bag from her bedroom with its big oval cheval glass, the tallboys with their exciting smells of glacé kid and lavender and faded perfume and the gritty pungency of ostrich feathers; my grandmother's canvas trunk from her enormous bedroom running across the front of the house with its fireplace and its sofa and chairs for private teas with friends. They all embarked in their several taxis and I returned to the gaunt empty house feeling very morose and sorry for myself. Suddenly it hit me with an almighty wallop. Alone! The whole of 6 Pembroke Gardens. A party! A good old dinkum Aussie party. Whacko!! I ran to the telephone.

The following night about twenty of my young friends male and female descended on 6 Pembroke Gardens led by a demon pianist who at once fell upon the Steinway and within a few moments had an admiring throng leaning over the keyboard while I circulated with the beer. But the drawing room at first proved to be a pretty off-putting place in which to have a party. The sharp spindly furniture was not conducive to lounging. The Burne-Jones paintings didn't exactly look disapproving, but they looked so ethereal, so drained of red corpuscles, so remote, that the voices of the beery couples insensibly dropped as they regarded them. We pulled up the rugs and tried to dance to the HMV handcranked portable but it wasn't until the beer had been well and truly gulped in Aussie fashion and couples started to catch sight of themselves in the gilt convex mirrors that the party started to get off the ground.

By midnight the joint was really jumping and couples were starting to sneak out into the hall and up the stairs. I was instantly sobered at the thought of their trying to use my grandparents' rooms for illicit purposes, and I bounded up past an interlocked couple in the Semi Turret to the bedroom floor. The bedrooms were intact, but somebody seemed to be in my grandfather's study. Silhouetted

85

against the lighted room beyond was the figure of my grandmother!
My heart skipped a beat. After an ageless interval during which I
heard beery voices drowning out the wonderful piano from among
the spindly chairs and King Cophetua's Beggarmaid, a voice said
tremulously:

'Oh, Mister Graham.'

Only Annie! What a relief! I went forward and shut the door
behind me.

'Annie. Why did you come up?'

'I didn't come up, Mister Graham, I came down!'

I noticed for the first time that she was in a Sherlock Holmes-ish
mouse-coloured dressing gown.

'I couldn't sleep. Oh, why didn't you tell me you was having
people in?' Annie's eyes gazed up at me in tormented indecision
from behind the pebble lenses, while her mouth worked and the
teeth slipped and skidded. Her sparse wisps of hair were scraped
back tight into the bun so that her forehead looked like the skin
on a kettledrum. I blurted out,

'Annie, I'm terribly sorry. I just didn't think.'

She nodded. 'And now I'll have to tell the Mistress.'

I gripped her fiercely by the arm. 'No, Annie, no you don't. Why
couldn't this be just a secret between you and me?'

Beery catcalls came floating up the stairwell. People were calling
my name; what kind of crisis was this? Was I just being missed?
Was the beer running out? Were—foul thought—the grandparents
arriving? I yelled that I was coming and then I grabbed Annie again.

'Annie,' I said earnestly, 'You look terribly tired. I think you need
a good drink of beer.' She simpered a bit.

'Oh, Mister Graham.'

'Come on,' I said. 'Just you and me together.'

Both her hands went up to her mouth and she looked stricken.
Her head started to shake.

'Not here. Not here, sir, in Master's study. I couldn't do it.'

'How about in my room then?' I asked. Before she could protest,
I hurried her upstairs, sat her down on my bed and poured her a
foaming stein of beer. 'Chin, chin!' I said, raising the bottle and
sighting at the moon along its telescopic barrel. Annie giggled.

'You are a one,' she said.

'Between us, eh?' I leered.

86

'Oh yes,' she said giggling.

'Here, Annie, here's the rest of the bottle. Take it into your room, eh? And we'll try not to keep you awake. The grandparents aren't coming in, are they?'

She grinned owlishly, 'Oh no, sir. Not till Monday afternoon.'

'Fine then,' I said. 'We've got all weekend. I'll clean up the shambles in the morning. Now off you go to bed.' I patted her arm. 'It's our secret,' I said.

'Yes,' said Annie blinking behind the glasses and twitching at the mouse-coloured dressing-gown. 'Our secret.' Then turning suddenly on me as she entered her room, and brandishing the bottle aloft in one hand, she suddenly barked, 'Better be, hadn't it?' She shut the door with a slam and a giggle.

I went downstairs and after a while people began to leave. When they'd all gone I cleared up the mess. There wasn't much really; no cigarette burns, thank God, just a few beer glass marks and stamped out stubs. But I had an uneasy feeling that somehow the ark of the covenant had been profaned. Annie never breathed a word and the grandparents, if they suspected anything upon their return, never said so. But I had a notion that my welcome hung by a thread and that I ought to get out of 6 Pembroke Gardens as fast as I could and for good and all.

Chapter Seven

ROAD TO KANGAROO VALLEY

I T wasn't all that easy, partly owing to a certain indolent streak and partly to the fact that Mother rather touchingly wanted to show me to various friends and relatives. It was about six weeks before I could get free and, though my puritanical side fretted at not being up and about, my other side certainly enjoyed a glimpse of a London 'season'. Hyde sallied forth in tails, with social-conscience Jekyll firmly battened under hatches in the sub-conscious. Perhaps at that age this is understandable, even though it was the days of the unemployed and the Jarrow marchers.

Mother, who was appalled by the fusty undergraduate remnants I had brought with me, outfitted me handsomely with both dinner-jacket and white tie and off I went to dinner parties in SW1 and SW3 with bright young things; to receptions at 9 Bruton Street, Claridges and the Mayfair; to dances with the music of Debroy Somers, Harry Roy, Carroll Gibbons and their respective orchestras. What I principally remember about that mad scurry were the wonderful late June nights when the sky stayed silvery bright until ten at night, and by half past two in the morning the starlings were already twittering.

Then came the country houses. I went first to Little Stoke on the Thames near Wallingford to see my exciting politically renegade cousin, Oliver Baldwin. It was an extremely comfortable, not to say luxurious, bachelor establishment, with male servants and smoked salmon and *crème brulé*, which I noticed that Mother, sustained on frugal 6 Pembroke Gardens fare, wolfed as eagerly as I did. Oliver was at that time Labour MP, socialist orator, broadcaster, gossip columnist, *bon vivant*, *épateur* of the bourgeoisie and general thorn in the side of his long-suffering father. To a youngster, of course, such attitudes were immensely intoxicating for they seemed to set the seal of approval on rebellion and snook-cocking. In a rather indiscriminate unthinking way I conceived an immense admiration for Oliver who was also very kind to me. I somehow didn't see the irony —or if I did, I relished the paradox—of this well-upholstered socialist quaffing brandy in his country house while going into ecstasies over the social realism of a current jazz hit *Buddy, can you spare a dime?* which he made me play and sing to him over and over again.

Next came Parliament Piece and its hostess, Violet Wyndham, who appreciated my playing of *Heat Wave* (of course I'd picked that up, as I told all and sundry, at the skirts of Ethel Waters herself). It was a marvellous weekend of thick lush foliage somewhere in Berkshire, thick roasts and melting pastries, thick brocade and satin evening dresses and silk-lapelled dinner jackets. I was appalled at the ease with which the wild colonial boy was slipping and slithering into this sybaritic life where everyone seemed to have enough money, where the fat of the land became a reality, and not a meaningless cliché; exemplified in linen sheets, bath towels as big as carpets, clothes 'laid out' on the bed and amontillado in a black tie. The only approach to the reality I had once known was provided by a tennis party. It was, regretfully, on grass and not the good old Aussie asphalt I knew; but I instantly found that my journeyman Aussie skill far outmatched that of the effete English. However, they were playing for fun and I was playing to win, as well as for fun. This was somehow wrong. In my agony and embarrassment I skied a ball and it went high over the tall yew hedge and into the kitchen garden.

'That's all right, sir,' I yelled at my host, 'I'll get it.'

'Don't bother,' he shouted testily. 'Use this one.'

'Okay, sir,' I cried cheerfully and proceeded to belt that one too across and into the kitchen garden.

'Don't worry, sir!' I yelled again. 'I'll get it.'

My host's empurpled face glared at me as I leaped lightly into the gooseberries. I could tell that I wasn't really a social success.

Mother sighed and decided to try again. This time it was to be Stanway, the home of the Earl and Countess of Wemyss and March. Stanway, Winchcombe, Glos., not far from Honeybourne, not even very far from Evesham, in the heart of the Cotswolds. I'd been there before as a five-year-old, and I carried with me in the second-class compartment of the champing GWR, and later in the be-rugged open tourer across the hills from Moreton-in-Marsh, vague memories of mullioned windows, warm yellow stone walls, slanting magical sunlight through deep trees, and dew in the morning. The reality for once was not far different, for Stanway was a real country house and the Wemysses real aristocracy though depatricianized and made familiar in our eyes through Mary Wemyss' lifelong friendship with my grandmother.

The beginning, it is true, was inauspicious. There is nothing so exasperating as a second-class railway carriage with its straw ticking covered in red buttoned carpetbag, when you *know* you ought to be travelling first because your hosts can afford to. I pointed this out to Mother. Her unanswerable reply, as we rattled through Didcot Junction, was that, as she was paying the return fares, she would decide how we would travel. Of course, if I wanted to travel first (personally she wouldn't dream of it; it was a waste of money) I was always welcome to pay the difference. I was silent and subsided morosely into the copy of the *New Statesman* with which, by an ostentatious flourish, I was advertising my kinship with the underdog while supping at the fleshpots of the landed gentry. A not uncommon means of salving the conscience at that time.

The be-rugged tourer—an ancient and noble Daimler—was the curtain-raiser. Stanway, when we reached it, was a Tudor mansion with diamonded chimneys set in rows, warm sandstone walls, mullioned windows, lych gates, dower houses, tithe barns, a private chapel and all the paraphernalia of as near a feudal relic as I was to see until I visited India twenty years later. I had to pinch myself to keep awake. A footman showed me to my room. I had a private bath not quite as large as a fives court. My exiguous smalls were laid out neatly for me on my bed; patched underpants and all. The bath was 'drawn', the heavy cretonne curtains pulled tight, to shut out the divine English evening and the divine heady English garden smell.

We dined at an endless table with candlelight reflected in the gleamingly polished oak. The hall in which we dined was so tall that you couldn't see the roof, only the hammer beams that supported it. A canopied fireplace as big as a suburban railway station gaped at us. Pikes and spears, chainmail, hauberks and breast plates flickered in the evening light. All the accoutrements of the English weekend in the grand style were there: gentle tennis; smoked salmon sandwiches in the rose garden; word games and dumb crambo in the evening to keep the mind well limbered up; sedate walks in the Cotswold glades; and over all the charming absent-minded hospitable kindness of Lady Wemyss. With her full skirts sweeping the ground, her multitudinous veils, her elusive key ring and housewife, her aristocratic beak and her shrewd kindly eyes, she has been forever enshrined as Lady Emily Leslie in Mother's book *Wild Strawberries*. I will go further. If you take equal parts of Stanway, the late J. L. Garvin's house near Beaconsfield, Beaconsfield village during the war and childhood memories of Rottingdean in Sussex you have a very fair approximation of Mother's Barsetshire immortalized in thirty-seven separate novels.

I was intoxicated by all this, but uneasy too. Not only were the acrobatic, highly allusive word games beyond my capacity, but I was also secretly ashamed of myself for wasting my time at English country houses when I ought to be out helping the socialist cause or combating the Nazis. The papers were full of Dollfuss, the new Austrian chancellor, and of how Hitler, the new German one, didn't care for him. Mussolini was sending troops to the Brenner. I chafed as I sat in my gorgeous bedroom eating eggs and bacon on a tray and devouring the *Sunday Times*. What right had I to be enjoying these things?

Mother and I both returned to London in a pretty testy mood: I, annoyed with myself for spinelessness and fleshpot eating; Mother, annoyed at me for my oafish behaviour. However she decided to try once again, and down we went this time to Oxford for a long week-end to stay with P. E. Matheson, a retired classics don and contemporary of my grandfather's who lived in a modest house on Headington Hill. Ah, this was more like it. A springless bed in an academic-spartan house; crackling humorous conversation and personally guided tours of the Oxford colleges, conducted at terrifying speed by old Matheson himself.

I would come down to breakfast to find him scrubbed to within an inch of his life and his face covered with tufts of cotton wool where he had cut himself while shaving. He had one of those lean, alert, pink and bony faces, and one of those stringy turkey-gobbler necks that seem destined to present bumps, nodules and sharp edges to even the most skilful shaver. He looked to me as if he had been cutting himself shaving for the past sixty odd years, and his watery blue eyes beamed out with gristly determination from an absolute forest of scrapes and nicks. While I ate my pallid three minute egg (served in the old-time nursery fashion with thin fingers of bread and butter), and drank strong tea in a 'father's cup', he puffed away at his pipe and outlined our activities for the day.

These were certainly formidable, but not to him. He knew the whole rabbit warren of Oxford like his own hand and he carried me along with him at a brisk trot through quads, up staircases, across bridges, down alleys until I was ready to drop, at the same time keeping up a rapid drumfire of historical anecdotes, statistics, and asides. We missed out All Souls, Keble and the women's colleges, but we 'did' just about everything else, including the splendours of New College, the opulent spaciousness of Christ Church, the cool dank antiquities of Merton and the bland self-importance of Magdalen. Neither the Bodleian nor the Sheldonian nor the Radcliffe Camera escaped our eyes; to say nothing of the statue of Dr. Fell and the bust of Shelley and the Morris wallpaper in Exeter. I was exhausted.

'Never mind,' said Mother. 'Tonight you'll see another side of Oxford life. Mr. Matheson's taking you to dine in Hall. At High Table !' she added with awe in her voice.

It turned out to be the Hall of New College and, under Mr. Matheson's wing, I was very small potatoes at a High Table which included the Warden, H. A. L. Fisher, together with Professor Myres, Professor Margoliouth, John Buchan and Robert Lynd, at that time writing 'middles' for the *New Statesman* as 'YY'. I was greatly subdued by this company, despite the sprightly proddings of Mr. Matheson, the natural kindliness of Buchan (primed no doubt by Mother as to my adoration of his Richard Hannay books) and the vinous benignity of Fisher at whose home we had stayed in Sheffield many years before and whose wife Lettice was an old friend of Mother's. But it was all too much for me and I subsided into a strangled silence varied by occasional blurting outbursts of painful gaucherie.

When the port arrived, however, my embarrassment gave way to an honest indignation. For the bottle, in order to negotiate the corner of the High Table, was placed on a little wooden railway, hooked to a silken rope and thence solemnly hauled up the slope by the next man. To see these elderly dons, their faces flushed with wine, boozing away aided and abetted by this sybaritic, this decadent device, filled me with censorious annoyance. Better the crudities of Australia or the bitter cold of Canada than thus to waste my substance in this odious manner. Mother, perhaps without knowing it, confirmed my view, for afterwards she gave a sharp and witty description of the men arriving after their port to 'join the ladies', as seen by one of the ladies. According to her, Herbert Fisher's face was beet-red; Robert Lynd looked as if someone had wiped his off with a damp cloth; my own innocent young eyes were bloodshot, and the only man who appeared normal was John Buchan. I hated it that Mother should think of me in this way and I slunk off to Magdalen where my old Melbourne friend Ross Campbell, now Rhodes scholar for Victoria, had rooms. Over Chablis and rusks—all he had—we decided to visit Paris for a week of innocent sinfulness, and under cover of this device I was at last able to leave 6 Pembroke Gardens.

But meanwhile, what about a job? Buoyed up on full board and lodging at 6 Pembroke Gardens and by the remains of 'Uncle' Graham Peel's insurance policy, I was protected from the harsh realities of this Depression year, and while this did give me a paralysing sense of guilt it failed to give me what I really needed: a good kick in the seat of the pants to pry me loose from dependence.

Of course there was always the immortal music. Through my *Australian Musicmaker and Dance Band News* contacts I made the acquaintance of Stan Patchett. One of the very early connoisseurs of jazz, a collector of old Brunswick and Parlophone recordings ten years before the jazz clubs and twenty years before LP, Stan was a simple, kindly, generous and utterly dedicated jazzbo. He was the pioneer of a cult and a profession since popularized by people like Leonard Feather and Norman Granz. He lived, worked, ate, slept, spoke and dreamed jazz, or 'swing' as it was just then beginning to be called. He lived in a two-room flat on an upper floor in Clarges Street, this posh address being provided less by his own earnings as a jazz addict than by those of his wife who ran a cosmetic business. She was always kindness itself in the way of beer and sandwiches on the bottom of a double bed when a fresh batch of Stan's impecunious young friends came bursting up out of the Green Park tube station.

They were both Australians and this was another bond. It made things that much easier for me. I showed the immortal music to Stan. He told me with devastating frankness and entirely unconscious charm that it was no good; but, typically, he didn't want me to let him be the judge. He would introduce me to others, more knowledgeable than he was, and perhaps . . . who knew?

Stan certainly tried, and so far as I could see, for my blue eyes only. We went down to Datchet by train to spend the day with Reginald Foresythe (and his 'New Music'). The great man told me as kindly as he could that my stuff was no good. Under Stan's solicitous eye it was like a painless injection. Never mind. Let's get another opinion—maybe a publisher. No, not Irwin Dash; he's Reg's publisher. Someone else. So we played (or rather I played) the stuff to Peter Maurice. No go. Maybe, said Stan, we should 'present' it more. How about a singer? So I got hold of Andrea Warren (née Troubridge) through Mother's Old Boy net; a young woman of a flower-like beauty and a clear true soprano. She very kindly consented—on both our behalfs—to appear in full evening rig at eleven a.m. on the stage of the Windmill (with me at the keyboard) and run through half a dozen of my immortal compositions. Or rather, she meant to, but the impresario stopped us both—out of sheer compassion—when two numbers had been sung. Not quite what we want. Go away and work at them a bit. Andrea never bore me any ill-will, but I thought, well, now really the next time I *must* 'present' it myself.

Next time proved to be in the Gargoyle nightclub in Soho and once again it was Mother who provided the entrée through David Tennant, one of its founders. I sat at the piano and played and sang while a group of brassy theatrical women, who were supposed to be listening with bated breath, talked and smoked and clinked martini glasses as I performed my stint. It was excruciating and I don't know how I did it; but to prove that my music really was immortal—and also to get a job—I was prepared to do anything.

'Has he stopped?'

'Oh, do go on, darling.'

'Play us some more.'

I suddenly caught sight of Mother's face through the twilight smoke of a London summer evening. She was really suffering. With me; perhaps more than me.

'Thanks awfully, deah. Not *quite* what we want.'

No, it wasn't, but in the end it did land me a month's work doing a turn in a café off Leicester Square. And with the few quid I'd earned, I was ready to go off to Paris with Ross and also ready to concede that the career of a jazz composer and/or pianist was not for me. Before I went there came a piece of electrifying news. My father was coming over. He'd taken me at my word, and would visit me in London and my brother Colin in Brussels, where Colin was at that time in the gas business. My father expected to be on this side of the water for a month. He would arrive on the *Empress of Canada* next week.

* * *

I discussed the matter with Ross as we jounced about in our third-class carriage on the boat train from Calais. I'd sent a card to the Russell Hotel 'to await arrival', explaining that I'd be away and suggesting to my father that he go direct to Brussels. Ross thought it was a wonderful idea, very romantic and all that. Why didn't we both go on from Paris to Brussels and all have a great big party? Terrific! We laughed like drains, and turned to *Paris Soir*. The headline said: HINDENBURG S'AFFAIBLIT.

We spent a week in Paris savouring all the inevitable delights. Not only the Casino de Paris, the Eiffel Tower and the Louvre, but a most foolish excursion by 'taxi' with a 'guide' to a room where a totally unexpected champagne cork popped—at our expense—across a sea of promenading breasts and buttocks. The bill flourished was so staggering that we paid it at once and ran, thankful to be able to still manage the onward trip.

'Skinned!' we yelled into the uncaring night and the lime-juice glare of the arc lights on the plane trees along Boulevard St. Michel. 'Oh boy, are we a couple of bloody fools!' The alarm and excitement —it lasted all of six minutes—had cost us the equivalent of ten English pounds. We went soberly to our rooming house on the Rue Gay Lussac and next morning took the train for Brussels.

Brussels proved to be at once exhilarating and matey: more easily grasped, more provincial, in fact more our style. We got hold of my brother and his friend Bobby Hayne and all went out beyond Uccle to the local Luna Park where we stabbed our heads through holes in plasterboard scantling to emerge as 'De Familie Yo-Yo': a ghastly memento to that intermittently popular toy. We listened to my father sing *The Self Banished* and the *Twa Sisters of Binnorie* and *Der Doppelgänger* in a tremulous full-throated deep-chested bay. His rich treacherous voice had not lost its power to grab your intestines and tie them in knots against your will. Listening to him breached social fortresses, made castles crumble and found you alone on the

darkling plain filled with a nameless dread. It was a voice that un-
manned you : the rich gritty bray of the authentic bard.

The Iserentants—Mayou and Victor—in whose modest lawyer's
and artist's home the performance took place, regarded him as a man
from Mars, though his communication with them and their Belgian
guests was, being wordless, instantaneous and deep. I wished irra-
tionally, among the chintz-covered pouffes and studio couches, with
the cottage piano and the salmon coloured walls hung with Mayou's
paintings, that Mother could hear him. Impulsively and perhaps
rashly I sent her a postcard next day describing the occasion.

We all travelled back together by the Ostend packet and my father
stayed on for a few days at the Russell Hotel, seeing old musical
friends, Hamilton Harty, Maggie Teyte, George Reeves. Once, so he
told me in a moment of unwise relaxation in his room in that
monstrous place of vitrified gamboge tiles, he telephoned Mother. I
was agape.

'What did she say?'

'Well, ye see, she said nothing.'

'Nothing?'

'I just said "May I speak to Angela please?" I didn't like to say
Mrs. Thirkell. And she said "Who's speaking?" And I said "It's
Jim."'

'And then?'

'She hung up.'

'Oh dear!'

I was terribly disappointed for my father, though he seemed to
take it philosophically enough. Match-making notions skittered
through my immature young mind, but instantly foundered on the
fact that Mother was already married. To George Thirkell back in
Australia. Australia and Canada.

'Mother, my father called you up!'

'I know.'

'He told me he did.'

'Well, so he did.'

'He said you hung up on him.'

'So I did.'

'Why?'

'I didn't want to speak to him.'

'Why not?'

Road to Kangaroo Valley

'Because I didn't that sweater you're wearing has a hole in it, better let me darn it for you before you take off for Hogarth Road.'

*   *   *

Hogarth Road it was to be. Earl's Court S.W.5. Not with Ross Campbell who had returned to Oxford, but with another Australian friend who was trying to break into the London theatre. Then, as now, Earl's Court was chockful of Aussies. Kangaroo Valley in fact. But first I had to say goodbye to my father.

He was leaving from Southampton on the *Empress of Britain* bound for Quebec, whence he would make the clattering journey on the high iron five hundred miles into the heart of midcontinent and 'Toronto the Good'. I found myself half-envying him. Colin and I went down to Waterloo Station to see him off and afterwards we sent a wire to the ship, Colin's idea: 'Best wishes for voyage and the next hundred years.' It was agreed that Colin would visit Canada next year. As I grasped my father's firm brown mottled hand with the twisted little finger, and the big amethyst signet ring, and looked at his craggy, benign and evasive face, I said,

'I might come out again myself. Just to see you,' I added.

His reply was both conventional and, as I now recognize, Canadian.

'You'll be very welcome. Very welcome indeed.'

My brother and I watched the train snake off towards Clapham Junction, sketched brief salutes, and parted; he back to Brussels and I to the upstairs flat in Kangaroo Valley. From that moment on we reverted to our own names and Thirkell vanished into oblivion.

All started off well in our walk-up flat. It had a 'front room' glaring across thirty feet of vacancy to narrow-chested grey brick terrace houses, and two bedrooms that gave out on the Underground. Had we but known it, this was almost exactly at the spot where the murderers placed the body on the roof of the train in *The Bruce-Partington Plans*, and were foiled only by Holmes' superhuman gimlet-eyed vigilance. And a bathroom. A great luxury this, or so we were told by the concierge, a beet-faced ex-pugilist who clearly regarded all 'colonials' with much suspicion.

'I suppose it's a bit out of the ordinary for you to have a couple of Australians here,' we ventured.

'Out of the ordinary? Blimey, we 'ad a bloke with a turban once.'

D

Finding a Father

We tacked our sheepskins to the wall, my MA and Roy's LLB; and I started to work at the café off Leicester Square and he at the Q Theatre with Frank Birch.

But first there had to be distractions. For if we were frank, we had to admit that neither of us was entirely destitute. I was still pulling down the remains of Uncle Graham's insurance policy at the rate of £3 a week from the PO Savings account; Roy had funds of his own which ran to a beat-up two-seater. Since we didn't know how long we'd be in England there was the temptation to do a bit of sightseeing once a few weeks' temporary work had pulled us in a few extra pounds. We toured the Lake District together in the beat-up car, marvelling at Grasmere and Rydal Water and being too young and impressionable to turn up our noses at the tourist gimmicks and the 'Teas with Hovis'. Roy went down to the West Country and I went over to Brussels to stay with Colin. We devoured the art galleries, including, perhaps typically, the Musée Wirtz with its melodramatic romantic 'horror' paintings, and excluding—inexcusably—the Van Eyck altarpiece in Ghent. During the course of a flying visit to Aachen, a sour-looking fellow in a landwehr cap and a swastika brassard clipped us for 2 Reichsmarks for the Wintershilfeswerke. Hitler, a newly chosen Führer of the newly proclaimed Third Reich, seemed to cast a shadow over everything. Europe, even England, began to seem stifling.

And then one drab foggy day in November when the streets and the air seemed full of floating greenish slime, I caught a glimpse, down the long corridors of the Tate Gallery, of a new rosy world of startling brilliance. When I eventually reached it, it turned out to be Seurat's *La Baignade*. It was my introduction to the Post-Impressionists and I plunged in right over my head with a fine blend of passion and ignorance. For weeks I haunted the galleries and started the long road back from Post-Impressionism and Fauvism to first principles. It was typical of my untutored enthusiasm that I should approach what was to turn out to be my career through the back door. I should have started out with the Van Eyck altarpiece and ended with Post-Impressionism, but I travelled the road in precisely the opposite direction. I floundered a great deal, for I had no one to teach me, but I had a set of values of a sort from an avid reading of Clive Bell and Roger Fry, and I plunged gaily on.

Christmas was coming and suddenly the theatre loomed for both

of us. Through the Q we'd somehow got a lead to Norman Marshall's
Gate Theatre at the foot of Villiers Street and it was rumoured that
none other than the great Hermione Gingold was looking for material
for sketches. We worked like demons and 'Ging' took a liking to our
stuff. When the Gate Revue—the intimate theatre of those days—
opened for the Christmas season, our sketches were in and our names
on the programme along with those of 'Ging', Walter Leigh, that
wonderfully gifted composer of light music, and Hedley Briggs, the
stage designer. It was wild and wonderful with rehearsals in the
chilly fog; bottle parties in Eric Maschwitz's flat; footlight romances
and bitchery among the cast; greasepaint and smelly dressing-rooms;
applause and cat calls; sweat and distant glory. When it was all over
I had enough to plunge into Europe once again and gobble up the
galleries; but on my return Roy greeted me with a long face.

'We've got to leave Hogarth Road.'

'Why?'

'I'm going to Luton.'

'What ever for?'

'The play's going on the road. It's a big chance and we might get a
London opening.'

I nodded glumly. How could I support, on my dwindling resources,
a flat or bedsitter on my own? It was cold and raw and the streets
were grey and the unemployed panhandling outside Earl's Court
station.

At this point, quite ludicrously, came a letter from Oliver Baldwin
very kindly inviting me to stay with him at his uncle's villa near
Algiers. I laughed sardonically. What would I use for money? I
didn't have any of my own, and I was absolutely determined not to
ask Mother. But I did want the sun and I did want to shake off
scuffed old sooty London. I thought again of sunny Canada. Cold
yes, but surely sunnier than this? I wrote to my father telling him
I'd like to come out. I wouldn't be a burden to him. I assured him
I'd be self-supporting (on the dregs of Uncle Graham's policy and
unspent Christmas presents from parent and grandparents). But just
the same I would like a job. Could he kindly canvass the openings?

Meanwhile the Hogarth Road partnership dissolved and I waited
in a fury of impatience. Roy went off to Luton. Oliver went off to
Algiers. I took a lonely bedsitter in Cambridge Terrace for a month.
I'd give Canada just that long to make up its mind about me. My

father's letter was cautious. He was glad I was coming; he'd be happy to put me up; he would do what he could for me. It seemed there might be an opening for a leader writer on one of the Toronto dailies. On an assignment basis to begin with. Of course there wouldn't be much money in it to start with; but a young fellow . . . land of opportunity . . . great future . . .

I was jubilant. A new country, a new job, almost a new personality. Mother received the news calmly and gave me a handsome going-away present. I think she would somehow have liked me to stay on in England and enter into the heritage which in her imagination was reserved for her sons, if only they'd been correctly brought up: a sort of Barsetshire life as an impecunious but attractive and above all biddable young country writer or interior decorator or estate agent. But alas—and it was in part her responsibility—I'd been raised in Australia and had the wrong set of values. I laughed in the wrong places; couldn't even recognize, let alone salaam to, the appropriate sacred cows. On the other hand I hadn't cost her a nickel since I was eighteen and didn't propose to now; so she heaved a dark brown sigh and gave me a quick warm half-embarrassed hug, and I was off.

On the *Scythia*, an ancient Cunarder bound for Canada? Well no, not exactly; you see the St. Lawrence is closed in winter, and the rail fare from Saint John, New Brunswick, is really more than I can afford. No, the *Scythia's* bound for Boston and New York and I'll take a bus up to Toronto. A bus? Heavens! Isn't it rather a long way? Oh, between four and five hundred miles, I guess. You guess? Aren't you becoming a Canadian a little prematurely? Well, one thing I'm not going to become is English, you sarcastic old . . . Anchors aweigh!

I landed ten days later in New York, having travelled third class in the iron belly of the old Cunarder, with a US transit visa which had cost me an ill-spared ten dollars and permission to stay for a month in Canada. The gargantuan towers of Manhattan slashed the sky as dramatically as a year ago and the great throb of the city reached me from the shore. But proceedings began with a near disaster in the immigration shed on the North River.

'What's the idea?'

'How do you mean?'

'This passport.'

Road to Kangaroo Valley

'It's valid, isn't it?'

'Sure, it's valid, but it says here you're a tutor, and your destination form says you're a journalist.'

'Well, that's right. I used to be a tutor, and now I'm a journalist.' (At least I'm going to be.)

'You shoulda put tutor on the form.'

'I'm sorry.'

'Okay. I guess you're the same guy. Away you go.'

I checked in at the old Dorp Hotel. They affected to remember me and the negro elevator boy smiled a knowing smile. But when I dialled her number I found that Pris was down in Florida. After a brief surge of unreasoning bitterness—in which I found myself thinking that Joan would never have behaved that way back in Melbourne—I went out on to Seventh Avenue; but it was blisteringly cold and I soon beat a retreat. I gave myself a few days at the Metropolitan, the Frick, the Museum of Modern Art and the New School for Social Research and then late on a late winter's evening I boarded a Greyhound bus for Toronto.

Under the Hudson by the Holland Tunnels and up once again on to the Pulaski Skyway and Newark. But then north and west through the Delaware Water Gap to the scrawny coal-pitted hills around Scranton and at last grey dawn at Buffalo with my eyelids stuck together and the whole bus smelling of sleep and sweat. But as we approached the American end of the Peace Bridge my heart gave a lift. For the magnetism of the great caterwauling tower-topped colossus I'd left behind me in the night somehow seemed feebler here. The sun burst through the clouds and over on the Canadian side late winter snow, fresh fallen, sparkled and glistened in the sunlight. A Union Jack stirred briskly at the masthead of the customs house and the quiet Canadians who examined my single trunk and my passport made no comments about tutors. Though I'd as yet scarcely set foot in this enormous country I had a queer sense of home-coming.

About midmorning, the bus decanted me in the Grey Coach Terminal in downtown Toronto. Waiting for me, with a smile combining just the right amount of cageyness and cheerfulness, was my father.

Chapter Eight

LITERARY LAPSES

THE name of the paper was *The Mail and Empire*. It was a morning daily and in contrast to the less sober evening papers, the *Toronto Daily Star* and the *Evening Telegram*, its heading was in Gothic. This distinction was shared with the rival morning daily *The Globe*; but the *Globe*, though it had a long and chequered history as an organ of political opinion, had fallen sadly behind in the circulation race. *The Globe* counted but a feeble 83,000 in comparison with the *Mail and Empire*'s healthy 112,000 plus. Of course neither of them could touch, or attempted to touch, the *Star*: 'Biggest circulation of any newspaper in Canada.'

The *Mail and Empire* was housed not inappropriately in a musty soot-darkened red-brick building with a gothic turret, which contrasted oddly with the vertical cement skyscrapers lining much of Bay Street, the city's financial thoroughfare. On one of the upper floors, behind a wooden railing, sat two secretaries looking out through the grimy windows obscured with dust. Beyond lay a door leading into the dark pine-panelled office of the Editor, Mr. F. D. L. Smith, who now examined me through thick-lensed horn-rimmed glasses across a large old-fashioned leather topped desk. He was pink-faced, almost bald, and surveyed me with that cagey expression that editors reserve for young men in search of jobs. His voice had the genuine unreconstructed nasal burr of the Old Ontarian or Upper Canadian. He looked opinionated, honest and shrewd.

'Not much we can offer a fellow of your literary attainments,' he twanged. 'I've read some of your articles and they're okay.'

'Thank you, sir.'

'But we can't pay here in Tronna the prices you'd command in The Old Country.'

Prices? I'd never commanded any in Britain if he but knew. Never sold anything except revue sketches, and a strong instinct told me to keep this particular talent dark for the time.

'On the kind of assignments we offer you wouldn't average more than seventeen fifty a week.'

$17.50! In good hard Canadian dollars. It seemed princely.

'That would be quite satisfactory, sir.'

'But there are compensations,' went on Mr. Smith. 'This is a young country with tremendous opportunities for youth.' He gestured at the wall map behind him: a geological map of Ontario. Above it was a photograph of the publisher of the paper. He lived in Montreal and was reported to be an extremely tough egg. He looked it.

'Up North for instance,' said Mr. Smith.

'You mean in Patricia, sir?' said I, anxious to show that I'd been doing my homework. He looked vaguely disconcerted.

'No; no. I mean the hard rock belt up North.' He pointed to the vast mineralized area above Lake Huron and the Ottawa River. 'Timmins, Kirkland Lake, Sudbury, Noranda,' he intoned the names with an almost religious fervour. 'Great things going on up there.'

'Yes sir,' I said, 'I hope to be able to get up North once I've got settled in here in Toronto.'

He nodded. 'Good. Can't start too soon. Well, look forward to getting your first piece Monday. Good day.' He rose from behind the desk to his full stocky height and extended a firm dry hand. I clasped it and rode down the rickety elevator to Bay Street. I was walking on air. $17.50. a week! Boy!

My father's surgeon, David Pratt, had arranged to take me to the Arts and Letters Club for lunch and we both drank to my success in the thin sherry which was all the club, in those days of the Ontario Temperance Act, was allowed to serve. Afterwards I wrote my first piece on the appointment of John Buchan as Governor-General of Canada and mailed it off in high fettle. But as I returned from the mailbox I was seized with a spasm of pain so violent that it doubled me up. Much to my embarrassment I found myself vomiting on the pavement. Someone kindly helped me up the stairs to the upper flat of 91 Dupont Street. Within an hour the shrewd probing eyes of the same Dr. Pratt were staring into the middle distance while he felt my belly. Within two hours I was in St.

Michael's hospital, and within three I was on the operating table, fully conscious, but numb from the waist down with a spinal anaesthetic while Dr. Pratt slit me neatly open and took out a very angry looking appendix.

Under sedation the next morning I asked for the *Mail and Empire*. There, swimming a bit before my eyes, was the piece on John Buchan. I thought it looked pretty good and the cheque which followed looked even better. I was in hospital for over two weeks, for in those far-off days the medical profession was still concerned about 'adhesions' and wagged many a stern finger at over-active patients, warning them they might suddenly collapse unless they lay very still and thus hastened their own recovery.

But I could write, and I did so. A faithful secretary typed the stuff out for free and my by-line appeared with commendable regularity. I was very proud. I seemed to have got started in this new country and this strange grey city—it was still March—when into the hospital came a buff envelope from the Department of Immigration. Would I kindly explain why I had overstayed my welcome in Canada? I was reminded that I had been granted entry for a month. Here it was, five weeks gone by and no record of my exit. It would be greatly appreciated if I would present myself, within twenty-four hours of the receipt of this letter, at the Immigration Office on Front Street, and furnish an explanation. It was not desired that I should become a Public Charge.

The letter hit my funny bone with such force that the nurse came rushing in, fearing for my stitches no doubt, as well as for the peace of mind of the other patients. My father called up the Immigration people, and, to do them justice, they extended my period of entry to six months and very handsomely wished me a speedy recovery. This was rapidly achieved, helped by a convalescent week at a farmhouse among the sleepy Caledon Hills where the pink maple buds, heralds of the full leaf, were just starting to burst from the ends of every twig and branch in sight. I returned to Toronto, limping dramatically but greatly bucked; and the stream of leaders continued. I was on my way. Within a month I was overwhelmed by a disaster of entirely unexpected magnitude, in part of my own creation.

Inspired by the vision of trees in the countryside and distressed at the way the Ontario Hydro and others were lopping and mutilating the great elms and maples which lined Toronto's suburban streets, I wrote a piece on the glory of trees. During the course of it I had some fun with Joyce Kilmer. *Trees* had long been—it still is—one of my unfavourite poems. The posture by which a tree is supposed to lift its leafy arms to pray while at the same time keeping its hungry mouth pressed close to the earth's sweet flowing breast had always seemed to me as ludicrous as the metaphor is distasteful. During the course of the article I said so. I did not know in my ignorance that Joyce Kilmer was a Canadian. I had unwittingly ridiculed a sacred cow. This I might have got away with; but I compounded the error by egregiously describing Joyce Kilmer as the 'authoress' of the poem. Not only was Kilmer a Canadian; he was a man.

The article was printed all right but the following day I received an urgent summons from F. D. L. Smith. The telephone and write-in complaints, he told me, had been considerable. These he was prepared to deal with; after all there was such a thing as Freedom of the Press. But although the article had been warmly commended by an organization known as 'The Men of the Trees', it turned out that the publisher in Montreal had not been amused. Mr. Smith was sorry, he really was; but they couldn't use my stuff any more. Orders were orders. I was greatly perturbed.

'You mean I'm fired?'

'You could put it that way,' said Smith dryly. He rose to his feet. 'I'm sorry this has happened,' he said. 'I like your stuff and I'd like to go on using it, but . . .'

'No use whistling against thunder?'

He gave a short laugh.

'That's one way of putting it. Anyway, I've spoken to B. K. Sandwell on your behalf and he'd like to see you.'

I was flustered. 'That's very kind of you, sir, I don't know what I've done to—'

'Skip it,' said Smith testily. 'You know BK's the editor of *Saturday Night*, don't you?' I nodded.

'Well, if you know that, you know that it's a weekly and that it has a literary and cultural section. I think you'd fit into it very well. Make a real contribution.'

'Thank you, sir.'

'Not a bit.' He was starting to sweat at the collar. He wanted to get the interview over, or over with. 'You go round and see Sandwell,' he said.

D*   105

'Thank you, sir. I'm sorry about Joyce Kilmer.'

'So'm I,' he said with a grin. 'But it can't be helped.'

Good old F. D. L. Smith. One could have a worse send-off than that, I thought. I went back to the flat and made an appointment to see Sandwell the following Tuesday.

*　　*　　*

'Smith tells me you set the cat among the pigeons over at the old *Flail and Vampire*,' said Sandwell when I was ushered into his very modest glassed-in office in one corner of the Consolidated Press Building, at the moment trembling with the weekly 'run'. I gave a big grin. He waved me into a seat with fluttering hands and I tried to take stock of the man who for twenty years held aloft a torch of literate comment in English-speaking Canada.

Bernard Keble Sandwell when I began my association with him was just on sixty. He had an amused flexible mouth below an enormous proboscis—almost as large and knobbly as that of Sir John MacDonald, the first Prime Minister of Canada, with which it was often compared. Weak but acute blue eyes and a mane of wavy white hair completed the picture of a man who, though the editor of the most influential weekly in English-speaking Canada, was at heart a don. From the flexible mouth issued the classic donnish bleat, rising, on the rare occasions when he was annoyed, to a bray. He also had the don's tigerish pounce on grammatical and syntactical solecisms, and was a tremendous stickler for precision, which he said was the product of thought. Muddled thought meant muddy writing and his comments on the weekly copy—provided it was filed early enough to be commented upon—were as rich and malicious as those of a Latin lecturer on a weekly 'study'.

Sandwell also believed in style. His favourite adjective was 'urbane' and there were those—especially among the newspaper fraternity— who thought that he made a fetish of urbanity at the expense of gutty prose. During the period of his Editorship the circulation of the paper hovered around 30,000 (in a country with a population, at that time, of about 10-11 millions) but its influence was far greater than its circulation. Though its name was *Saturday Night*, it appeared on Wednesday evening. Its format was that of a newspaper printed on glossy stock, with 'futura' typeface, and it was divided into three 'sections' much as Sunday papers are today. The first section contained political and economic comment and editorials on national and international affairs; the second section was devoted to literature, the arts and, somewhat incongruously though importantly, social notes. The third section was devoted to business and the stock market and its column of advice to investors, 'Gold and Dross', was reputedly what really sold *Saturday Night* and pulled in the big advertising accounts. If so, this was but one more example of the ingenious Canadian talent for making money support culture.

The paper was profusely illustrated with excellent photographs beautifully reproduced on the high glossy stock. You might compare it to an illustrated version of a British journal of opinion such as the *Spectator* or the *New Statesman*, but with a touch of Sunday supplement. What made it remarkable was that it was then the only such journal in Canada, and indeed its survival, which owed much to Sandwell's talents as an editor, was something of a tribute to the determination of English-speaking Canadians, in the face of overwhelming competition from United States weeklies, to maintain a journalistic identity of their own. It cannot always have been easy and later, as I grew familiar with the ways of the paper, I was to learn something of the pressures to which Sandwell was subjected; both by American competitors and by Canadian advertisers.

Sandwell was a courageous editor. Behind his urbanity, his slightly mocking scepticism and his almost professorial and highly un-newspaperlike Attic irony, lurked a tough and resourceful champion of editorial freedom of speech. He also had a skilled journeyman's familiarity with offset, photo-engraving, the screen density of blocks, leading out, and other recondite aspects of the profession. Because of these characteristics young men were much attracted to BK and he in turn loved to argue with them and to give them a leg up by printing their stuff. Among those to whom he gave a helping hand were Yousuf Karsh, the internationally known portrait photographer, Robertson Davies, now Master of Massey College, University of Toronto, but for some years Sandwell's Literary Editor, Maxwell Cohen, Dean of the McGill Law School, and the novelist Morley Callaghan. He was about to give me a helping hand.

'Well now,' he said, leaning almost too far back in his editorial swivel chair and gazing at the ceiling. 'What are we going to find for you to do?'

He suddenly bent his pale blue eyes at me as from a great height and a wry smile played about his mobile lips. He scratched his ample white hair in perplexity.

'I'll do anything,' I said.

'Anything?' His brow—he had almost no eyebrows—arched in mock commiseration.

'Well . . .' I temporized with the long-drawn monosyllable. Sandwell reached nonchalantly among the papers at his desk and chucked me a card.

'The Ontario Society of Artists has its annual spring show at the Art Gallery. Do me eight hundred words—neither more nor less—and get me a few eight-by-ten glossies from Baldwin, he's the curator, as possible cuts. Good day.'

He rose abruptly with a dismissive gesture from the editorial chair, and I muttered confused thanks which he waved aside with a deprecatory hand. I found myself in the street with my ears buzzing and hardly able to believe my luck. An art exhibition. This was where my frantic boning-up on European galleries would come in useful. But did I know enough? No time left to worry about that. I knew I could write and I hoped that this would make up for my lack of art knowledge or of the local scene. Prayerfully I boarded a Dundas street-car and alighted at the Art Gallery. Though I didn't know it, my career as an art critic and later as art editor of *Saturday Night* was about to begin.

I wandered through the exhibition of the Ontario Society of Artists making copious notes; but it was easy because both the job and the paintings stimulated me. I was fascinated by the broad bold sweep, the vivid colours and the dynamic patterns of the landscapes and by the 'social realism' of the portraits and figure work. I wrote my eight hundred words and greatly to my surprise Sandwell printed it exactly as I had written it, even including the rather quaint, to Canadian eyes, habit of prefixing the name of each artist with a 'Mr.', or 'Miss'.

Further commissions followed but now it was June and by that mysterious law enshrined since earliest times by Ontario (or perhaps Upper Canada) habit in a land where the seasons are very sharply divided, all exhibiting activity came to an abrupt stop. Sandwell was sorry, but after all it was the 24th of May; The Queen's Birthday (Victoria), and we all knew that on that date straw hats came out and art dealers closed up. He liked my stuff. 'I feel I have been fortunate in connecting myself to a good pipe line,' he was kind enough to say. But no more work. I felt that with Sandwell's help I'd cracked the art world in Toronto and that there was something useful as well as stimulating and modestly profitable for me to do. To put it a bit naïvely—and the young have perhaps the right to be naïve—I thought I could 'make a contribution' to the country of my adoption, as Smith had said. Sandwell smiled and didn't disagree, for which in my heart I thanked him. But after the 24th of May there was just quite simply nothing to write about.

Sandwell then said he was sufficiently sure of my talent, and of the interest I'd created in the world of art—'come to think of it,' he mused, 'that would be a good title for your column' (my column!)—to make a definite offer of the post of art critic when fall brought round the new exhibitions. But meanwhile, he smiled his regretful will-o'-the-wisp smile and handed me a cheque for $42.50. It was the biggest cheque I'd ever received in my life, and at Depression prices was probably worth about $150 in today's money. I went to the offices of the Greyhound bus company and for the sum of $33.80 secured a round trip ticket from Toronto to New Orleans.

*   *   *

It really wasn't as quixotic as it sounds, for my father wasn't charging me lodging, and as my wants were few, I was in funds. On top of this the feeling that I had no job now, but a definite job to come back to in the fall, filled me with newborn confidence. But there was also, to be honest, the siren beckoning of my brief jazz past, cut off in its prime perhaps.

Oughtn't I, before I settled down to the sober life of an art critic, oughtn't I to give old Satan blues *Just one more chance*? Any way, even if I oughtn't to, wouldn't it be fun? I scurried around to F. D. L. Smith and told him of my intentions. He commissioned articles on New Orleans and its relationship with the early Canada through the Sieurs d'Iberville and de Bienville. Matt Cleary of the Toronto *Star* said he'd look kindly on my first-hand impressions of Basin Street, though to be frank it was a bit off—wasn't it—to be going *south* in summer? Most folks went north. Up to the summer cottage, or The Lake. A number of my new-found friends made the same observation, but they wished me luck; and all my father said, when he came down to the bus terminal to see me off, was, 'I hope you'll be back by the tenth of September because Colin is coming over for a visit.'

I hadn't forgotten of course. This was to be The Great Reunion when my father would present us to his Toronto. We had now agreed that I should call him James, the fatherless and sonless interval of almost eighteen years being too great to be bridged by 'Dad', and 'Father' being too stuffy. Accordingly, and full of my newfound Canadianism, I said, 'You bet, James,' and climbed aboard the bus.

Jet planes and diesel electric expresses have taken the romance out of the long-distance bus. But in the days of the Depression—unless you were brave enough to 'ride the rods' under the belly of a fast freight train: a pastime of truly appalling danger—it was the best and cheapest form of locomotion and also by far the most democratic and friendly. Adjoining bus-seats forced companionship on you for a far longer period than does the trans-oceanic jet. For the great Greyhounds travelled across the continent and you might be a couple of days and two or three nights jammed against your neighbour, apart from routine meal and 'comfort' station stops. The fact that this neighbour, far from being the girl of your dreams, was usually either a talkative matron or a taciturn and meaty gent in shirtsleeves, didn't matter much; for through conversations with them, or from their mere proximity, one gathered some essential raw material about life in Canada and in 'these United States'. Also in the days when university professors were on $5,000 a year or less and the only people who seemed to have any money were bankers, the cross section of bus travellers really covered most walks of society: automobile workers, doctors, small businessmen, retired people and itinerant farm hands. The essential mobility of North American society, both in terms of social change and physical movement, found its exemplar and its symbol in the big inter-urban bus. And to a lover of the new world, the rubric Compagnie des Wagons Lits et des Grands Express Européens could never compete with the sonorous intonation over the public address system:

'Bus now leaving for Hamilton, London, Windsor, Detroit, South Bend, Gary, Chicago and points West! All aboaaard!!'

Then the night departure from a terminal, poised equivocally between the smart and the sleazy parts of town; the interminable slewing of the great bus round exigent corners flanked by darkened skyscrapers thrown into sharp shadow by the wakeful blaze of rooftop neon ads; the uncertain descent from the foetid bus at some unnamed 'comfort station', in the middle of the night, but the nearby 'diner'— a roadside eatery in the shape of a pullman car—ablaze with light in contrast to the single lonely old negro dozing over a paper and a broom at some lonely terminal on the Great Plains; the sharp pneumatic hiss as the bus jerked to an abrupt stop at one of a thousand unguarded railway crossings, the idling of the motor and the regulation opening of the bus door while the driver obeyed the tilted cruciform injunction : 'Stop ! Look ! Listen !'; the excitement when a train pounded by, siren blazing out the lost-soul wail silenced now for ever by the bleat of the diesel; 'coffee and' (i.e. and a dough-nut) at an all-night greasy spoon, or ham and eggs at an early morning roadside café. These themes were repeated endlessly yet with subtle variations.

In Chicago, Mark Hambourg and his wife were staying at a South Side hotel while he lectured at a summer school at the University. The pianist was an old family friend and I had a standing invitation to dine with them. I figured the free meals would be worth the cost of a room in a cheesy Loop hotel; and besides you couldn't very well 'do' the Art Institute in an afternoon. My rumpled linen suit looked very shabby in the Hambourgs' hotel suite, but they were kindness itself and gave me two enormous feeds. Had I looked up Mark's brothers Boris and Clement in Toronto? Well no, I hadn't had the opportunity yet, you see : been trying so hard to get into the art world that there hasn't been time yet to get into the music world. But, my dear boy, surely your father . . . ? Well, yes, I suppose so (though perhaps they were rivals for the slim purse of the Toronto patron?). I'll write to Boris, said Mrs. Hambourg, and Borina, his wife, you'll find her a real delight. 'Thank you so much,' I said, but oh dear, I thought, here's yet another obligation as I sailed off into the Illinois night in yet another bus.

I spent a week in Dallas—thanks to the courtesy, indeed the tolerance, of casual shipboard acquaintances. Mac and Nin—he a Texan, she an exiled Englishwoman—put me up in their suburban home and lodged and fed me and put back the weight I'd lost and the sleep I'd missed, and generally performed those simple nameless unremembered acts for which friendless lonely young men are so more than ordinarily grateful. Howard Dealey of the News, whom I met at a party, commissioned articles on a Canadian's impressions

of Dallas. Seeing I was only a landed immigrant of six months resi-
dence I didn't feel that my opinions would reflect much of the
Canadian point of view, but brashness (and the need for cash) won
the day.

On I trundled, much re-invigorated now, through a flat landscape,
stabbed with orange flares and reeking of methane and petroleum.
Heat—August Mississippi delta heat; William Faulkner heat—had
us by the throat, smothered and suffocated us in endless scarves of
warm damp miasma. The bus rolled on, night became day and day
night. Our coats and ties were off, our shirtsleeves up, our tongues
hanging out, our shoulders, seats, temples and armpits sweating
profusely. The whole bus was a living moving stinking testimony to
the perils that beset those who fail to use Amplex or Mum.

And then one evening we were high up on the Huey Long Bridge
spanning a new Mississippi grown enormously broad and swirling
seaward, contained by levees as tall as church steeples. Embayed in
the river's giant curve and protected by those enormous dykes lay
the city of Basin Street. I dumped my bags in a cheap downtown
hotel and before starting out to do the town called at General
Delivery. There was a letter from my father saying that Colin's trip
had been advanced by a week and he did hope I'd be able to get
back for the celebration. I perched on the jangling springs of my
cheap little bed and read the letter again. Here it was August 20th—
his birthday incidentally. He was due in Toronto August 31st. And
here was I 1,800 miles south and west of Toronto. Buses average
about thirty m.p.h.; say sixty hours if I went flat out? But what
about stops? Refuelling? EATS? Comfort stations? Could I make
it or should I give up the attempt and deprive my father of his hour
of pleasure and perhaps of triumph? I've rarely been so torn in my
life.

In the end duty won. I wrote my father telling him I was speeding
up my trip; then set out to explore in two days the town where I
should have spent a week. I found it easily enough, perhaps a bit
too easily. In the basements of the Vieux Carré and under the lazy
iron filigree work dripping from the wistaria-smothered verandahs
were little combos that hadn't changed much since the days of Jelly-
roll Morton and King Oliver. I heard *Basin Street Blues* on a rackety
snarling trumpet, *Beale Street Blues* on a smothering trombone.
Banjos still plunked though it was now the middle thirties. The string

112

bass thumped in plangent rhythm. The front was off the cottage upright and the moth-eaten felts of the hammers jumped and jived while fans slowly slurped their bourbon through thick scarves of smoke, and feet beat insistent rhythm. Both the melancholy and the scarcely restrainable sexual excitement were there and the waiters undulated among the crowds with deceptive languor. I looked about as much part of the picture as a steam-roller on a golf course. But I loved it and was sorry when the inevitable night departure bus trundled out past the old cemeteries with the tombs above ground against the ravages of Old Man River, and rounded the heel of Lake Ponchartrain and on over the border into Mississippi.

* * *

I was eventually able to present myself, a bit sweaty and bristly under the chin, at the Union Station in Toronto in time to greet Colin as he stepped off the train with my father, his eyes aglaze with his first view of North America.

'Howdy stranger,' he said, 'how's about a Pittsburgh stogie?'

I was tongue-tied. Off he went with my father to stay at the little flat in 91 Dupont Street while I went off to a room at the house of Lady Mary, Mrs. L. A. Hamilton. The Great Reunion had begun.

Chapter Nine

A GRAND REUNION

I CAN quite see what was in my father's mind. He wanted to present his two grown-up sons to an audience which knew only of him. Hence—we having been absent from this audience ever since it was assembled—he regarded us as in some sense an extension of his own personality and as an additional justification for his achievements in Toronto social and musical circles. We were essentially on show for his glory and enhancement. Personally I didn't object to this at all; I thought he rather deserved it. In any case he was paying the shot. But it did mean that we were both presented, in essence, as people who we were not.

I was quite prepared to admit that my father might have been wrongfully divorced by my mother. I was also prepared to accept the fact that he who had never lifted a finger in my direction in the seventeen years between the divorce and the confrontation should, as it were, bask in *my* refulgent splendour, earned and developed by me (and my mother) away from him, and with which he had had nothing whatever to do. In fine, I was prepared to play his game, to let the adoring acolytes and the genuine friends think of me as someone who reflected credit on my father, but who also repaid, by implication, the immense trouble he had spent—or would have spent, poor man, had he been allowed—over my education and development.

In brief the mysterious past of James Campbell McInnes (insofar as it was known to Torontonians) was to be amply vindicated by the appearance, fully armed, from the brow of their respective Minervas, of two tall, reasonably presentable, moderately intelligent young men. By their fruits shall ye know them, etc. All this seemed fair enough, if just a trifle phoney, if smacking of just the faintest whiff of the mountebank. But what I was not prepared for was the lugubrious

114

constraint which surrounded the visit: the posturings, the humbug and the mysterious reticence, all of which were to blow up in my face with an almighty bang just as it drew to a close.

First on the programme was The Presentation. For this purpose the roof garden on the Royal York Hotel had been reserved—at Heaven knows what price—for nine o'clock on a Friday evening. The Royal York, erected in 1929, was the noblest monument to the enterprise of the Canadian Pacific Railway; but in those days it was still sufficiently new to command awe as well as respect. 1,200 rooms, 1,000 baths, 23 storeys of skyscraper ending in an Italianate arcade surmounted by a brief muted mansard roof: the small but necessary nod in the general direction of the Loire château style to which both big railroads had committed themselves. It was enormous, efficient and impersonal. Here, 300 feet above the Union Station, the tracks, the docks, the harbour, the Islands and the sultry summer spread of Lake Ontario—a freshwater sea; here, poised above a myriad lights all flickering oddly in the twenty-five cycle southern Ontario current of those days, my father, my brother and myself assembled in white tie and tails for the Great Event.

Soon the elite of the Toronto musical and social world began to disgorge itself from the banks of express elevators and to trickle slowly across the carpeted lobby into the roof garden: the men all in white tie and tails; the women all in floor-length evening dresses with a profusion of mink or silver fox stoles. As neither my brother nor myself knew a single soul we contented ourselves with bobbing and smirking and uttering the usual banalities; but it was clearly a tremendous occasion for my father and he was enjoying every minute of it and we were delighted that he should. He looked very handsome and majestic and his deep resonant voice, pausing just this side of the fruity, conveyed a wonderful impression of plenitude and graciousness.

As the room filled up, white-coated waiters began to circulate with soft drinks and petits fours and canapés, while the background air was made harmonious by the strains of the recently formed Toronto Trio, all of whom had at one time or another studied with or accompanied my father. As the evening wore on and the room became fuller and the buzz of converse louder, so our throats began to be more parched.

'See if you can rustle up a drink,' whispered Colin. I deserted the receiving line and, innocently passing to the bar, demanded a Tom Collins.

'No hard liquor here, sir,' said the maître d'hôtel bending a stern eye upon me.

'Can I have a glass of beer then?'

'Sorry, sir.' The man shook his head. 'Beer and hard liquor served only in the bedrooms.'

I had a bright thought. 'Did my father by any chance reserve a bedroom?'

He gave a slow solemn shake of his head. So that was that. I returned with the sad news to Colin, foiled by the Ontario Temperance Act or perhaps by my father's deliberate decision, for I remembered my earlier conversation with Fred Ince.

By ten thirty guests who had started to arrive at nine were leaving, and by eleven the Roof Garden of the Royal York Hotel was once again empty of all save we three and one or two faithful followers. I felt a tremendous sense of let-down; and I supposed in my ignorance that the guests must have felt the same. To get dolled up to the nines, come all the way into town simply to stand about for an hour and a half drinking orange juice and ginger ale: surely this was an intolerable imposition? Yet the look on my father's face told me it had been for him an immense success, and at the same time made me feel that I was harbouring mean thoughts. What I hadn't realized of course was that most of the people were in the know as to the fences which my father had built around himself, both at his work and in his relaxation. And if I'd only known Toronto as well as I subsequently came to know it, I'd have realized that I had no need to feel sorry for the guests, the great majority of whom, once locked safely behind the doors of their glossy secretive mansions, would have taken off their shoes and poured themselves good stiff hookers of rye. But I made a resolve then and there that the visit would be rounded off by a less sedate party, to be given by me in a studio setting, which I thought I might be able to secure through one of my new artist friends.

* * *

The following day we all boarded the train bound north for the Muskoka Lakes and the home of the Jackson family; Bala. Ontario is a land of lakes, and those which fill the thousands of furrows that the glaciers scraped in the pre-Cambrian rock as they retreated north at the end of the last Ice Age, are of an undeniable beauty. It is a beauty of melancholy and emptiness rather than the romantic beauty of the hilltop tarn or the dramatic splendour of the mountain lake. These can be found in Quebec, and of course in British Columbia, in great quantities. The Canadian poet Earle Birney, himself admittedly a British Columbian, speaks of 'raped Muskoka', and though these lakes have the passionate devotion of the Ontario householder to whom they represent freedom, large horizons and unspoiled nature 'right at your doorstep', to a stranger their melancholy becomes tedious, and in the end monotonous. Because the shores are so low there is a tremendous expanse of sky and an equally enormous expanse of water split by a thin tufted horizon line. Consequently there are no dramatic shadows of mountain and crag; no deep fissures penetrating soundless gorges. It is an inland seascape innocent of features until the immense void of the Canadian sky—high and thin—starts to cloud over. Then the drama of the sky is faithfully reflected in the water, and turbulent nature rages out of control, blotting out the headlands and whipping the quiet waters with angry gooseflesh. But in the end it is the emptiness and, since there are tens of thousands of lakes, the sameness that tells.

It so happened that Bala was a not over-prepossessing entrance to this paradise. For one thing it was on the CPR main line from Toronto north to Sudbury and hence had grown up as a sort of small entrepot, a market summer village rather than a resort town. For another we were not really bound for the 'vacationland of the North'; because the Jackson family, far from being vacationists, were local folk who lived off the tourists and vacationists during the brief warm summer. During the rest of the year they simply existed, or else came down to Toronto to get a job after the fall freeze-up until it was time to go north again after the spring break-up.

'From freeze-up to break-up you'll find me down in Tronna.'

The village of Bala had a summer population of about 5,000; but in winter this sank to 300, and the summer station built out over the lake on stilts to accommodate 12-car long trains of revelling vacationers, moved half a mile north to its lonely snow-bound duties.

Bala just about was the Jacksons. Lorne was head of the local hydro; Wilfred ran the only movie house; Stewart did all the local haulage. 'He is the Carter Paterson of Bala,' said my father. The general store and a small hotel were run by Burgesses who had married Jacksons. They were loyal hardworking citizens of this tiny community and, when the farming possibilities had collapsed owing to the penury of the soil, they'd stayed on to exploit the relentless old pre-Cambrian rock in their own modest way. They struck no gold, copper or nickel, as their luckier neighbours did further north. On the other hand Bala, and the Muskoka region generally, never sank to the derelict status of other Districts on 'The Shield' which had died on their feet before the First World War and were threaded with abandoned railway lines and broken down shacks and the empty shells of once busy townships where capeweed and golden-rod grew on the main street.

We passed the weekend, courtesy of the kindly Lorne and his wife Mabel, hugger-mugger all four of us in his tiny house, two to a bed. We went paddling inexpertly in a canoe on the Musquash river, we went on leafy walks, liberally menaced by ferocious mosquitoes. We rowed sedately, avoiding the lip of the dam over which Lake Muskoka tumbled headlong on its eventual way to Georgian Bay and Lake Huron. We watched the trains go by; watched too the smart set of Toronto's fast upper crust gunning their gleaming power boats away from the jetty to sybaritic pleasures on remote wooded islands, dimly seen in the cardboard cut-out Japanesey distance. We talked and listened, principally to my father, over innumerable cups of tea; and we yearned uselessly for a single glass of beer. On the train back to Toronto—our father very proud of having shown us his Canada, and I a bit anxious too that my new home should appeal to my brother, for I was proud of the start I'd made—Colin sprang a surprise. He had a little spare cash. He and I were going on a quick trip to Montreal and New York to get away from the adoring camp. My father acquiesced cordially. It occurred to me that maybe *he* was getting a bit fed up with *us*.

Colin and I had four days in Baghdad on the Subway—still in those days (along with London) the cultural Mecca of English-speaking Canada. Our culture included everything from the Metropolitan Museum and the Frick to a boat trip round Manhattan and an evening at Minsky's where in company with a couple of thousand other randy males we saw the immortal Gipsy Rose Lee do her bumps and grinds.

We returned to Toronto with only two days of the Visit to go.

118

A Grand Reunion

During our absence my plans for a real party had been maturing rapidly. Mindful of Mrs. Mark Hambourg and the kind Chicago invitation, I'd approached brother Boris who had turned me over to his wife Borina who clearly controlled the purse strings. Yes, they would be glad to let me give a party for my father in the main salon of the Hambourg Conservatory. She had known my father long and favourably. She was delighted at this development. Musicians should stick together. A distinguished 'cellist like her husband; a distinguished singer like my father. I was doing the right thing. Of course there would unavoidably be a bit of a mess to clear up afterwards and, well, in short: ten bucks. I gulped a bit and paid it out; then went off to outlay at least four times that amount in drink.

It was a great party; everybody said so. I invited all my artist and newspaper friends and their wives and girl-friends and the younger musicians and friends of my father. The welkin rang and the liquor disappeared with exemplary speed. About eleven we left the party to put Colin on the boat train for Montreal. We waved boozy farewells, and I gazed longingly after the rear lights of the departing train; not because I wanted to go to Europe with Colin but because I was a romantic fool about trains. When I turned to take my father's arm to accompany him back to the party, or back to 91 Dupont Street—I wasn't sure which—he was nowhere in sight.

Chapter Ten

'TORONTO THE GOOD'

THEY found him in a small hotel at the West End of Toronto, docile and drained. I was much subdued by this experience, for it seemed to me that I was in part to blame. I didn't feel that I could consult my own generation on this touchy subject, so I spoke to Lady Mary who I felt sure would respond.

'Campbell's not like other men,' she said, looking at me through her bi-focal hexagonal rimless glasses, and with her usual quite unconscious mixture of severity and affection. 'He really just can't touch it. One glass—even a sherry—and he's off and away into some dark private world of his own. He really just doesn't know where he is.'

'That's what Fred Ince told me.'

'Yes,' she said shortly. After a pause she added with some asperity, 'Fred Ince might also have advised you not to invite your father to that farewell party. You may not know it, but there were plenty of his dear friends from the old days who were just dying to see him kick over the traces.'

'Well, I don't think I'm to be blamed for that.'

'I'm not saying you are. I agree that you couldn't have excluded your father; it would have been too cruel. And he'd probably have come along anyway. But it wasn't good for him.'

She pulled a crumpled yellowing handkerchief from the sleeve of the stained black barathea dress that covered her gawky suffragette's figure. She took off the hexagonal glasses and squeezed her kindly pouched grey eyes with a finger and thumb of a big bony work-roughened hand. I looked at her with my own mixture of affection and exasperation.

'What do you think I ought to do, then?'

She remained silent for a while, polishing the glasses absently with the crumpled handkerchief and staring out of the smeary old French window at the used car lot across the street and the big elm trees that were starting to yellow. Finally she cleared her throat.

'I've known your father a long time. Almost fifteen years. In fact,' she smiled dimly and revealed her big fine crooked teeth like old ivory, 'I took over from Lady Falconbridge—a real "Lady" by the way. He needs looking after. When he came back in 1918 he was,' she searched for a word, 'very badly bruised.'

I nodded. 'Yes. I know a bit about that. It's been haunting me—from both sides—almost since I can remember.'

She moistened her lips with a grey tongue. 'I'm sure it has, my dear boy, and I'm not going to assess the rights and wrongs. Your father has the most terrifying temper when roused; a black, unreasoning Celtic rage.' Unexpectedly, she threw back her head and laughed heartily. 'I've been on the receiving end of some pretty brutal tongue-lashings myself, I can tell you. Your mother may have had something to put up with.'

The Indian maid came in with the tea. She'd been born in a reservation in the bush about 400 miles north of Toronto and had slippery raven-black hair, a smooth slabsided expressionless face—half mongol, half Mayan—and sculptured lips masking decayed teeth. She put the tray down silently on the stained walnut coffee table between the two imitation high-backed damask Barberini chairs and slid deftly out. Her carpet slippers, though they looked big for her, made no shuffle. Lady Mary started to pour.

'Campbell has to be protected from himself,' she said, 'and other people have to be protected from him.' She passed me a cup and gave me a level grey-eyed look over it. 'I know you don't particularly take to this—this—gaggle of adoring people who surround him. I often think it's rather like trying to get to someone through layers of cotton wool. But I think it's the best thing for Campbell. He has to operate at half speed, with the boilers damped down; or else his whole machine goes wildly out of control. As you've seen.'

I said, 'Do you think any harm has been done by the party? I mean to his reputation?'

She thought for a while, over strong and very loud sips of tea; then cocked her head slightly, as if listening for some sound—perhaps the cracking of a reputation.

121

'No, I don't think so,' she said. 'This is of course an extremely censorious city. A very cold self-righteous city. But the ranks have been closed; very few people know of it. And those that know won't tell, will they?'

'Are you looking at me?'

'Not in that sense, boy. I don't think you would speak about it—wittingly. But you're new to this town; your background has been very different from—not mine, I'm English originally too; nor his—obviously. But theirs. And it's they who are in control. You might—' she hesitated and rubbed a bony cheek in her great craggy generous face.

'I might what?'

'You might, through resentment or high spirits or sheer youthfulness or exasperation with their cagey ways, try to break the pattern. I wouldn't. He's better as their prisoner.'

'You mean I have to be party to this pretence?'

'It isn't exactly a pretence—unless you want him to tear himself to pieces.'

'No, Lady Mary; of course I don't. It's just that—well look here: my father's a fine singer, a bard if you like, a poet; and here he is surrounded by a lot of equivocation and humbug. People pretending he's someone he's really not; someone quite different from the reality.'

'How do you know what the reality is?' she asked harshly. 'You've only known him for six months. And you're young.'

'Well, for Pete's sake, don't hold that against me, I hope.'

She put her great gaunt hand on my knee and gave it an affectionate pat. She looked at me quizzically through the hexagonal glasses.

'I'm not ever likely to do that. I love young people. That's why I like having you here and that's why—since you've raised the subject—I ask you only a nominal rent. But—how can I put it without offending you?' She gazed up at a corner of the high ceiling. Iron radiator pipes ran naked up the inside wall and in the cornice above them cobwebs undulated gently in the rising heat. 'Let me put it this way. Ask yourself whether, having sought your father out—and we're not denying the worthy motive for your action—you have the right to try and make over the pattern that he, and his friends, have so carefully established for him over the years; that has made him able to resume his career; and which could be broken so easily and would be so hard to mend.'

She leaned back in the uncomfortable Barberini chair and aligned her strong gaunt hands on the lion's claws, which made the arms. 'There, I've said more than I meant to.'

I shook my head. 'No, Lady Mary, you haven't; and you've given me a clue. I agree with you. I must go along with this; must acquiesce. After all, when in Rome.'

'Or in Toronto.'

'Yes. I quite see that I mustn't upset the apple cart. And from that point of view it's good that I left 91 Dupont Street.'

'That was why I invited you here. Your coming to Toronto has been wonderful for your father. But your continued presence, at close quarters, is too rich for his blood.'

'You don't expect me to *like* all these people?'

'Heavens no. Just be tolerant, that's all.'

'I like you.'

'Oh, I'm quite different from them.' She laughed, in a rough mannish sort of way.

She was too. She'd been born Constance Bodington in England and not very early in life had become the second wife of L. A. Hamilton, a Canadian railway surveyor some years older than herself. He brought her to Toronto just before the First World War and she at once threw her tempestuous energies, her physical toughness, her passion for lost causes and lame dogs, above all her gauche jerky kindness, into alleviating the lot of the Toronto underprivileged. She was big and gawky and terrifyingly persistent: a wonderful wearer-down of pompous clerics; an unrelenting extractor of funds from cowed businessmen; an inexorable caller on civic politicians; and a passionate lover of the music of Bach.

She was elected a councillor of the city of Toronto; she became chairman of the Yorkville Library Association; she ran her summer home for indigent artists and musicians out on the shores of Lake Ontario; she was co-founder and treasurer of the Bach Society; she conducted free classes in German and Italian; and she filled the rackety old house on St. Joseph Street with a succession of lame dogs and tame cats: refugee 'cellists from Austria; English remittance men with a gift of the gab who were down on their luck; unemployed Italian waiters; poverty-stricken painters; young clergymen whose faith had been shaken. It didn't escape my notice that she assumed that I belonged to one of these categories.

30 St. Joseph Street was a mixture of Toynbee Hall, the Dolmetsch establishment at Haslemere, and the New School of Social Research in New York. One learned to love music, especially and perhaps too especially Bach; one imbibed vaguely Fabian socialist principles; one saw the Golden Rule being daily enacted. And though tough and endlessly resilient in the pursuit of social justice or of favours for others, Lady Mary was unutterably careless of herself. She dressed like a scarecrow in rusty black and smeared old greys. She ate when and as she could, although she ran the ramshackle old house on time for her husband, 'Lock' as she called him; L.A. to us. His real name was Lauchlan Alexander, and he exemplified the virtues and defects, the visions and the prejudices of pioneer Upper Canada.

When I knew him he was close to eighty, with stiff white hair, thick-lensed steel-rimmed spectacles and a circulation so poor that when he sat in his stocking feet in front of the cannel coal fire of an evening, smoking greasily up the narrow chimney, his socks would start to singe long before he became aware of it.

'Careful, Lock, your feet are burning,' Lady Mary would say.

'Eh?' He was very deaf.

'YOUR FEET ARE BURNING,' she would repeat in a loud monotonous bray.

'Eh? Hah, he! So they are. Forgot all about it. Just telling Graham here about the early days. The early days.'

He'd been born in Penetanguishene—Penetang for short—at the foot of Georgian Bay on Lake Huron. It was the extreme edge of the pioneer farm country just where the pre-Cambrian shield slices it off neater than a knife, and granite supervenes. He was an Anglican and a teetotaller—though he didn't mind Lady Mary having an occasional bottle of our local sherry made from the pungent Catawba grape of the Niagara Peninsula. He had retired on pension, and to nurse his carefully guarded investments, long before I met him; but his early manhood and his middle years had been a period of great adventure which he never tired of recounting nor I of listening to; for he had been a land surveyor on the CPR.

There was then, and there still is, a Hamilton Street in Vancouver, the reason being that L. A. Hamilton helped to lay out the city in 1886. When Vancouver celebrated its half-century the city fathers invited L.A. out to the coast to participate in the event as an honoured guest. He was too old and frail to go, so they made him a Freeman of the City. He was immensely proud of this honour and used to show the parchment at the drop of a hat. To me it seemed entirely miraculous to be sitting in the scuffed old living room at 30 St. Joseph Street actually talking to the man who had laid out Canada's third largest city; who had tramped the bush from the original terminus of the CPR at Port Moody, slogged through the virgin forest with transit and theodolite, put in benchmarks and pegs for the streets, supervised the first land sale; and helped to preserve Stanley Park as a chunk of the original 'forest primeval' right on Vancouver's doorstep.

L.A. had known all the CPR great and he had a special admiration for Sir William van Horne. 'He was the fellow who really got things done,' he used to say of that wonderful American-turned-Canadian who watched trainload after trainload of ballast and fill disappear into the muskeg north of Lake Superior; who laid rail on the Prairies at a rate of up to five miles a day; who finally retired to an enormous fortress-mansion on Sherbrooke Street in Montreal which, before his death in 1915, he filled with valuable paintings, including, incredibly, a van Gogh and a Marie Laurencin.

'But I liked the Prairie best,' said L.A., rubbing his steaming, indeed his smoking wool socks together. 'It was like the sea. A Manitoba maple, maybe no more than twenty feet high, it'd make you jump when you came in sight of it; like a steamer on the horizon, kind of unexpected, you know.'

He helped to lay out many of the towns created by the CPR as it crawled westward: Brandon, Regina, Moose Jaw, Swift Current, Medicine Hat. Being shrewd and hard rock and of Scots-Ulster descent, he also bought the odd lot here and there for himself; and as the Prairies surged into life in the twenty years before the First World War, he was able to add to his savings and to augment his pension by selling them off. Not that he ever told me this; he was far too close. I learned that from Lady Mary; warm, gullible and truthful, with a heart as big as a whale.

On the face of it you couldn't have found two people more ill-assorted than Constance and L. A. Hamilton: she, warm and open-hearted, he, shrewd and tight-fisted; she fond of reading Axel Munthe and Huxley; he the Bible and the stock market quotations (a not

uncommon choice in that part of the world). Yet there were like-
nesses; both were frugal and both had a passion for—of all places—
Italy.

They had visited Italy twice and had brought home the Barberini
chairs and a couple of soi-disant Caravaggios which looked very
exotic in staid Toronto. L.A. had at one time thought he'd like to
retire in Italy, but he'd given up the idea because, he said, 'they're
so servile'. Which didn't prevent him bringing back to Toronto an
Italian man-of-all-work who cheated with the marketing money,
flapped round the furniture with a feather duster, and otherwise
seemed to spend much of the time yarning in the kitchen. He had the
bright bogus-honest eyes of an auctioneer in an antique store and
when rebuked used to say, 'Ah excuseta me. Toronto eeza so differ
from Taranto. A joke no? Ha ha.' After a while even L.A.'s patience
wore thin and the bright eyes returned to Italy leaving only the
chairs behind.

As for the frugality, it was in part forced on Lady Mary by L.A.
He kept her on short commons for running the house and he himself made savings on the most ludicrous matters. He kept putting off
having the front stoop mended until one Sunday, coming home from
church, he shoved his foot right through a rotten board and was
held there until extricated by me. On another occasion I was alone
in the house one very cold winter's day when the front door bell
rang. When I opened the outer storm door it was to find L.A., his
face blue with cold, almost collapsed on the top step. I steered him
through to the inner warmth, permitting myself a shocked

'You really shouldn't be out on a day like this, sir; it's eight below.'

He leaned puffing thinly against the hall radiator while I helped
him off with his overshoes. After a moment he emitted a strangled
grunt.

'Heh heh ! I was downtown. Needed a haircut. Heard there was a
place on the corner of Wellesley where you could get it for ten cents
less; so I walked.'

'You walked a mile and a half up Yonge Street in this weather?'

'Yes,' he croaked. 'Funny thing was, when I got there the place
was closed.'

That was L.A. all over. He couldn't help it; and indeed he could
laugh at it. He used to tell the story of a friend of his who was
being buried and nobody could find a good thing to say about him,

until one fellow piped up with 'Well you know, you gotta say one thing for McCluskey; he didn't spend any dough'. At which the mourners nodded sagely; it was the highest praise they could bestow.

But Lady Mary was also frugal by nature except in the things of the spirit, and here she was brimful with the special brand of competent capable generosity that overwhelms with its kindness. Both my father and I were in turn the beneficiaries of this engulfing kindliness. She never spared herself in any cause that she deemed worthy and during the period that I lived at 30 St. Joseph Street, gradually clawing my way into the Toronto artistic, radio and literary world, the tumbledown house was rarely empty.

The Bach Society held its executive meetings in the dining-room and a part-time secretary was installed in one corner, perched on a kitchen stool so that she could use her typewriter on the sideboard. When a committee man used the funds for unauthorized entertainment at the Mott Hotel (we learned of it through his egregious self-complacency in placing an item in the social column of the *Mail and Empire* announcing that 'covers were laid for fourteen') Lady Mary only clucked a little and shook her head.

'We'll have to raise some more money that's all. Just because we've been deceived in this man, we mustn't lose sight of our main object.'

Once again the secretary mounted her stool, this time to cut stencils. Fred Ince lent a multigraph machine which was installed in the scullery and anyone who happened to drop in was enlisted in that endless chore of volunteer societies, 'addressing, folding and stuffing'.

Meanwhile the faded old drawing room, gaunt as a barn but as large, had been given over to the rehearsals of a newly formed concert trio. These musicians came every afternoon at four and we folded and stuffed to the interminably repeated strains of Schubert's Trio No. 1 in B flat major as the boys scraped and sawed themselves into practice for the opening night.

Though the Hamiltons' house gave the appearance of extreme decrepitude on a scale of vanished nobility, and of scrimp and save, it was in point of fact only one of three establishments. As soon as the snow started to fly, about mid-November, old L.A. would pick himself up and pack himself off to Florida where he had a small farm at a place quaintly named Kissimmee. Usually he was accompanied by his unmarried daughter and his niece and her husband,

and occasionally—when she absolutely couldn't get out of it—by Lady Mary herself. And there he stayed until Easter. Then, after a couple of months at 30 St. Joseph Street, it was time to go out to his 'summer place' at Lorne Park.

This was about twenty miles west of Toronto in gently undulating lightly timbered country, some of it in fruit trees and some in pasture. Since it is the mise-en-scène of Mazo de la Roche's *Jalna* novels it is probably better known to the world at large than most other parts of Canada; though to someone like me who believes in the rock, the lake and the pine, it is in no sense typical. The farm lay about two miles inland from Lake Ontario, here like a fresh-water sea and overlooked by steep wooded bluffs. The farm at Lorne Park was split by the main east-west line of the Canadian National Railways. This made its operation something of a hazard for, in common with most of their companions in the Ontario of those days the level crossings were unguarded, naked even of a warning wig-wag. There was nothing but the usual St. Andrew's cross on a pole with the legend:

RAILWAY CROSSING   STOP   LOOK   LISTEN

Although everyone of course obeyed this injunction, yet ours was a busy line and, while the freights were easy enough to judge and apprehend, the speed of an approaching express was less easy to assess. Trains coming towards you at eighty m.p.h. have a way of looming up much faster than you think, and more silently. This was particularly hazardous when we were driving cattle across the tracks. However no casualties were sustained during my visits, though musical conversations were frequently and unnervingly blasted apart by the banshee wail of an approaching train. With its subsequent roar and rattle the locomotive often seemed to be headed right into the living room.

The farm was as ramshackle, as sparsely furnished and as over-flowing with the milk of human kindness as 30 St. Joseph Street (and presumably Kissimmee). Dotted among the white-pine and maples, and overlooking a tiny ornamental sheet of water with a derelict wooden bridge and a thin coating of green scum, were half a dozen little frame cottages. At any time during the brief but intolerably hot and humid Toronto summer you would find most, if not all, these cottages and shacks occupied by beneficiaries of Lady Mary's bounty.

BERNARD K. SANDWELL, TORONTO, 1934

Here a violinist practised while his wife cooked the beans over a single burner on an electric hotplate; there a university student in a T-shirt and shorts tapped out his thesis on a portable and slapped at the huge Lorne Park mosquitos; here an artist, seated on a canvas chair on his exiguous verandah, immortalized the scatter of frame houses under the solid spreading maples; over there a couple of girl singers in cotton dirndls and pony-tail hair-dos rehearsed madrigals to a cracked cottage piano. At one and at six the Indian maid beat a tattoo with a hammer on a triangle suspended from the back stoop by a piece of fencing wire. 'Come and get it!' All trooped in to yet another of Lady Mary's enormous meals of beef stew and corn on the cob. She never charged anyone a cent.

The Depression was still very much with us, and in and near Lorne Park and its nearby market town of Port Credit was a group of academic spartan young marrieds who kept alight the twin torches of culture and social justice in darkest Ontario of the darkest Thirties. To them as a bee to a honey pot I flew. None of us had any money and all of us were working at part-time jobs; but there were week-ends when we could all double up together in each other's modest lakeside houses and contribute either half a dozen beer or a 'mickey' of rye (12 ozs.) to endless bull sessions. We discussed Heywood Broun and the American Newspaper Guild; the recently formed (and almost as soon still-born) New Writers' Group; the fuss everyone was making over Dionne Quintuplets; the latest pronouncement of the comic demagogue who was at that time running our local affairs; the general decadence and gloominess of Europe; and always the thrilling political battles of our favourite statesman, Franklin Delano Roosevelt.

Often we met at Dick Blue's storey-and-a-half cottage on the road from Port Credit to Cooksville. Dick was an Englishman who had married a Canadian girl and after losing his shirt on the Stock Exchange had come out to Canada to repair his fortunes. At the time I met him he'd been in Canada about ten years but was as unreconstructed a stage-Englishman as you'd meet anywhere; complete with checked yellow waistcoat, tweed 'country suit', bristly United Services Club moustache, pipe and basset hound. When in his city clothes he even wore pearl grey spats though this was neither as English nor as up-to-date as it might seem, for many prudent Torontonians wore them, carefully tucked inside their overshoes or galoshes. His

E

general get-up made him about as inconspicuous as a bloodstain on a clean shirt.

Dick revelled in this conspicuousness and was not above striving to impart a slightly raffish air to it by sporting a beat up (but lovingly polished) Essex convertible two seater, and acting as if his modest house at Port Credit was a country seat. To this end not only the checked waistcoat and the green or scarlet ties, but also the hiring of an elderly and ham-fisted 'butler', Robert. He was just about the most incompetent manservant who ever existed, but under Dick's direction he played the part of the cheeky old retainer to perfection.

'And good afternoon to *you*, sir,' he would say hobbling out of the back quarters in his shirtsleeves with a frilly apron tied on in front. "'Aven't seen you since last week, sir. A regular Night Owl. Hyuk—Hyuk—Hyuk! Gimme ya bags.' And he would dissolve into a reedy chuckle while he bathed you in waves of cheap rye, and his rheumy old eye dared you to rebuke him for familiarity.

Robert used to burst into the guest room, whether you were dressed or not, wheezing the morning news. 'I see where the Premier's made a dope of himself again.' Or else, leaning on a mop-handle while he told you the latest 'doings' in Port Credit village. 'Yas. I 'ear Mr. and Mrs. Tonkin are broke up. Yas. It was Mr. Oldham from 'Amilton, they say.' A leer. 'Or else Missus Tonkin an' 'er young man from Oakville. Hyuk-Hyuk-Hyuk! They'll be the death o' me yet.'

Robert's shopworn pseudo-Dickensian jokes and his all-licensed fool's rudeness would have driven most people away from the house; but to us—against the conformist Toronto background—he was an exotic plant. Furthermore Dick could play Chopin and Lully like a dream on his tiny boudoir grand. Many a roaring rye-fuelled social discussion—half the people sprawled on the floor and the rest on what few chairs there were—would be stilled by Dick's sudden slam of the piano lid, followed by a dreamy nocturne or spirited mazurka.

At such times his face underwent a complete transformation. His olive skin drew tight over closed eyes; his head swayed gently to the rhythm, and the light cut deep clefts in his noble sunken forehead. He ceased to be a comic Englishman in the colonies and became the lost lonely lovable soul he was. He played plenty of wrong notes; but that didn't matter, for it was the mood that held us. And when it was over no one wanted to go back to political wrangling unless it was the odd drunk. We'd lurch out of the overheated little cottage into fresh fallen snow, into the damp air from which soft flakes fell black against the night sky or scurrying white in the yellow beams thrown from the house. We knew Dick both in affluence and in need, for he was a born gambler and was up and down like a jack-in-the-box. But whether he was driving a Willys-Knight ('The Queen Mary') in lemon gloves, or whether he was drinking a solitary beer with me, in a threadbare overcoat, in the dreadful 'beverage room' of the Mott hotel, he never varied a millimetre from the incurable optimist and the incurable romantic.

The finger-wagger, the woman who was always saying, 'Well, now just what do you mean by that? Define your terms', was Mary Carver. Mary, the wife of Humphrey Carver, an architect and town planner, who had come to Canada in the late twenties, had been born Mary Gordon. She was one of the six daughters (there was also a son) of Rev. Charles W. Gordon of Winnipeg, otherwise known as Ralph Connor, author of *The Sky Pilot*, *The Man from Glengarry* and many other works of outback muscular Christianity popular in the years immediately before and after the First World War.

Mary had inherited her father's immense curiosity about the world, and she was spry, alert and enormously kind. With her brow furrowed in a perpetual frown you never felt, when Mary said, 'Come along now, define your terms', that she was laying for you a donnish trap. You felt simply that she really wanted to know and you did your best to explain because you knew that, once the explanation was forthcoming, Mary would arc across the wordy circumlocutions in a brilliant intuitive spark generated by Prairie shrewdness and the wild winds that blew across the barren lands. Often when you went out to help her with the glazed ham, the potato salad and the corn on the cob it was to find her gazing abstractedly out of the kitchen window, her brow wrinkled, the knife in imminent danger of slicing off a finger.

'Now I wonder what he meant by that?' she'd say.

'Never mind, Mary, let's have some beer.'

'But I *have* to know. It's important that I know!' and her marvellously attractive and lively plain-Jane face looked up at you with a devastating clarity that made you feel unworthy because you knew that *you* couldn't tell her.

At this point Humphrey would propose an innocent sing-song round the cottage upright. Because he was six and a half feet tall— a real lodgepole of a man—we always agreed, pantomiming extreme terror; though, as so often with tall men, he was really a very gentle fellow. Like many of his generation, he was a tremendous devotee of Gilbert and Sullivan. It was always a surprise to me that Mary and her sisters who, whether married or single, were constantly dropping in and out, knew these ditties far better than Humphrey did, or I did; were word perfect in fact. It was only later when I got to know Canada really well that I discovered that the loyalties of certain of my English-speaking compatriots were awkwardly divided between their native land and the 'Old Country', that they were still colonials at heart, and that they would often slip, quite un- consciously, into talking of Canada, *in Canada*, as 'out here'.

'Out where?' you would challenge them rudely. 'Where are we out from?'

There'd be an uncomfortable silence until someone observed sheepishly, 'Well, the Old Country, I guess.' How different this was; this describing one's own country as 'out here' from the Americans' description of Europe as 'Over there'.

Since it was still the Depression and we were still young, we were all for social reform, not a very hardy plant in an atmosphere of in- dividualism and get-rich-quick. But the really appalling poverty and hardship of the early Thirties, especially in the Prairies—and espe- cially in contrast to the almost legendary affluence of the Twenties —had stirred consciences to new depths. Led by clergymen, welfare workers, professors, dirt farmers and a surprising number of first generation English Canadians or even English immigrants, the League for Social Reconstruction burst into flower. It was an awkward name and showed, some of us thought, a distinct doubt in the minds of those who had framed its manifesto, as to whether the word 'social- ism' would be acceptable to Canadians any more than it had been to Americans. But it was soon shortened to LSR and those initials were an exciting beacon to young men and women without jobs; to graduates clerking in department stores for $17.50 a week; to dirt farmers on the Prairies who had driven the famous fuel-less model T Ford pulled by a horse; and to embittered youngsters who had ridden rods on transcontinental freights.

Some of those who attended the bull sessions of the LSR used the nonconformity thereby conferred as a special means to cocking a snook at Toronto. Since 'Toronto the Good', as it was widely known throughout Canada in those days, had given me my first steady job, had kept me in funds, had provided a rehabilitation centre for my father and had proved for me the gateway into Canada, I was disinclined to take a poor view of the city. Not so my friends, all of them Canadians; and though many of them Westerners, many of them also Torontonians. The silent venom which they poured on the city, the loud splenetic rancour with which they cursed it, used to astonish me. I thought Toronto was a bit smug and self-complacent, a bit hypocritical and certainly a great place for a humbug to make an easy living. But these were the virtues (or characteristics) of Anglo-Saxon and Anglo-Celtic protestants of the middle class, especially in new countries. Having lived in Melbourne for over a decade I didn't think Toronto had much to teach me about humbug and self-complacency. But my friends thought otherwise. They just hadn't a good word to say for the town. Montreal was exotic and Gallic; Quebec was history; Winnipeg was brash and vigorous; Vancouver had the scenery. But Toronto, Toronto the Good, Hogtown, Babylon-on-the-Humber, what did it have?

Well, I thought it had quite a lot. Its three quarters of a million people supported by far the best symphony orchestra in Canada; in fact for a while they had two of them running in competition. It had the biggest and best museum in Canada and a very fine art gallery. It had four daily papers and was the centre of the Canadian publishing business. It had, in those days, deep tree-choked ravines where a man could wander in silence without sight of a house for miles down rustic lanes and watch the squirrels and chipmunks and listen to the birds much as they must have been in Fenimore Cooper's America or the country of Ernest Thompson-Seton's *Lives of the Hunted*.

Of course certain of the publicized virtues were harder to live up to. Toronto was 'a city of churches', and indeed you could hardly help seeing them, for they were on almost every other corner. But did this imply piety or churchiness? Toronto was 'a city of homes' in contrast to sinful Montreal where people, one was told, dwelt in apartments. True enough; but the homes, especially in the West End and off the Danforth, were of a paralysing sameness. The city struck me as worthy, hardworking, self-centred, shrewd and pretty pleased with itself. It wasn't like Paris or New York or London; but then it wasn't like Adelaide or Belfast or Cleveland either, though it was more like them than it was like the first three. It was perhaps a frustrating place for a young man to spend seven years of his life, but not a stifling place. The reason for this was that, even as Paris sums up France, so Toronto summed up the virtues and drawbacks of the pioneer society of Upper Canada from which it was descended. And though the drawbacks were distasteful—censoriousness, smugness, frugality—the virtues were not inconsiderable either, hard work, tenacity, shrewdness, reliability.

Since for me Toronto was the place whence I jumped off into the Canada that I've known and loved for thirty odd years I regarded it with affection. But perhaps it was not from Toronto that I jumped off. My leap was rather through the vivid swirling canvases of the Group of Seven and their followers. Right through them and out the other side into the 'true north strong and free', into a potent myth and an equally powerful reality.

Chapter Eleven

TRUE NORTH STRONG AND FREE

URING the first months in Toronto I didn't go North at all, except for the staid weekend of Colin's famous visit. This hardly counted since it was heavily hemmed in by parental strictures and the need for good behaviour. Further, this particular bit of North was so very much an extension of Toronto—our Brighton, on a Northern Lake as it were—that it didn't really seem like a new country. Certainly not like a majestic land nor the home of a powerful myth.

The phrase 'Up North' or 'Going up North', though it was clearly freighted with heavy meaning for Torontonians, and was indeed a highly emotive phrase, at this time meant nothing to me at all. Insofar as I apprehended the phrase, it was as a bleaker alternative to 'Down South'. Yet until I had apprehended it, the essential Canada—the land of the emotions, myths and symbols; the only land shared by our two founding races and shared by them alone—remained totally unknown. As usual it was left to the artists to enlighten me. One day B. K. Sandwell sent me to cover an exhibition by the Canadian Group of Painters. This name naturally roused a good deal of resentment among other groups. Who were these upstarts to arrogate to themselves the name of the nation? And wasn't the very word 'Canadian' a piece of claptrap designed to hide the fact that they just hadn't thought out who they really were? A patriotic scoundrelism in fact. As I looked at the paintings I thought the Group had every right to the name. Most of the canvases were great swirling linear compositions, brightly if flatly patterned, vivid in colour if lacking in subtlety. They were, above all, romantic paintings. Unlike the reticent understatement of the classicist, these paintings rushed right up to you, eyes wide with wonder, hair dishevelled, clothes in disarray; they gripped you by the lapel, shouted in your ear, tried to climb right into your lap. Their message was: 'This is our country. Isn't it overwhelming? Don't you love it?'

The painters deliberately took you on a sort of Cook's tour of Canada: the cod drying on the flakes among the lobster pots at Peggy's Cove in the Maritimes; a church spire stabbing lonely and stark into a clear silver-blue sky from the rolling melancholy contours of Quebec; the Ontario north country with its sparkling lakes, endless sombre curtains of spruce and mournful vistas; the bald prairie with grain elevators like ships at sea; great tangled masses of mountain; and over all the tundra and the barren lands. There were urban scenes, it is true; but they were usually of slums: Belle Epoque forerunners of social realism. But mostly it was the empty land.

It was assertive painting; maybe a bit too assertive. It underlined everything; spoke in italics, but spoke too with tremendous gusto. It told you essentially of the Canada that lies to the north of the strip a hundred miles wide and parallel to the United States border, which then contained about eighty per cent of all Canadians: a sort of demographic Chile. It spoke essentially of the reason why, after two hundred years of settlement, Canada was still in those days a 'corridor lying along the 49th parallel threaded by steel rails'.

But its idiom was not naturalistic. It was heavily patterned and highly decorated, and to this extent stylized in a romantic mode. Looking back one can now see that its technique derived in large measure from the Art Nouveau which gripped Paris and later New York in the days immediately before the First World War. The tangled cast iron curlicue entrances to the Paris Metro with their tortured lettering and horror of straight line, have much in common with paintings like Tom Thomson's *Northern River* and J. E. H. MacDonald's *The Tangled Garden*.

Perhaps the famous New York 'Armory' show of 1913, with its first glimpse of the Post Impressionists and the Fauves—not to mention the social realism of John Sloan and Saul Bellows—may also have had an effect. The members of the Group of Seven are on record as suggesting that all of these influences were at work. But perhaps the main thing to remember is that the artists were all in their late twenties and early thirties during these years and that when they formed the Group of Seven in 1920 they had worked together, and together endured the public acrimony that pursues the avant garde, especially in provincial Anglo-Saxon protestant societies. Some of them had fought and painted together in the First World War, and all of them were deliberately determined to try and see the Canadian North in a new way. They announced as much in their public manifestos.

The Group of Seven—though it disbanded thirty-five years ago —is still a magic name in Canadian painting. At the time of this particular exhibition the Group was also a tremendous force for aggressive nationalism—Canadianism it was called—and had a strong appeal to all those under fifty who wished to assert our personality. The fury which this style of painting aroused among the traditionally inclined had to be seen to be believed. It so happened that I found myself directly on the receiving end of a blast of official invective from no less a person than Sir Wyly Grier, President of the Royal Canadian Academy.

Carried away by the Group show I had written an enthusiastic encomium which Sandwell had printed without change in *Saturday Night*. The next week I had to go to Montreal to cover some shows and in emerging from a large commercial gallery I ran slap into Sir Wyly. He literally shook his cane at me.

'Ha, McInnes!' he said, brandishing the weapon in the narrow entrance of the Metcalfe Galleries on Drummond Street. 'What's this I'm reading in *Saturday Night*?'

'Indeed, Sir Wyly,' I said mildly, 'to what do you refer?'

Sir Wyly was a man of less than normal height with a small white waxed moustache and rimless pince-nez. He trembled with chagrin and also, as I later discovered, with outrage, for he'd been born and raised in Melbourne, coming to Canada as a young man, and he couldn't understand how someone like me (who if not born in Melbourne had at least been raised there) could so betray our common—and as he believed—establishment-minded heritage. I stood looming over him with my unavoidable six foot two. He bristled. He was in a grey tweed coat with a beaver collar, grey spats, overshoes and a blue Homburg hat which he didn't bother to take off, while I removed mine with an ostentatious flourish.

'I've been reading your column,' he blustered. 'You take a very biased view. Of course you're a very young man.'

I bowed distantly. Sir Wyly eased himself past me in the airlock

E*

between the outer and the inner door of the Metcalfe gallery. He brandished his cane once again.

'I'm surprised Sandwell prints your stuff,' he said.

I replied with some hauteur, 'I have Mr. Sandwell's complete confidence. If you are dissatisfied, Sir Wyly, I suggest you write to him.'

As I made to sweep out with majestic indifference he called after me, 'Be fair to the Academy, sir! Be fair!'

I thought I detected a faint note of pleading in the voice and, as I'd not yet covered the annual show of the Royal Canadian Academy, I assumed that Grier was not only resigned to my doing so but anxious that I write a good report of the goings on. I paused, and observing rather pompously, 'You may rest assured, Sir Wyly,' swept out into Drummond Street where snowdrifts, dry as borax, were piled four feet high in great banks outside the buildings, where shoes creaked in the hard-packed snow, and the air rasped at one's throat like a file. I'll show him, I thought.

When the Royal Canadian Academy exhibition came on I covered it with what seemed to me just the right mixture of sprightliness and irony. BK didn't think so.

'I think what we need,' he said, pulling at his pendulous lower lip and gazing at me with his deceptively mild blue eyes, 'is a little less about the Academy and a little more about the paintings. After all most people know the RCA is full of old hats, but they don't know what this year's crop of pictures are like.'

He tossed my copy back at me across his desk. 'Try again,' he said mildly, but with a sudden stirring at the back of his melting blue eyes.

'Yes, sir,' I said, adding cheekily, 'I might perhaps unearth an Augustus John, would you say?'

'Let's say a Munnings-and-ginger-ale; possibly an Orpen-and-soda.'

BK was like that. Immensely protective of his young writers but absolutely firm on standards, both of style and of commentary. When I told Herbert McManus, the managing editor, he gave me an ironic look from under tufted eyebrows and twanged,

'Coming from BK I'd say that was just about equivalent to being clapped in irons.'

Yet, though BK would stand no nonsense from his staff, neither would he allow them to be intimidated. A few weeks later the gallery of a large department store put on an exhibition by two showy and meretricious central European journeymen. I said what I thought of them and in due course the piece appeared. I thought nothing of it, believing, in my innocence, that the truth will out. I learned later, though informally, that an official of the company had called and asked for a retraction, or that I be disciplined. Failing that, he hinted, the store's advertising might be curtailed. BK simply said 'Thank you' and hung up in his face. This was a pretty brave thing to do in the Depression years, on a paper struggling for advertising, and with a store in Toronto which had branches in other large Canadian cities. But that was BK all over.

BK thought my enthusiasm for the Group of Seven and the Canadian Group of Painters was a bit excessive, but being committed to building and constantly repairing the dyke of Canadian nationalism against the flood of American culture always lapping at the brim, he gave me my head. As I wrote more it became, I think, more balanced; or at any rate less intolerant. But as I studied more of these big powerful canvases I wanted to meet the giants who had painted them. This turned out to be quite easy: something which always astonishes the young who are innocent of the fact that the old love praise and approbation even more than *they* do. All of the original members, except Jim MacDonald who had died in 1932, were still with us and at that time in their middle fifties, and at the height of their powers.

The first one I met was A. Y. Jackson: Alex Jackson, the bachelor doyen of the Group. He lived alone in an enormous studio in an unexpectedly modern building down the slope of one of the many ravines which split Toronto's asphalt carapace, and where there were trees and quiet. The Studio Building was square, stern and uncompromising, with great areas of unadorned north windows and the rectilinear simplicity of an early Frank Lloyd Wright. What made it remarkable was that it had been built just before the First World War at a time when gingerbread curlicues and tortured art nouveau filigree had been all the rage.

The origin of the building was as remarkable as its style. An early friend and patron of the young artists who were later to become the Group of Seven had been a Toronto doctor with a summer place in Georgian Bay, a passion for the North Country and a fairly lucrative practice. His name was MacCallum. To his drive and

passion were added the taste and wealth of an original member of
the Group who happened also to be a millionaire. Lawren Harris was
a member of the Harris family whose partners were the Masseys.
The profits of the farm implement business can rarely have been put
to better use. The Masseys are better known and their philanthropy
has been on a bigger scale, but Lawren's contribution to the erection
and maintenance of the Studio Building, and its rental at nominal
fees to rising young artists, was in its own way a gesture as notable.

Alex Jackson's studio was on the third floor. He invited me to
'come in any time' and by any time I soon discovered that he really
meant any time. Being myself a lonely young bachelor with a ten-
dency towards romantic hero-worship I soon began to frequent Alex's
studio, indeed to infest it. I must have been a perfect nuisance. If
so, he never let on.

Slow, laconic, puffing a little as he padded slowly from the corner
where he hid his cups and plates behind a brown burlap curtain,
over to the square birch table, where he ate his beans and bacon, he
kept up an intermittent drumfire of commentary on the world of art
and its denizens.

'Anything you need you'll find,' he once said after I'd sat silent
for forty minutes watching him at work on a canvas. 'But you must
sense the need of it.'

Alex was the darling of all the Toronto ladies; the perennial
bachelor who at fifty looked seventy (and at eighty looked sixty).
He had a bent and broken nose, a loose friendly mouth filled with
long narrow wonderfully strong teeth, a tonsure of grey hair over
a pink healthy scalp, with an unruly tuft sticking up to make him
look like an elderly Tintin, though his gait was more like that of
a bear. He was a very steady, very prolific painter. Perhaps not 'inspired' in the sense that his friend and colleague Arthur Lismer was.
The struggle to resolve contradictions, the genuine furor poeticus
filled all Lismer's canvases with a rampaging protest. Alex Jackson's
were much quieter, but tremendously strong with great sweeps of
colour built up from within. You felt the bones of mother earth—
and there's an awful lot of mother earth in Canada—beneath the
outward flow of rhythmic contour. You felt also, though his landscapes were bare of people, a strong sense of men against the sky;
a brooding tenseness as of a man, or perhaps a nation, 'on the mark'
at the start of a race. Not a hundred yard dash but a thousand

metres. And waiting for the starter's gun. Waiting. Alex's passion was like the curses that Macbeth had to endure: not loud but deep. In the banked fires of his emotions he was like the land that he painted and loved, but perhaps like its dwellers too; strong, shrewd, laconic.

After a while he'd pull back from the canvas, sensing that the light, which seemed consistent to me, had subtly faded. With slow deliberation he'd go silently about the business of wiping his brushes, scraping off his dirty smeared old palette, allowing me to wheel the easel over into a corner while we split a quart of beer. Then he'd 'have to get some grub'. This meant he was on his way downstairs and out the back to the little tumbledown shack, crouched under the rear windows of a steam laundry and a block of sleazy apartments, and mercifully shielded by a couple of large scraggly maples. This shack had a special significance for Alex Jackson, as it had for all members of the Group of Seven. It was the place where Tom Thomson had spent the winters between spells of guiding and painting 'Up North'. The reason Alex went there was prosaic enough. Tenancy of the shack had fallen to Keith McIver, a mining engineer and prospector, and in its warm winter snuggery these two lonely but self-contained bachelors could eat comradely meals in the wholly comprehended silences of the elderly. It was tacitly understood that I would not penetrate this sanctum and I never did.

Every artistic group, every movement, needs its saint or avatar. The Group of Seven found theirs in Tom Thomson. For a Canadian hero his career and personality were just about right. He was born a farm boy, drifted from job to job including a spell out in the Pacific North-West when it was opening up at the turn of the century. When he was thirty he began to show considerable talent as a designer and engraver, and he entered a commercial art studio where his dexterity made him a most valuable member of the art room. But whenever he could, he'd get away from Toronto with his paint-box and his little 8" × 10" birch panels, and go sketching. He started at the end of the tramline but gradually went further afield until he finished up in Algonquin Park in Northern Ontario. Here the man and the place and the talent met in happy conjunction. His sketching became prolific; his palette lightened; his brush became sure, swift and immediate. He gave up his job and with the help of his friends —including the same Dr. MacCallum—devoted his entire time to painting. In spring, summer and fall he was a guide, forest ranger and fisherman in the Park, painting whenever he could. In the winter he came down to Toronto and worked up some of his sketches into canvases, spending much of his life in this same shack, known by the time I came to Toronto as 'Tom's Shack'. In the midst of this tremendous spurt of creative activity he was mysteriously drowned on Canoe Lake in Algonquin Park in the summer of 1917. He was just forty.

Well, of course, the elements are all here. Even if Thomson's painting hadn't been as good as it was; didn't have that alternation of brooding melancholy with stark line and vivid sparkling colour; hadn't made such a direct overt and indeed naïve appeal to the Canadian psyche: he would still have been the ideal hero for the movement to have. In lay terms, and for English-speaking Canada, Thomson comes as near to leading the pantheon of national heroes as anyone I can think of. French-speaking Canada has its own pantheon of hero-priests, who are ours too—Breboeuf, Lalemant, Joguès —to whom it may point with pride and from whom we can all draw honest inspiration. And we can all share the political great. But among the artists and musicians and writers Thomson is a rare nationally loved and nationally revered figure.

And what did he do? At a time when Canadians were in one of their recurring moods of self-examination he rejected alien ways of looking at the Canadian physical heritage. He went up North, into the bush, and painted Canada as he saw it. 'This,' he said—(and it was all the more powerful because he didn't say it but simply painted it)—'This is your heritage.' The audience caught the implication: be worthy of it. And then in less than ten years it was all over. The legend of course enshrines the might-have-been as well as the achievement, and in this sense Thomson was at once more and less than he appeared to be. Less of a painter perhaps and more of a symbol; a messianic figure in sweater, tuque and hunting boots, with his paint box slung on his back, paddling swiftly up the silent reaches of a northern river into the slanting sun beyond the next headland.

The effect of this legend on me was very strong, and I determined to get out of the great grey city and into the North, both in the sense of rock, lake and pine, and in the sense of seeing more of these canvases. My opportunity came through Pegi Nicol, and Harry McCurry. The conscious cuteness which turned Margaret Nichol into Pegi Nicol gives only one clue to her vivid personality. She was cute of course; cute as a button, wayward and exasperating, and also a bit of a tease. But she had a wonderful way of seeing the world without eyelids. She could take a group of children playing in a slum street, a tangle of narcissus bulbs in a flower pot, a view of smoky steaming winter Montreal from St. Helen's Island in mid-St. Lawrence, and put on them all the stamp of her own personality: a series of disjointed writhing images, never at ease, full of bubbling enthusiasm; a brilliant and cascading profusion of figures like the endless talk of an Irishman over a whisky. A Pegi Nicol in a gallery proclaimed itself immediately because of its completely individual quality; much as one knows, after a bar or two, that it is Chopin's music because it is so personal that it can be by no one but him.

This wayward teasing elfin creature married a great big wrestler of a man from New Brunswick. He calmed her by force. In fact he once shouted her absolutely silent following a party to which everyone had come dressed as something from the Southern Hemisphere. She brushed herself off, went home and turned up for elevenses the following morning with perfect composure. This was widely regarded as the Taming of the Shrew. But no one could ever subdue her painting.

She just went gaily on, cocking her Peter Pan haircut out of her eye, talking in a high thin faerie voice and wearing 'bohemian' clothes of her own design; the sort that artists pride themselves upon as being timeless, along the well-known lines of Elizabeth Hawes' *Fashion is Spinach*: ponchos and shifts and sandals and swooping hats in one piece of felt. But which somehow never look quite right. And meanwhile the canvases grew and one day she walked into the hospital where I lay with a stubborn hernia and said, while her husband remained inarticulately sympathetic,

'You look terrible.'

'I feel terrible.'

'This room's awful. It's the most awful room I've seen. I'm going to paint you a picture.'

'Thanks very much, Pegi.' Thinking she wouldn't.

And then two days later she sidled into the ward, fortunately just after the daily bed-bath, and placed a square paper parcel in front of the brown stained hospital mirror, beneath the inverted porcelain bowl that hung from the hospital ceiling.

143

Finding a Father

'I've brought you a painting,' she said and skipped out twitching her mantle blue, while there lingered, among the dreary hospital smells of formalin and carbolic and sour sweat, a wafted trace of *Mon pêché*. I stared for a moment at the square package and then rang the bell for the male nurse. He came sneaking in holding a forbidden cigarette cupped in one hand behind his back. His close-cropped hair was red and his neck was scarred with perpetual acne.

'What's up?' he said sourly.

'Please untie that parcel. There's a picture in it. I'd like you to prop it up against the mirror.'

'Picture, eh?' he said suspiciously starting to rip off the paper and cellophane. 'What kinda picture? You speak to the matron?'

'Oh, just undo the package, will you?'

'Want to watch out what you show in the ward. One o' the nurses might take a fit. Heh heh.'

He ripped off the last of the paper and gave a noncommittal grunt. I felt a sharp sense of disappointment. There, propped against the mirror was the head of an unknown woman in dingy green and choleric pinks. A powerful portrait, but perhaps not one to live with. I had a sudden thought.

'Turn the picture round.'

'Please?'

'Okay, please then; but turn it.'

Freshly painted, with the oil still glistening, was spring in Toronto. Tumbledown mansard roofs, old bricks splashed with red ochre, bits of ragged blue sky; the whole seen through a tangle of maple branches and twigs with the sticky new buds bursting from their pods and surging right out into the stuffy carbolic-sweaty ward and filling it with that heady air that comes from the Canadian north in the instant pause while the ice cracks, the sun pours down, and just before the trees burst into leaf. Spring! Leaping into the Canadian arena like a young lion. Monday it's winter, Tuesday it's spring, Wednesday it's summer. Pegi had caught the transient moment.

'Hey,' I said to the male nurse, 'I think it's just about time you let me up.'

The buds bursting on Grosvenor Street in mid-town Toronto were one thing. Among the sad tiptilted apartment blocks, the grimy old red-brick lofts, and the staid bay-windowed mansions in tuck-pointed yellow-brick, they were life itself. But out on the edge of town different miracles were happening. Spring was spreading across the undulating fields so fast that the green flush was like a negative limning in a developing tank, or the shadow of a cloud in a high wind. Down in 'The Village' you could get an inkling of what it was like, for the trees there were old, and taller than the high tension wires, which was rare in Toronto. The Village was a derelict area between the affluent downtown skyscrapers and the rather prissy residential district that abutted on the University. It was the decayed core of Toronto, a scabrous wasteland of enormous half-empty prodigal parking lots; of half-finished buildings abandoned after the Crash with their twisted iron guts still spilling in frozen fatuity out of the gaping concrete rectangles. The original shacks still stood: urban versions of the thin-chested farmhouses of the 1880's and 1890's. In the stunned aftermath of the Crash, no one could be bothered pulling them down.

With the onset and deepening of the Depression smart, or smart-aleck, bohemia moved into the low rental shacks. These had no basement: a pot-bellied Quebec heater, its convolution of pipes held free of the ceiling by bits of twisted picture wire, supplied the heat. Bohemia quickly converted them into book shops, antique stores, small art galleries, picture framers, silversmiths and turners of pewter, bookbinderies, small smart cafés—without a licence in those drab temperance days, but where you could eat stick bread, gossip and drink bootleg rye out of a hip flask. And there they flourished flanked by the sleazy rooming houses along Laplante Street and overlooked by the yawning yellow cliff of the General Hospital.

But what made The Village were the trees: great skinny elms, tall maples as dense as a green nimbus, here and there a scraggly poplar. They spread cool depths of shade in the acres of concrete sidewalk labelled 'City 1933' or 'Jones Pvg Co 1934'. If you couldn't afford to go up town to Hog's Hollow or over to the Island, The Village was the place to keep cool or maybe to hear the rustle of spring.

In the days when cars were still only one to a family—abject poverty by North American standards—Hog's Hollow offered the temptations of Paradise at the end of a five cent tramcar ride. You ground north for eight solid miles on the Yonge Street car with its trailer and the stolid conductor sitting at his 'Pay Enter' seat while the passengers did all the work. Up the slow hill that marked the edge of an ancient pre-glacial lake; one and a quarter miles to each 'section' of land carved back from the shore of Lake Ontario by the hard-bitten pioneers. Past Queen and Dundas and College; past Bloor and St. Clair and Balliol (pronounced Balloil by the conductors); past Maple ('Maybow next! Maybow!' 'I want Maple, conductor.' 'I just called it, din you hear me? Maybow!') Past Mount Pleasant—with the cemetery—and Eglinton and Davisville, and eventually the 'radial' took over from street car; a mammoth with a cow-catcher riding on rails set high on sleepers instead of being buried in the pavement. But here you stopped and, hand in hand, skittered downhill with a picnic lunch into the deep peace and solitude (until the mosquitoes found you) of the cool piney woods, while the poor unfortunates in cars zoomed high above your heads on the Avenue Road viaduct.

Or if you were feeling really romantic, as well as poor, you could take the SS *Sam McBride* across the harbour to the Toronto Island, and it cost no more than a tram fare: five cents. The Islands were totally unexpected in relation to the gaunt grey canyons of downtown Toronto. Low, sandy and treed principally with willow and poplar, they lay about a mile out from the foreshore and extended about two miles along from East to West to form a natural lake harbour which had originally attracted the English to found Fort York. These islands were really no more than deposits of mud and gravel from the Don and the Humber rivers and from the chalklike Scarborough cliffs nearby, swirled west and south into a sandbar by the winds and currents of Lake Ontario.

But once the *Sam McBride* docked you were in a quiet world of leafy glades, innumerable still channels crossed by pseudo-rustic bridges, and the welcome shade of great weeping willows with clotted blackened stems. The city seemed miles away, and yet if you turned your back on the Island there it was, a fistful of very impressive skyscrapers reared up against the northern sky. A faint hum drifted across the water as from a purring dynamo in a distant power-house. Pretty dramatic eh? you'd say to American friends. Not quite up to New York or Chicago of course. But—a bit like, say, Cleveland, eh?

The main island was split by a wide tarmac walk off which little frame summer cottages nestled among the willows. Delivery was by launch through the swampy channels for in those dear dead days no cars were allowed on the Islands, another source of heavenly relief. The tarmac ended in a promenade or 'boardwalk' on top of the rock-and-fill mole which protected the 'seaward' side of the islands from the fierce and capricious storms of Lake Ontario. It was fun in a way, but to anyone who had known the sea there was something queer and flat about a freshwater seascape, even if its horizon was limitless. It was too much a pale echo of something that it couldn't aspire to be. I had a feeling—powerfully reinforced by the Group of Seven canvases—that the real Canada lay elsewhere.

Pegi Nicol again. The morning after the great party she announced that she and her husband had decided not to go up North with Ken Mayall and therefore there were spare seats in the car. Forgetting about my hernia and my adhesions I joyfully accepted the offer and next morning we started off on the 300 mile trip north to the Temagami forest reserve. Ken Mayall was a forestry engineer who had graduated from the timber-cruising of student days to become a practising ecologist undertaking land-use surveys for the Ontario government. He was a short stocky sandy-haired bachelor who peered myopically at the world through pebble lenses, but who was skilled enough in the ways of the wild to spot a nesting vireole on a tree a hundred yards off or a bear crouching in the lee of a white pine.

We took off in his beat-up convertible up Yonge Street which ran ruler-straight to the North Pole, said the wags, adding that of a winter Sunday morning you could fire a cannon up it without any danger to life or limb. The buds were bursting all right on the maple trees, and the bright almost chemically green leaves were squirting out of the twigs like Japanese water flowers, making thousands of tiny green parasols against the sombre backdrop of pine and spruce. The air was balmy in the high sixties; creeks chuckled under culverts and in the lee of tangled hedges little swathes of laggard snow melted almost visibly, like butter in a frying pan.

About mid-afternoon the pre-Cambrian rock sliced up through the farmlands and we entered a sharp crackling land of browny-pink stone and mournful conifers and views of innumerable lakes, grey or blue depending on the colour of the sky. The air started to have plenty of bite; and the vistas at the top of low undulating rises looked sharper and more distant. We hit North Bay at dusk and when we woke next morning there was frost on the ground and the mercury stood at 26.

North Bay was in those days the end of pavement. You entered 'The Gateway to the North' on tarmac from the south; but you left

it, north, east or west, on gravel. The town had a history going back
to the days of Champlain who had portaged his canoes across the
height of land between the Ottawa and Georgian Bay—La Mer
Douce as he called it. But it looked to me like a real frontier town:
all frame houses and bumpy sidewalks and raw scars of earth. Almost
at once we climbed over a scarp and spent the rest of the day on an
unbelievably narrow roller-coaster gravel and dirt road, full of chuck
holes, big loose stones that whipped up against the sump with an
alarming clang, blind turns, steep hills and a curtain of virgin forest
on either side, the feet of the trees still choked with snow.

Not a bird, not a flower, not even the blood-red sap beneath the
skin of the wintergreen or the pussy willow. At Temagami we were
told the ice had just 'gone out', but the water below the little dock
was already filming over again as the sun sank behind the low
forested hills, and Ken decided that as we had twelve miles to go
down the North-East Arm we'd better look slippy and chance it that
the shore at the forester's shack wasn't too encumbered with mush
and ice.

The lake was immensely cold and silent and the sky freezing and
distant as we chugged along. Our outboard disturbed nothing on the
sombre banks; either forest to the water's edge or great slashing
towers of rock. The place seemed dead, yet at the same time tingling
with awareness. The crisp inter-planetary air caught at your throat.
Big stars hung blazing lanterns in the yellowy-greenish sky; and
when we reached the little wooden dock opposite Bear Island, there
was a skittering among the dead branches lining the shores. Somebody who didn't like us was leaving in a hurry. We waded ashore
through eighteen inches of ice cold water, tied up the boat, unhasped
the locked front door of Mayall's log cabin and entered a cold dank
interior smelling of old blankets and ski-wax. Within an hour we
were fed and bedded down before a roaring fire while outside the
mercury stood at 17 and the aurora sent great crackling curtains of
greenish light undulating across the night sky. It was the 18th of
May.

Though we stayed at Temagami less than a week, like the Group
of Seven I fell in love with the North Country. We lived the shame-
less, bearded, blasphemous life that young men live when they're
alone in the bush; but we loved the crisp clear mornings, the sparkling vistas of blue-flecked lake, sun dancing on the waves, stony

crags slipping down beneath the water, silvery-blue skies as deep
as the world's great morning. And when we stopped doing things,
there came the old, corny, but accurate Robert Service, 'the silence
you most could feel'. We were back in the land of *The Last of the
Mohicans*, a man dwarfed against the secret silences of the forest
and the implacable hostility of the last remnants of the ice age.

Then one day spring suddenly came to the north country. The
mercury ran up to 70; the log cabin became stifling and naked silver
birch burst into green flame almost as you looked at it. We struck
camp and headed south to Toronto where the trees, in Ontario's
'banana belt', were already hiding the street lamps and the high
tension wires and meeting in an interlacing network above the
suburban avenues. But how hot, dull and sweltery it seemed.

*   *   *

In the wake of the Group of Seven a great swirl of amateurs boiled
and bubbled. Churned up by the threshing screws of the Seven as
they ploughed their way across the Canadian intellectual muskeg,
they bobbed and curtseyed in a series of exhibitions where enthusiasm and faith rather than talent or competence were the criteria.
Among the worst of painters and the best and kindliest of men was
a highly successful tycoon whose normally beady eye became glau-
cous or moist in the presence of the canvases of the Group or the
landscapes that had inspired them. Each summer, he went up to his
cottage on an island in Georgian Bay and each fall he would invite
artists and amateurs and friends to his yellow brick house in Toronto
to see his paintings and to make such comments on them as might
be permitted by his hospitality, or encouraged by its bounty.

Distinguished artists would pause, dark brown glass in hand before
one of his wavy rocks, rocky waves, or reinforced concrete pine trees,
and say judiciously and innocuously, 'Yup. Got something there.'
His skies were leaden blue, his trees grey cement, his water as con-
vincing as cast iron, and his rocky promontories as solid as cardboard; but it was the enthusiasm that counted. A genial mine host,
the tycoon would stroll benignly from group to group, thick slug of
rye in hand, modestly disclaiming any talent or inclining a humble
head before some particularly nauseating bit of feminine gush.

'Yes,' he'd say to anyone who would listen (and it was surprising
how quickly the friends melted away when it was apparent that he

149

was about to give out), 'what I tried for there was an effect of light. Yup. Alex Jackson liked that one quite a bit.'

And as the years rolled by, the pile of iron-hard sketches burgeoned in his basement and in the attics of those to whom he'd been kind enough to give a painting. But he himself rolled on undeterred by the praise of fair-weather friends: a great big ungainly moose of a man in old-fashioned loud bright-brown tweeds, incongruous pearl grey spats over pickled brogues, and a disarming undergraduate's shock of black hair falling in a cowlick over a deeply lined forehead. Only the eyes remained without illusions. They were crinkled at the edges, but the steel blue irises behind steel-rimmed bi-focals saw the world steadily and saw it whole: and knew that his paintings were just no damned good at all.

'What're you doing for the summer?' he said to me one of these showy evenings. 'Why not come up to Georgian Bay with us and see the real Canada.'

'Well,' I said rather ungraciously, 'I have to work.'

'Surely BK will let you cruise with us up where the Group of Seven had its cradle? It should be worth it to the paper with the stuff you're writing, shouldn't it? Eh? Honey Harbour. The Giant's Tomb, Go Home Bay, the Western Islands. I guess those names mean something to you, don't they?'

He was leaning over me with a dark brown glass in his hand, his great ruddy slab-sided face all crinkled up with pleasure and alcohol. I thought of those sweeping canvases of the Group with their vistas of open sky and slashing great rocks and platinum-blue lakes edged like rulers with a tattered fringe of wind tossed pines. I thought of the excitement I'd felt at Temagami. I thought of the tame scraped-over clutter of Bala, with the CPR freights clattering by in a billow of dust and the roaring speed boats and the smell of hot-dogs and frying fat. Certainly not *my* true north strong and free.

'There might even be a couple of articles or radio broadcasts in it, for you,' said the tycoon. 'Think it over.'

'I've thought it over,' I said. 'I'll come.'

At Midland, by the end of steel, over where the Jesuit priests Bréboeuf and Lalemant had been martyred by the Iroquois, a snub-nosed ferry was waiting. They were using cannel coal in the boilers and the prevailing westerly sent a rich cloud of glutinous black smoke billowing over the graves and ruins of Huronia. I threw my grip through the air and over an iron lattice, and a tow-headed student in a blue striped T-shirt, working his way through college on a summer job, caught it inexpertly. It hit the iron deck with a smack and a corner burst open revealing underwear and pyjamas. I snapped at him irritably but his 'Geeze. I'm awful sorry, sir' took the wind right out of my sails.

'That's okay,' I said, rammed the offensive smalls back in the trunk, inserted my tartan scarf over them and toted the bag up to the front of the ferry just as an Indian in a greasy sweatshirt cast the final rope off a bollard. It snaked into the scummy water and the snub-nosed ferry took off into a fresh breeze and towards the 'open sea'. Soon the low wooded slopes and lakeside marshes slid behind and we began to thread our way through a labyrinth of whale-backed rocks and islands.

I found myself on a semi-circular slatted wooden bench painted a tired chocolate. In front of me a latticework galvanized iron guard-rail curved back on either side. Below was a small well-deck crammed with packaged goodies for the summer cottages on the run: canned soups and cornflakes in cardboard cartons; big hams in plastic bags; white sacks of flour; crates of iceberg lettuce and grapefruit from far-off Florida. In among the cartons the Indian, his hair smooth as black liquorice straps, gazed sloe-eyed at a pair of whimpering husky dogs. His olive face with its flattened nose was impassive, but the leather thongs to the dogs' collar were taut and the Indian's knuckles showed white. Spray was breaking over the dogs as the boat eased itself out of the harbour to the open water in among the whalebacks, and they weren't liking it.

On the slatted seat on one side of me was a six-year-old girl in a suede windcheater sucking on a yellow popsicle. On the other side was an old fellow in a five-gallon straw hat, the crown battered and broken, blue jeans, dirty white sneakers and a filthy old sweater full of holes over a tieless shirt buttoned high on the neck. His hands lay on his lap over the scrappy jeans; thin, almost translucent dark brown, heavily veined and knuckled. They looked like the hands of an oldtimer. His head was sunk on his chest and the rising west wind fluttered the wisps of white hair in his ears and played over the gnarled gravelly peaceful old face. I turned my attention to the whalebacks.

It was a landscape unlike anything I had ever seen and it was

151

both sinister and exciting. The midsummer evening sun raked across the tops of the reddish brown islets of rock. Sometimes they looked like whales, at other times like a flotilla of submarines with a twisted windblown pine for periscope. Sometimes, when the clouds caught them, turning the inland sea to a pitted pewter, they looked like nameless monsters raising themselves very slowly from the primaeval ooze. Then the sun would get down below a cloud and bathe the old stone walruses and seals with red-gold light, and at once the landscape would open up, island on island, until the 'sea' was reached. Beyond that, like a bit of fluff on the horizon lay the Western Islands, twenty miles off. And yet of course it was no more the sea than Lake Ontario, though grimmer and more majestic, with its rock and pine, than Ontario's chalk and sedge and sand.

The boat nuzzled a flat rock, held there by its motors. I saw the tycoon beckoning below and beyond him a little rocky harbour with half a dozen power boats, a couple of outboards and a dirty old inboard which looked to me capable of about three knots. It turned out later this was an over-estimate. Beside him was a lean girl in corduroy slacks and a turtle-necked sweater. I threw my trunk to the tycoon and the girl caught it and grinned. My foot was scarcely on the harsh abrasive rock when the stubby steamer backed, shied like a bronco and ploughed off north trailing a rich cloud of smoke from which fell oil smuts.

'This is us,' said the tycoon. 'And this is my niece Jane.'

'Hiya.'

'Hi.'

We came to the dirty old inboard. Another Indian boy waited for us to stow ourselves in among the hams and roasts and canned goods and a couple of small orange crates undulating gently in a slop of oily bilge. Then he cranked the little fly wheel with a bit of dirty rope and off we chugged out into the open. The tycoon sat up front in an oilskin and pretty soon the girl and I found we needed them too, for though the sea looked calm to its horizon line twenty miles away, the west wind was whipping it up and we had to make for one of the islands across the white caps which flung spray in our faces at each bump. Not being salt it wasn't sticky, but it was wet. We crouched in the stern and after a while we got in the lee of a big bare island. On top of its highest, barest point was a big boney house shaped like a box. It was anchored to the skyline: literally anchored by great wire hawsers strung from each corner and tightened right across the top of the roof. It was the most desolate, uncompromising hunk of weathered wood I'd ever seen. It ought to have been down east on the Maine Coast and painted white. But here it was, a thousand miles from the sea, and not painted at all.

'Here we are,' said the tycoon. He leaped nimbly ashore for all his sixty odd years. Jane and I followed. The Indian boy took the bags to the house and the inboard to the boatshed. Before washing for supper in a tin basin by the light of a small kerosene hurricane lamp, I looked out through the window: no glass, only a board folded up against the outer wall on to a large hook, to be let down when the westerly blew. It was blowing now, and the cheesecloth flyscreens, as symbolic of rude frontier comforts as the double-seater privy reeking of chlorate of lime, were starting to puff in and out like the fins of a giant ray. I decided the window needed closing. I got it down, but only after a wrestle with the rusty iron hook. When I got back inside the westerly had blown out the lamp. Through the chink I could see the remains of the sunlight lying in a long yellow smear across the distant horizon. Above it was a towering mass of clouds that seemed to boil upward in the dusk like explosions of a volcano.

I had a week at the island. It was mostly helping the tycoon paint his terribly sincere and wonderfully awful pictures; or sometimes trolling for whitefish among the inner islands. With Jane I got precisely nowhere. She was interested solely in outboards and was away in them alone for hours at a stretch. The sun was surprisingly hot and in the lee of rocky outcrops among the pungent juniper bushes and the dry moss you could quickly acquire a tan, or a burn. But once the westerly began to blow the whole firmament split apart. Rain came slanting down in great driving sheets; the Georgian Bay pine, permanently bent by the wind, now bent double; the horizon was blotted out and the world contracted to a grey oasis in the surrounding gloom, through which the wind wailed and sang, and through which, too, one could dimly descry the waves tossing in fury and sending spume careering upward into the high rocks and the branches of the trees. Here it was exhilarating; on the outer islands it was terrifying.

I managed to persuade the girl to go with me to one of the outer islands to fish. Vague ideas of a Lake Huron arcady lay at the back of my mind. We took the inboard because the tycoon said it was easier for a greenhorn to operate than the nervous and skittish outboard. He didn't tell me that it was also practically unmanoeuvrable and with its three knots speed quite incapable of keeping a heading once a gale started to blow.

In the middle of trolling for whitefish the westerly blew up out of nowhere. We started to ship water at an alarming rate. Jane set me to baling fiercely while she took over the rudder—claiming, quite rightly, to be more at home in the old boat and more familiar with the terrifying squalls than I was. The squall developed into a full gale which roared about our ears so that we could barely hear shouted words of encouragement or command from one end of the boat to the other. Rain lashed us savagely and then gave place to hail which really hurt and pounded on the sides of the dirty old boat with all the bite of a snare drum in a war movie. We seemed to be drifting broadside with the oncoming waves slapping over the gunwale greenish grey in the murk.

Thunder growled somewhere in the clouds; but since clouds, rain and lake were alike one indistinguishable mass of bruised purply-grey it was hard to tell whence it came. I went on baling frantically. Lightning split the sky wide open and sizzled into the water less than 300 yards away. I was pretty close to panic now but the lightning also revealed a low treeless island to which we were drifting at far too fast a clip. If not swamped then smashed, it seemed. But after heroic straining the boat gave a grudging sluggish response to the girl's rudder strings. It was enough to allow us to just miss a sharp point of rock and skid round it on to a gravelly spit on which we landed with a jarring thud that threw us out of the boat.

We hauled the boat up a foot or two, both of us lashed by drenching rain and the girl's hair draggled down to mingle in her turtle-neck sweater, like a horse's mane into its steaming blanket. We tied the boat to a stout old gnarled juniper bush, veteran of a thousand 'blows', and scampered across the island to the lee side. Here we crouched, soaked to the skin, teeth chattering and fingers blue with cold while the storm slowly blew itself out and any thought of dalliance was utterly banished from our minds by the peril.

When a watery sun at last rode a silver disc behind dissipating storm clouds all she said was,

154

'Lucky it wasn't an easterly or we'd have been blown fifty miles clear over to Michigan.'

'Do you have a US visa?' was all I could manage.

'Don't need one. Canadian citizen.'

That's right, I thought. Better do something about that. She tossed the wet stringy mop out of her face and gave a tight grin.

'Come on,' she said, 'Let's get the boat started.'

When we reached the boat it was half-buried in sand and driftwood, so I took off my shirt and waved it in the air and after about an hour the tycoon came bouncing across the still choppy water in the outboard.

'Kinda worried about you two,' was all he said as we clambered aboard.

The last two days were a sullen anti-climax, yet when I got back to Toronto and saw with dismay its prim self-satisfied suburban streets, its half empty canyons of grey cement with rubbish swirling at the intersections, and its tame ravines, I realized that I'd been bitten by the same bug that had attacked the Group of Seven. I would never be entirely happy in the city again.

* * *

I commented on this one winter night to Harry McCurry, at a party given by Alex Jackson in the Studio Building. Harry was a chunky fellow in his late forties with grizzled greying hair, a clipped moustache above a humorous mouth, and a glass eye almost as blue and as gentle as his own one; the sort of kindly eye that didn't make you want to claw your way up the wall or dream about Old Pew. He grinned when I started to criticize the 'banana belt'.

'You're just fed up with Toronto. Don't blame you. Hog town, that's what we call it in Ottawa. Why, the country you love—that you've just discovered for yourself—is right at our back door. You don't have to go a couple of hundred miles to find it, like you do here. Why don't you pay us a visit?'

'I'd like that very much.' McCurry was Deputy-Director of the National Gallery of Canada and this could be a big help to my column; reduce my areas of ignorance anyway. The next thing he said made me redden with pleasure.

'The Director and I've been reading your column in *Saturday Night*. It's good stuff.' He fixed me with his friendly eye. 'Why not come up and spend some time with us at the Gallery? We might be able to help each other.'

I thanked him expansively but left things up in the air. When I got home next day there was a letter with OHMS on it and the coat of arms of Canada gilt and embossed. Postmarked Ottawa, too. Heavens, I thought, McCurry must have put through a long distance call right after our conversation. What a wonderful guy! I tore open the envelope. Out fell a letter signed by someone called F. L. C. Pereira whom I'd never heard of. It appeared that he was writing on behalf of His Excellency Baron Tweedsmuir of Elsfield, C.H., Governor-General of Canada. Their Excellencies knew my mother and it would greatly please them if I could spend the next weekend but one with them at Rideau Hall in Ottawa as their guest.

Well! Mother again. And poaching on father's territory, too, in a way. Ought I to accept? Well of course I ought. For one thing a request from Vice-Royalty was a command, wasn't it? And what about Harry McCurry and the National Gallery? Why not kill two birds with one stone? I wrote off an appropriate reply. Fortunately the GG's invitation coincided with a special week-end ski excursion to Ottawa and I bought a coach-class return ticket which entitled me to a seat, but not a berth. Having sat up all night, dozing fitfully between jerk-water stops, I staggered blearily out of Union Station in Ottawa, and into the friendly though deferential grasp of a uniformed chauffeur and his limousine.

Chapter Twelve

GROUP OF SEVEN

THE Tweedsmuirs turned out to be pleasantly affable, if just a shade distant. I gained the impression that perhaps Mother had been twisting their arms. Rideau Hall—a comfortable limestone mansion with the most enormous pediment heavy with armorial bearings—was warm and cosy. Outside the snow was piled high in deep powdery drifts. A mountie patrolled with a beaver hat well down over his ears, and the sun shone brightly out of the most innocently crystal-blue sky in the world. The temperature was not so innocent; it hovered between −12 and −20 degrees fahrenheit, that is from forty-four to fifty-two degrees of frost. This meant that when you went out your feet on the hard packed dry snow squeaked like a dentist ramming amalgam into a wisdom tooth; the hairs in your nostrils grew icicles every time you breathed in; your ears tingled sharply as you banged them to keep the frostbite out of them; and the cold after a while penetrated right to your loins and your belly.

But it was dry, crisp and jolly, especially on the ski-slopes below Rideau Hall, outside its forbidding and rather un-Canadian wrought iron fence. Here the locals emerged from the tilted frame houses of New Edinburgh to hurl themselves down the snow-covered slopes to the ice-filled Ottawa River: frozen solid and as virgin white as any unused damask table cloth. Across the river, scarps and edges and nodules—scarcely hills—crouched in the cold bright sunlight. Beyond them there was in those days almost literally nothing except rock, lake, muskeg and tundra until you reached Hudson Bay and the Arctic. This was indeed 'the true North strong and free'.

Inside it was a bit different. Apart from me, we seemed to be an English (or Scottish) enclave. In addition to H.E., courteous but remote, and his wife, friendly but preoccupied, there were Alastair Buchan, acquiring the robust Canadianism which later distinguished him, and Michael Adeane, quiet, courteous and shrewd-eyed. If it didn't seem exactly like a bit of Olde Englande, it didn't seem very Canadian either. I chafed a bit, especially when we were all bidden to play Monopoly—an asinine and tedious game—with a wealthy neighbour.

On the final evening Lady Tweedsmuir, primed no doubt by Mother, asked me to sit down and play. 'They all laffed when I sat down to play' as the old ad in *Popular Mechanics* had it. A little, though not much loth, I sat down at a forbidding grand plastered with cabinet photographs in repoussé silver frames of the royal and near royal. T.E. listened politely while I ran through a few current hits. I stopped. Silence. This was even more unnerving than the performance at the Gargoyle. Finally the following conversation ensued.

Her Ex: And what was that last number you played, Mr. McInnes?

Self: Well, Ma'am, that was 'Don't save your kisses, just cast them around.'

Her Ex: I see.

At this point the G.G. rose and we all of course rose too. With a brief circular handshake he swiftly left the room with his head carried down and forward as if on the scent: of Richard Hannay maybe. Afterwards we played word games and drank cooling draughts of fruit juice, and Lady Tweedsmuir very kindly asked my advice regarding the Canadian paintings on the wall which were almost all of the late 19th century brown gravy school. So that although, *in the end*, a jolly time was had by all I couldn't help feeling that H.E.'s sudden departure had to do with my advising those present not to save their kisses. Really I suppose he was off to his study to weave for us all yet another absorbing tale of high adventure; but when I left next morning I still felt a bit uneasy as the aide ushered me into the fur-rugged car while a stone-faced mountie held the door open with a judicious mixture of toughness and deference. Within an hour, having installed myself in a rooming house run by a Mrs. Precious, I was down at the National Gallery having the time of my life among their collection of Group of Seven canvases.

In those days the Gallery was and had been for twenty years

housed in one end of the Victoria Building. Its co-tenant, against whom it constantly strove not to be elbowed right out into the street, was the National Museum. Then, as now, the average man was more interested in the skeletons of mammoths, snakes preserved in bottles and the geomorphology of the Canadian Shield than he was in painting and sculpture. The space accorded to the Gallery reflected this mournful fact, as did the method of reaching it. For unless you happened to arrive at very precise public hours, the way to the Gallery lay through the Hall of the Dinosaurs and the entrance, dimly descried through a forest of diplodocus and tyrannosaurus bones, proved, when reached, to be dwarfed by two dioramas showing the world in the Silurian and the Devonian ages.

Having pulled open the glass door further barriers appeared in the shape of a brass turnstile, 'temporary' partitions of scantling and monkscloth (erected about 1919) and, if you were bound upstairs, Mr. Fraser the liftman. Since the Victoria Museum had been constructed long before the days of lifts, they had been forced to install this one naked in its free-standing vertical cage, in much the way that elevators are installed in the older Paris apartment blocks. It was easy enough to approach the cage, but it had the disadvantage of being almost always empty. By craning your head you could usually see the electric cables dangling somewhere between the second and third floors, and you'd know that Fraser had jammed the door open with his tall stool and gone to have a natter with his crony Gagnon in front of Neri di Bicci's big altarpiece among the putti of Della Robbia. They were almost certainly talking about fishing.

So you leaned on the bell push and after a very long while you'd hear a clank far up the tunnel of the cage and then the whine of the motor as Fraser started to descend. When he reached the bottom he'd be in a testy mood and to assuage him you had to start a bright, cheery conversation about fishing, otherwise he'd stop the elevator four inches or so below your floor uttering, a deliberate fraction too late,

'Mind the step! Oh gee, that's too bad; did you hurt yourself?'

If he were in a friendly mood it was even worse because he'd then embark on a fish anecdote and of course he'd need both his hands. This meant stopping the lift with a jerk between floors while you waited in a frenzy of impatience so that you could get to Miss Ingall, the tall, angular good-natured spinster, who was the Director's secretary and who was already tapping her foot on the floor above. Eventually Fraser would let you go and 'retire' to the top floor for further gossip with the other compleat angler. Fraser worked as a liftman in the Gallery for thirty-eight years, never arriving a moment before 8.45 nor leaving a second after 5.30. Then he retired so that he could fish seven days a week instead of two, and all evenings. In some ways the perfect petit fonctionnaire.

Gertrude Ingall's friendly face broke into a wonderful toothy grin and along you went to the Director's ante-room. This room, like those in most buildings where outside appearance is the prime consideration, was grotesquely malproportioned. Its greatest dimension was its height and life in it was like working in the bottom of a well. The work space was further constricted by the usual serried ranks of filing cabinets painted Public Works pea green. To the side of the cabinet nearest the door a newspaper cartoon was stuck with scotch tape. It showed a picture of a girl talking to a burglar. The caption read, 'Better hop in the filing cabinet; they can never find anything there.' Always good for a laugh. The buzzer buzzed, Gertrude held the door open and you went through to the Director's office.

The Director was not Harry McCurry, who was the Deputy; he was Eric Brown. He was one of the leanest as well as the kindliest fellows I ever met. The beanpole figure, usually dressed in English tweeds and a pullover, was topped by a crest of smooth blondish-grey hair brushed straight back from a high forehead. Beneath it was a face almost comically lean and ascetic with a very long thin droopy nose, the asceticism belied by a receding chin and a pair of very clear shrewd pale blue eyes. 'Brownie' sported a monocle and had never in twenty-five years lost a trace of the high pitched slightly nasal English accent which, together with his asthma, he had imported into Canada from England in 1910 when he became the first full-time paid Director of the Gallery.

When I met him, Brownie was in his early sixties and he was the unsung hero of the national movement in Canadian art. He had come to Canada as a young man in his late twenties. His brother was Arnesby Brown R'A, painter of, among other things, Aberdeen Anguses knee-deep in luscious grass under a scintillating sun. Perhaps partly because of this Brownie had refused to be intimidated by the old guard of the Royal Canadian Academy or the industrial mandarins of Montreal and Toronto. These men were apt to assume

THE AUTHOR WITH SOME MEMBERS OF THE GROUP OF SEVEN, OTTAWA, 1936

Group includes: *Front row, left to right:* MAUD BROWN, ERIC BROWN, H. S. SOUTHAM, BESS HARRIS, DOROTHY McCURRY

Back row, left to right: HARRY McCURRY, DONALD BUCHANAN, GRAHAM McINNES, DUNCAN CAMPBELL SCOTT, THREE MEMBERS OF THE ORIGINAL GROUP OF SEVEN—LAWREN HARRIS, A. Y. JACKSON, ARTHUR LISMER—AND LAWREN HARRIS, JR.

that the riches which had enabled them to collect the cream of the inferior Dutch 19th century painters entitled them to advise Brown on how to build up the Gallery's permanent collection. Brownie, though to) shrewd a civil servant ever to put himself in the wrong, took no notice whatsoever of these people.

He picked Canadian paintings because they were good or significant or both; and in doing so became the strong right arm of the national movement in Canadian Art. He arranged the big exhibitions at Wembley in 1924 and at the Musée du Jeu de Paume in 1927. These shows, by putting the seal of international approval on the Group of Seven, grudgingly convinced many Canadians that it was, if not respectable, then something to be proud of. He 'discovered' certain key figures in Canadian 20th century painting such as Emily Carr of the swirling forest in British Columbia and David Milne, the spare, wry, laconic observer both of the back country and the city slum. He helped young artists, he encouraged young writers and he also built up the permanent collection.

Brownie's intimate knowledge of artists, art dealers and galleries especially in Britain was such that, over a period of twenty odd years, on an annual budget which never exceeded $135,000 and was sometimes as low as $25,000, he built up one of the finest small public collections in North America. One didn't compare it with the New York Metropolitan or the Art Institute of Chicago: but a collection which included fine examples of the work of El Greco, Rubens, Rembrandt, Holbein, Veronese, Titian, Botticelli, Gainsborough, and Bronzino was certainly not to be overlooked. All these treasures were housed in the tail end of the National Museum, in poorly lit, un-air-conditioned rooms, backed by dirty monkscloth and shielded from glare by pieces of hanging canvas. In these primitive (iditions he built up not only the collection but the catalogues, the workshops for restoring, and the shipping facilities for innumerable travelling exhibitions across continental distances.

Ottawa is a city where the climate can be severe. It may be twenty-eight degrees below zero and the air so dry that as you shuffle across a carpet to greet your guest the welcoming handshake is signalized by a blue spark half an inch long. Or it may be in the high nineties with a humidity of close to a hundred per cent. Brownie had to care for the collection under these conditions in the rickety old shell of a building and on almost no money at all. He did it by sheer professionalism of the highest order which included gathering round him a group of devoted assistants of whom the chief was Harry McCurry.

Harry, it turned out, had come into the Gallery from the Customs section of the Department of National Revenue. He had no higher education but he knew the intricacies of civil service procedure, and could always figure out a way of legitimately 'getting round the King's Regulations'. He was also a passionate lover of the North and of the Group's painting. His wife was a niece of Archibald Lampman, one of the poets who struggled for a national idiom at the turn of the century. She was also a singer with a rich contralto and had a great admiration for my father. These were unimpeachable credentials.

Harry occupied a large airy room next to Brownie's; but Brownie's had more character. Being in a corner of the building it ended in the cylindrical walls of a very High Victorian turret, in the midst of which was placed his desk. From behind this he rose now to meet me, his mouth in a friendly lopsided grin below his probing nose, his monocle dangling from his waistcoat by a black string.

'Let's go and look at *Judith and Holofernes*,' he wheezed. 'I'd like to show you something. Little problem of attribution.'

'Oh,' I said, as he held the door open for me against the pneumatic closer. It took all his strength. I felt I ought to have opened it for him. 'Isn't it genuine?'

'Oh, it's genuine all right,' he said, scratching his left ear with a lean finger as we moved towards the elevator. 'But Edelstein thinks it may be two paintings. Now where on earth is Fraser?'

He looked quizzically at the empty cage. 'Have you got a match?' he asked.

I took one of the great big Eddy matches, the size of small faggots, that I carried round in my ticket pocket. They'd strike and flare on anything—a thumbnail, the seat of your pants. Brownie took the match, broke it in two, and very carefully inserted a small piece in the bell push beside the elevator cage. At once the bell started a high pitched buzzing. He backed slowly from the cage, wheezing with laughter, almost bent double.

'That ought to bring him,' he said.

Fraser hated anyone to 'lean on the goddam bell' as he'd often told me. This was one of Brownie's little jokes. The buzzing became louder and more insistent. Shortly there was an angry clashing of steel doors, and looped cables started to run down inside the cage.

'Here he is,' said Brownie. He turned his back and gazed ostentatiously at the ceiling. The elevator stopped. Fraser emerged from it very red in the face. He was a chunky little man with a blue chin and jowls, dressed in the regulation mud-grey uniform and cap.

'What's the idea,' he started, when he saw the Director who beamed, 'Ah, good morning, Fraser, run us up to the third, would you please?'

Fraser swallowed hard, jerked the broken match from the pushbutton and looked at it angrily. Brownie passed into the cage.

'Up please,' he said, looking into the middle distance. As we alighted he said to me but without looking at Fraser, 'Surprised at you, McInnes.'

I was dumb enough to turn around; I saw Fraser's lowering visage sink slowly out of sight. Brownie chuckled wheezily.

'You've made a friend for life,' he said. 'Come on and let's look at Judith.'

But when we got abreast of it—*Judith with the Head of Holofernes*, stark naked save for a strategically draped piece of gauze—he pointed to a couple of prim upright leather-bottomed ladder-backed chairs and we sat down.

'Look,' he wheezed, 'this is as good a place as any for a talk. Better than my office because Gertie's girls always listen in.' My face showed polite interest and mystification. Brownie went on like a Ford convertible with a leaky gasket.

'Harry and I have been reading a lot of your stuff in *Saturday Night*. We like it and we think you ought to do more than articles. We think you should write a book.' He looked at me along his eyes. I didn't know what to say.

'A book?' I repeated stupidly.

'Yes. A short history of Canadian Art.'

'I haven't the knowledge,' I said. 'I'd need time to research it, even if you think I've the talent to write it, which I doubt.'

He made a hole in the air with his forefinger.

'Just my point,' he wheezed. 'Just my point. Of course you need the time. We've spoken to the Carnegie people about you and they're prepared to put up five hundred dollars. Think it over.' He pulled his tall-drink-of-water up to its full height before I had a chance to budge. He looked quizzically at me down his long proboscis. 'Talk it over with Harry,' he repeated. 'We'd like you to do it.'

Almost on the instant he loped off leaving me staring at *Judith with the Head of Holofernes*, my mind in a tumult. Harry, when I sought him out, confirmed the offer. They figured it might take up to six months, with the research I'd already done to build up a cardex for my column. They'd give me a corner in the library and the resources of the Gallery would be placed at my disposal. I said I'd like to take the night to think it over, and I repaired to Mrs. Precious' room where the steam clanked and bubbled in the ancient radiators, and the cold made crystal stars on the misted windowpane; and where the mist itself was composed of one part tobacco, one part wieners and sauerkraut and one part stale bed linen.

Knocks on the door woke me at seven thirty and a raspy female contralto yelled, 'Phone! In the lobby!'

I'd not packed a bathrobe or slippers to save weight (an omission pointedly noted by the footman at Rideau Hall). I scrambled into an overcoat and shoes and clattered down the brass-bound lino treads to the corner where the wall phone protruded from a maze of scribbled numbers, the receiver dangling limply on its cord like a corpse on a gibbet.

'It's Harry. Hope I didn't wake you?'

'Oh, no, I—'

'We'd like you to join us at the Golf Club for lunch. Some of the artists are coming up from Toronto. Can you make it?'

'I'd be delighted.'

'Twelve thirty, then. See you.'

'I haven't decided—' but the phone was dead. He hadn't even bothered to ask me about the Carnegie grant. He certainly hadn't given me any chance to tell him. And a golf club in winter? What did this mean, and who were these 'artists from Toronto'? I shaved, gave myself a sponge bath in the bedroom basin and lugged my suitcase out into the paralysing cold. It was one of those days when your spit almost bounces off the sidewalk with a metallic clang. In the Union Station, where I checked my suitcase in a steel locker for ten cents, they had the hot air blowers roaring at full blast. The thermometer outside Bowles Lunch stood at eighteen below zero; the Gatineau Hills across the river looked near enough to touch and the smoke from the cement factory was like a rope hung down from the sky.

I got myself outside eggs and bacon and waffles and trudged a marrow-chilling half mile to the Parliamentary Library, where I devoured old newspapers of the period 1912-1917 until it was time to go to the Golf Club. The library was a charming circle of reading booths in warm honey coloured panelling: points in a star inside a sort of lay chapter house with lancet windows through which shone the innocent clear blue Canadian winter sky. Over us presided a bust of a youngish Queen Victoria in marble. Its period charm was in sharp contrast to the Golf Club which proved, when I reached it, to be a gloomy barn of a building, in 'Wimbledon Transitional', with heavy frowning eaves of sombre wood: a swollen and congested Surrey roadhouse against acres of desolate empty snow. It was dark inside after the blinding light so I heard rather than saw Alex Jackson's voice.

'Glad you could make it, Graham. Arthur and Lawren want to meet you.'

It is something very special for a young man when a much older man says he wants to meet him. Half of him is edgy at the possibility of being patronized; the other half is tremendously honoured to be even noticed, let alone made a fuss of. These were the giants of the legendary Group of Seven. Alex Jackson I knew, but Arthur Lismer and Lawren Harris were only majestic names. They both turned out to be a little larger than life, but reachable all the same.

Lismer was a tall, rawboned fellow with a penknife of a nose, a twisted smile, a pair of very lively grey eyes and a tangle of unruly hair which gave the impression, even in the morgue-like atmosphere of the Golf Club lobby, of being blown about on one of his own September gales in Georgian Bay. Harris was a handsome fellow with a slightly olive skin, and a mass of beautiful wavy white hair so fine that it looked as if it had been strained through muslin. His voice had an unexpected twang to it that seemed to come squeezing with difficulty out of a rocky cleft. Lismer's still had remembrances of England behind the vivid jerky colloquial Canadianisms. To my great surprise both men congratulated me warmly on getting a Carnegie grant, said they liked my stuff and was sure I'd write a good history.

'You'll make a contribution,' was the way Harris put it. This rang a faint bell. 'This country can always use people who have a contribution to make.'

Yes, I thought; well, that's one way of putting it, but before I had a chance to catch Harry's eye we went in to lunch which in deference to the principles of our host, who was Chairman of the Board of Trustees, was *bien arrosé* with Ottawa River water.

* * *

But later that afternoon, when we'd all returned to the Gallery for a look at the latest retrospective exhibition of the Group, I did catch Harry's eye.

'What *is* all this?' I asked him in the corner of his wide light office, my petulant query mercifully drowned by the rattle of tea cups and spoons as Gertrude and her girls prepared cuppas for the honoured guests. He twinkled his blue eye at me, but both his eyebrows shot up.

'Mean to say you haven't made up your mind yet?'

'Oh yes. I've made it up, but—'

'You'll take the grant?'

'Ah yes, but—'

'Fine. Then what's all the fuss about? When can you start?' He grinned. I let my hands fall to my side.

'Okay,' I said. 'It's just that I'd've liked to accept before being told I'd accepted by a stranger.'

'Meaning who?'

'Lismer and Harris of course.'

'You're too touchy. They're not strangers in the Canadian art world; and you should know that. Have a cuppa.'

I sighed but not too windily.

'When do I start?'

'It's up to you,' said Harry, slurping tea.

'The season ends by the 24th of May. I could come up right after that.'

'Fine! Gertie'll let you have your first cheque.' He moved off to line us all up for a group photo along with the Chairman of the Board.

'Just *one* more please. Theng yew! Thenks zealot!'

'See you're in good company now,' said a laconic voice at my ear. The fellow standing next to me was plain as a gargoyle, but a

distinguished one, a shrewd one; and his knobby lopsided face below
a tangle of black bushy hair drawn like a vee, grinned disarmingly.

'Buchanan,' he said. We shook hands.

'I don't mean this crowd,' he blurted with a dismissive wave of
the hand and slopping his tea. 'I mean you're in my company.'

'Is that distinguished?'

He shoved his tongue under his upper lip.

'You could call it that,' he said. 'I guess you and I are the only
two people in this room—maybe in the whole of Canada—who've
got research money from the Gallery.'

'What's yours for?' I asked, sensing competition.

'Oh, it's a life of Morrice. Just out this month. Tell you what.
I'll give you an autographed copy if you'll give me one of yours—
when it comes out?' He grinned again mischievously.

'That gives you an unfair advantage.'

'Wait till you read my book before you believe that,' he said.

I took an immediate liking to him and later he was the cause of
perhaps the greatest adventure of my Canadian youth. But right now
all I saw was the laconic twisted mouth, the gargoyle grin; and of
course I felt an honest admiration for a man who'd written a book
while I hadn't. When I found out he was five years older than me
I felt a bit better. But later that day when the book arrived and I
started to read it I felt just about the same again.

For the man was a stylist, with both a passion for accuracy and
a true feeling for painting. Morrice, who had died in 1924, was an
early post-impressionist or intimist; a friend of Conder, Bonnard and
Matisse. What made him interesting to me was that he was also a
Canadian, perhaps the first of our internationally known painters
and perhaps even now (with the possible exception of Jean-Paul
Riopelle) the best known outside Canada. I read Buchanan's book
at a sitting.

*   *   *

I moved up to Ottawa in late May, buoyed up by an unexpected
bonus. The University of Toronto had asked me to take over an
extension lectureship in art appreciation. The amount involved, $250
for 25 lectures, wasn't exactly princely, but the recognition really
delighted me. It seemed that I was maybe carving some sort of niche
for myself. Making a contribution? I persuaded Mrs. Precious to let

me have the room at a cut rate and I rented a bicycle to get around the Capital and out to the Gatineau Hills. In this I was counted eccentric in the extreme for, even though we were still edging out of the trough of the Depression, to be without a car of some kind, even a beat up jalopy or dusty fourth-hand old heap, was almost unknown. I encountered many curious stares as I bent puffing over the handlebars on my way to Britannia Park for a swim in the Ottawa, here a lake six miles long.

In two months the back of the job was broken and some of my preliminary findings had been published in the University Quarterlies. This was important not only for prestige but for payment. Many of the 'Little Magazines' of the thirties were so penurious or so convinced that you thirsted to see your name in print, that they paid nothing at all. This made them an easy prey to the amateur, the axe-grinder and the political special pleader. Their inability to pay was partly the result of regionalism, for the problems facing any small intellectual magazine that wished to 'go national' were extremely formidable.

The population of Canada at that time was not much over ten million of whom about 30 per cent were French-speaking. That left a potential English readership of about seven million. But the readership was heavily eaten into by US magazines which flowed in a steady stream northward from a country with about eighteen times the English-speaking readership of Canada. And our meagre seven million was spread out in little pockets all the way from Halifax to Vancouver like a few beads on a very long string. This meant that in practice most 'national' magazines published in English were based on Toronto, and their advertising, even among the 'little' magazines, was apt to reflect this. One magazine for many years ran an ad. for a steam laundry which simply said 'Dial Elgin 5211', a Toronto number. How a 'national' readership was supposed to figure that out had simply not occurred to the editors. Consequently I was very happy to be paid, if only at the rate of 1 cent a word.

By the end of June, too, things had started to close down and the summer lethargy had taken hold of urban Canada. The art world was dead and all the painters had gone sketching; the universities were on vacation; the newspapers appeared but the magazines were at half strength. The Canadian *fermeture annuelle* was under way and I started to get itchy feet. At just this time came a cheque from the *Winnipeg Free Press* for a couple of stories I'd sold them. I put the proposition to BK. If I went out West would he accept a series of articles on art galleries, summer schools, distinguished painters and what not? Yes, thank heaven, he would. The CBC chipped in with a few broadcasts. Harry McCurry wrote some kind letters of reference to professors and artists and curators.

I wrote to the editor of the *Free Press* and received a cheerful and cynical letter assuring me of a welcome but promising me nothing. 'All aid short of cash.' I bought a single colonist class ticket to Vancouver and climbed aboard a train bound once again for Midland. Only this time we steamed out on to the broad oily bosom of summer Lake Huron, headed six hundred miles north and west through the Sault Ste Marie locks right to the head of Lake Superior. We travelled for three days and two nights across these inland seas with crushing variations in temperature: 60 on Huron, 94 at The Soo, 48 on Superior. Huge lake freighters slipped by us in the oily fog-shrouded water: like sleek shiny cigars with a tip-tilted nose of a prow, and the smokestack and crews' quarters and life-boats all hunched up at the stern. Between them ran an endless iron porpoise full of wheat, or iron ore or limestone.

Then one morning low craggy hills formed through the haze. At their feet were enormous serried cylindrical towers, receding in massed and pillared majesty like some New World Ctesiphon. Terminal Grain Elevators. I stood at the Gateway to the West.

Chapter Thirteen

THE LAST BEST WEST!

THE West—by which was meant essentially The Prairies—held a very strong fascination, indeed an attraction, for most Canadians in the Thirties. They looked back nostalgically to what then seemed a golden era of expansion, and it was all connected with the peopling of the Prairies in a great surge of communal activity which lasted from the mid 1890s up to the outbreak of the First World War.

Canada then, old timers would tell you in the Depression years, really was going places. The slogans of the era, as they almost always do, seem to catch the authentic voice of the period: Come to the Last Best West; Canada's Thousand-Mile-Long Farm. For the first time in many decades the slow leak of population to the States—Canada's severed artery—slowed, ceased altogether, and finally and miraculously reversed itself. Americans began migrating up into Canada in search of their last frontier. And the immigration figure for the year 1913 still stands as an all-time record. In 1895 there were only about 280,000 people on the Prairies; by 1920 there were over two million and two new provinces, Alberta and Saskatchewan, had been created. What this meant in terms of tractors and schools, roads and churches, elevators and houses, railway and universities, sewers and libraries and electricity, to say nothing of the sheer mass of people, was a new national heritage. Exciting too was the thought of the millions of bushels of Number One Northern Hard that had turned Canada into the 'bread-basket of the world'. Less obvious perhaps, but as real, was the feeling of élan, of lift, of having arrived, that the period gave to Canadians.

Then came the First World War and the tap was turned off. The flow restarted in the twenties, though not as fast. In 1930 the tap was turned off again : effectively until after the Second World War. There was thus at this period in time when I stood on the boatdeck of the *Assiniboia* looking up at the great terminal grain elevator, a very real sense of a lost golden age. Yet there was also a feeling that somehow, despite dust and drought and hail and 'hoppers' and Russian thistle, 'The West' was still golden, would still surprise us all, was still a place well worth visiting if you wanted to get a lift out of life.

The Lakehead was the visible eastern end of this enormous cornu-copia of grain that had its origins 1,500 miles to the west in the foothills of the Rockies. To handle these massive grain shipments the CPR had double-tracked its main transcontinental line all the way from Winnipeg to the Lakehead; over 400 miles, most of it through trackless wilderness of rock, lake, spruce and muskeg. But even that was stopped now. The 'carryover', the stored wheat, was unsaleable in a world without ready cash; and a succession of ruinous droughts had impoverished the wheat farmer. 'Lucky to get feed and seed grain off my half section this year.' It was a great human tragedy, yet self-pity was the last thing to expect on the Prairies and certainly the last to encounter.

Very early in the morning after an all-night rattly train across the barrens I scrambled down from my hot little upper berth, where my face was eight inches from the ceiling, and ran to the washroom at the end of the car to see the Prairies begin. The sight was ex-tremely dramatic. After travelling for almost a thousand miles through the bush, with sombre greeny-black curtains on either side of us, the trees suddenly began to thin. A little later the rock plunged beneath the surface, and the trees ceased altogether. Then the sandy loam was overlaid with rich blackish-brown earth. The horizon was all at once five to ten miles away, with a country elevator in the middle distance looming like the Eiffel Tower, and the telegraph posts by far the dominant feature. All this took place within two or three miles, in four or five minutes. The Prairies had begun.

Winnipeg. An indescribable clutter of iron girders, wooden room-ing houses and fire escapes at the north end of the city, the whole area giving the impression that it had been thrown down in a hurry from a passing aircraft and somehow had taken root. I rode a rachitic old yellow street-car with a cowcatcher to a cheap hotel right near the corner of Portage and Main. This was symbolic of the hub of Winnipeg, and it looked as if it had a bad case of arrested development. Portage Avenue was indeed the 'widest main street in the world'; thrillingly wide, 132 feet. To reach the street-car island stops in the middle was an adventure. To cross the Avenue was a life's work. Yet somehow a street as wide as that needs buildings of a certain height to give it any sense of scale, and most of its length it didn't have them. Pioneers had ploughed this great wide swathe through the city so that it still kept the character of a prairie town, open to all horizons and skies.

Only at its northern end did Portage Avenue make visual sense. Here it bent to meet its thinner twin, Main Street. Junior skyscrapers (1918 vintage with heavy cornices) crowded together and the whole shebang fetched up against the squat uncompromising immensity of the Grain Exchange Building: ten storeys of heavy yellow brick blocking the view and proclaiming for all to see the character and profession of Winnipeg: the Gateway to the Prairies, the most land-locked city in Canada. Perhaps, apart from some Central Asian town, or maybe Minneapolis, the most landlocked in the world. Bang in the centre of the north American land mass: 1,500 miles from the Atlantic; 1,500 miles from the Pacific; 1,500 miles from the Arctic; even 600 miles from Hudson Bay. A wide breezy open city, and Portage Avenue undoubtedly a place down which to walk chin in the air, arms swinging and chest breathing deep. The Gateway to the Prairies; but at this time the Gateway also to a depressed area.

I put a nickel in the pay phone and called George Ferguson, associate editor of the *Winnipeg Free Press*. His secretary said he was busy but that he'd told her to say he'd be glad to see me at his home around six that evening. Greatly elated at this mark of favour I went into the library and read up on some back numbers of the *Free Press*. The *Winnipeg Free Press* occupied in those days a unique position in English-speaking Canada. Among liberals throughout the English-speaking world it disputed pride of place with the *Manchester Guardian* and was in Canada as prestigious in its own way as the *New York Times* in the U.S.A.

Its legendary editor was John W. Dafoe (perhaps a cousin-german of Daniel Defoe?), the grand old man of Canadian journalism and Canadian liberalism. He was still active in the editor's chair and still sweeping the snow off his own front porch, an oracle and elder citizen deferred to alike by politician, journalist, clergyman and merchant. He was the author of a biography of Sir Clifford Sifton, the giant of the days of prairie expansion between 1900 and 1915. He was a patron of young writers and original newspapermen, perhaps none of them more remarkable than Cora S. Hind, the farm correspondent in mannish leggings and gaucho hat, whose annual estimate of the wheat crop achieved an astonishing accuracy and whose word was hearkened to with respect even by the Council of Management of the Winnipeg Grain Exchange. Dafoe was an arbiter, along with Ralph Connor and Edgar Tarr, of the literary life of Winnipeg, at a time when literate political and economic talk and writing were almost the prerogative of the great prairie capital. Many people came to Winnipeg, or at least stopped off at Winnipeg, simply to see Dafoe and listen to his wise counsel. Ferguson was his heir apparent, and I considered myself very lucky indeed.

The taxi dropped me in one of the few cool streets along the banks of the Assiniboine: a true sluggish meandering Prairie river, deep sunk below muddy banks. The trees on the street were smaller than the hydro-poles; back east it was the other way round. I walked up a few steps to the front stoop of a two-storeyed house in gamboge-coloured tapestry brick. The front was open but the screen door was closed. I waited a moment, fancying I heard voices, then I rang the bell.

'Come on in,' yelled a powerful slightly gravelly voice.

'It's McInnes,' I said.

'We *know* that!' said the voice. 'Come on through. We're in the kitchen.'

I went through an empty living room that had a slightly musty shut-away smell, and into a dining room with the curtains drawn. I hesitated.

'This way,' yelled the voice through what sounded hopefully like the clink of ice cubes in a pitcher.

I turned down a corridor and entered a bright kitchen with the late evening summer prairie sun streaming in through the windows and into my eyes. Two silhouettes rose to greet me and a very capable hand shot casually out from the hip of the nearest.

'Ferguson,' he said. 'This is Chester.' I shook hands. 'I guess you'll need this.' He thrust a tall cool Tom Collins into my fist. 'Sit down,' he growled like a bear in a good mood. I sat down at a white enamel-topped kitchen table and looked at my hosts.

173

Finding a Father

Ferguson was a tough chunky four-square fellow of about forty. He had a massive head topped by short-cut thinning sandy hair. His face was slab-sided with a big nose, a mouth with a sceptical twist to it, and two very appraising grey eyes beneath big tufty brown eyebrows. He was in shirt-sleeves and a pair of linen pants. Thick hairy arms lay in front of him on the table, one fist locked round a Collins as he sized me up. I had a feeling he'd be tough in a tight corner, whether intellectual or physical; but that behind the hard gravelly voice lurked a lot of sunshine waiting to come out.

His companion was a tall, big man, very nimble on his feet. He had a ruddy complexion topped by a startling thatch of greyish-white hair, a sharp nose and twinkly blue-grey eyes. His voice sounded English to me, or as if it once had been. He too was in his shirt-sleeves and though he was leaner than Ferguson he was sweating more profusely in the humid evening heat. His name was Philip A. Chester and he was head of the Hudson's Bay Company. It was as if a very young and total stranger to London had been received by the Editor of *The Times* and the managing director of Harrods.

'Grab yourself another Collins,' said Ferguson. 'Mary's up at the lake with the kids and Chester's wife's back East. So the trimmings won't be fancy.'

'We're just a couple of grass widowers,' said Chester.

'None the worse for that,' said Ferguson, 'and I can promise you plenty of that tough intellectual Prairie conversation you hear about —if that's what you want.' He grinned.

'That's what you fellows from back East feed on, isn't it?' said Chester with his light lilting baritone.

I swallowed rather a lot of Collins.

'I think you're both kidding me,' I said very seriously.

Ferguson let out a delighted roar.

'This guy's all right,' he said. 'Well, if you can put up with a couple of middle-aged summer bachelors for an evening, there's plenty to drink and after a while Chester here'll cook us some ham and eggs.'

'I'll do that for you, sir,' I said. They both laughed again. 'Let's have your impressions of the West,' said Ferguson quizzically.

Green though I was, I didn't fall for that one. Instead I let *them* talk; and as the prairie sun sank slowly out of sight behind the listless Manitoba maples, the old Canadian problems began to be batted back and forth between us all. I used sometimes to think when I was a young man making my way in Canada that these people, distinguished in so many ways, were unique in one thing. You could get three Englishmen in a room and the talk would roam from marine biology to numismatics to cricket; three Australians and it would be the turf. But with three Canadians it would be Canada: our hopes, our fears; the eternal relentless friendly pressure from the giant to the south; our own bi-culturalism; the way we were strung out across 3,000 miles of continent like mileposts along a lonely highway.

After a long time night started to creep silently across the prairie and to cover us, and all our troubles, with a soft cool blanket of inevitability; to smooth out all the gritty lumps and craggy hummocks until all became painless, dreamless and simple—in a majestic sort of way. Or maybe it was the drink. We talked our way through six or eight Collinses, two helpings of eggs and bacon and finally, with the lees of the bottle, through the washing-up. I was feeling no pain. Around midnight I must have fallen asleep for the next thing I knew was Ferguson shaking me awake with a cheerful growl and Chester driving me back to my scruffy little hotel through the suddenly cooled night air where the arc lamps on Portage Avenue each pricked through its own circular halo of haze.

I thought then, and think now, that the way those two leading citizens took me into their home—and into their confidence—was the most wonderful introduction a young man could have to the country of his adoption. In among the frame houses and the interminable railroad shunting yards and the wide empty streets and the humpbacked cement sidewalks and the horizons beyond the city limits, stretching to eternity it seemed, I'd found the craggy contentiousness of Edinburgh and the amiable descants of Steele's and Addison's coffee houses. But since the frontier always lies westward, a couple of mornings later found me five hundred miles further on in Saskatoon; a speck on a map in the middle of the achingly endless prairie sea.

*   *   *

The glory of Saskatoon in those days was the Bessborough Hotel. It was in the currently fashionable skyscraper château style favoured by both railways. In fact, having been opened as recently as 1935, it represented the last splendid baroque flourish in the war between those two improbable knights, Sir Henry Thornton of the CNR and Sir Edward Beatty of the CPR, which had covered Canada with a rash of such hotels during the previous decade.

The onset of the Depression had put a stop to all that. Train services had been pooled in certain regions and hotels were half empty. In any case what use was a 260-room skyscraper hotel to a town of forty-odd thousand people in the middle of the prairies? This of course was not a question you asked the people of Saskatoon. They were very proud of the Bessborough, so named after a recent Governor-General, and they had a right to be proud because although it ought to have looked ridiculous—a skyscraper crowned with the mansard roof and turret, right in the middle of the pretty close to bald prairie (though purists in baldness would say that this lay 150 miles south around Regina the capital)—in fact it looked very impressive.

The reason lay in the site of the city itself. It was built on highish bluffs overlooking the broad tawny South Saskatchewan River; and the river had been crossed by delicately arched and well-designed concrete bridges. Framed in these, especially when its little plume of cleaned-up smoke was fluttering from the turret, the Bessborough looked both romantic and, in a curious way, inevitable.

Of course it was far beyond my purse. My hostelry was a beat-up old hotel in the centre of town with a lobby in dark stained wood; a worn Axminster runner leading to a reception desk in brass-bound plastic with a punch bell; behind it a tired receptionist in spring metal sleeve guards reading the sports page of the *Star-Phoenix*; and behind him a great cellular rectangle of pigeon holes each containing a key with a tag the size of an automobile licence plate. My single room (without bath) looked out on a well across which floated, or rather bleated, the strains of the ineffable Bobby Breen singing *Rainbow on the River*. But I could use the basement coffee shop of the Bessborough and it was here that I met Max Cunningham.

My introduction had been to Professor Spark at the University but he was out of town and his wife passed me on to Max who happened to be in town. This circumstance, as he soon made clear to me, was a complete accident. He should have been up at his art school on the lake two hundred miles north.

'You better come up with me,' he said. 'Have some coffee first.'

The Last Best West!

Max Cunningham was a Lancashireman who'd come out to Canada at the turn of the century. He'd been a rancher, a dirt farmer, a schoolmaster and finally ended up as an art instructor and himself a painter of certain prairie moods in a competent sort of way that didn't really say anything except that you felt that a nice guy had extended to the country of his adoption tender loving care. He was a rumpled sandy-haired fellow in his early sixties with a straggly unkempt moustache, deeply pouched pale blue eyes and the gnarled weatherworn hands of a farmer. In the art-moderne coffee-shop of the Bessborough with its crisp white napery and twinkling glass, he was dressed in a tie-less shirt buttoned to the neck, a leather vest fringed at the edges and a pair of brown corduroy jeans. On the chair at his side sat a bashed-in hat with a stained crown and a frayed sweat band.

'Car's right outside,' said Cunningham. 'Got to get back to the lake tonight. I could take you with me. We read your col-yum and the summer art school would like to meet you.'

'How far is it?' I asked. 'Believe me I'm not looking a gift horse in the mouth; I'd love to come. But I have to catch a train out of here for Edmonton Sunday night, and it's Saturday morning now.'

He thought that over, chewing the ends of his tattered moustache and looking into his empty coffee cup as if he expected to find a fifty cent piece in the bottom.

"Bout two hundred miles,' he said finally as if he'd reached a great decision. 'We can be up there by mid-afternoon. You can see the school and have a swim and supper. One of the young perfessors can bring you back after lunch tomorrow.'

I nodded. 'Fine, just let me check out of the hotel.'

'This hotel?'

'Not likely.'

'Ah, yes,' he said, smiling at an elderly waitress. 'Meet you in ten minutes, eh?'

I checked out of my room, parked my bag with the tired receptionist and went outside with a haversack full of overnight necessities. In a few minutes a very ancient high-riding Packard convertible oozed slowly round the corner. Stuck out from the back of it like a bustle on a dowager was a canvas-covered tool box caked with yellow mud. On either side of the car forward of the front door was a spare tyre secured round a stanchion by a piece of inner tubing. Down one side of the hood hung a waterbag. The rear offside window was broken and through it I could see moth-eaten upholstery with bits of kapok sticking out like the guts of a moose the timber wolves have been at. Cunningham's friendly creased face beamed from behind the wheel.

'Chook yer grip in the back,' he said with his trace of a Lancashire accent, 'and ride up front with me.'

I threw the suitcase in through the broken window, opened the door and settled myself in the worn bucket seat beside him. I nearly hit the floor. What was left of the springs held me with my head barely able to see through the windshield.

'Shoove my mac under you,' said Cunningham. He put the stately old wreck of a car into gear, rushing from low through to high in one single sweep of the shift. Very slowly we gathered speed.

'Have to go easy on the gas these days,' he said.

Within half a mile we were out of the city. Within a mile the pavement ended, and we continued the journey for the next three hours in a rich shroud of boiling dust, a lot of which filtered in through the open rear window.

'What do you do about that window in the winter?' I asked.

'No dust in the winter,' he grinned beneath his straggly moustache. 'Just snow. Course it gets a bit cold, so I stuff it up with cardboard when the snow starts to fly.'

We drove on in silence. The road, yellow gravel to the horizon, ran ruler straight. About every twenty or thirty miles it took a sudden inconsequential right-angled dog-leg turn, signalized hundreds of yards in advance by a big checkerboard sign. Probably to go round the perimeter of some independent fellow's half-section. The landscape was gently undulating but in vast sweeps between the undulations, the whole on an immense scale. In the middle distance combines chugged slowly through waving seas of wheat, and the light breeze blew distillate smoke from the tractor and chaff from the blower down in our direction. Into the car came the faintly acrid smell of freshly cut grain as well as a lot more dust. I started to sneeze.

'Hay fever, eh?' mused Cunningham, relaxed behind the wheel which dug an edge of its rim into his big paunch. 'Too bad. Lotsa people get it from the grain. But we're easing up into the parkland now. You'll be out of the hay-fever country by four o'clock.'

The Last Best West!

To me there was no change except that, imperceptibly, the rolling prairie was starting to acquire a few trees: manitoba maple, native poplar, here and there spruce. After an hour pavement suddenly sounded smooth beneath us and we cruised up the main street of Prince Albert.

'Last town on the way to the north,' said Cunningham.

It was a main street bordered with two and three storey frame and tapestry brick stores. It ended in an enormous truss bridge and inside this steel spider's web we crossed a very wide river more greeny-tawny than the one near the Bessborough.

'North Saskatchewan,' said Cunningham. 'They join east of here and go on down to Hudson Bay.'

It looked like a river that had already come a long way. About eight hundred miles as I later learned and almost eight hundred still to go. Beyond the wooden decking of the bridge, gravel started again and the road, running due north plunged into a forest of low cut-over bush: spruce and pine and native poplar. We could see the road up to five miles ahead cutting a notch in the scrubbily treed skyline.

'How far to the North Pole?' I asked.

He chuckled. 'You're in the Park-belt now. It's like this all the way north till the timber gives out—the land of little sticks they call it. Only difference is there's rock instead of this sandy loam. That's coming up in a few minutes.'

Sure enough soon big rocks began to show and the rest of our ride was once again in the country of the pre-Cambrian shield with its sparkling lakes and its great slices of granite outcrop, and its sombre curtains of spruce.

'Going to like our summer school,' said Cunningham. 'We founded it two years back. It gives the kids from the College and the high school art teachers a chance to study away from it all. Under canvas, but we've a big hut for feeding and another for lectures.'

'Lectures?'

'Yes, Les Hall's in charge. He's a perfessor at the College. They cook and feed and sleep and swim, and whiles they paint—that's my job to supervise—and whiles they listen to history and art criticism from Les. Here we are now.'

He swung the old car in on a dirt road that soon became just two wheeltracks through the bush. Our front bumper mowed down purple fireweed which scraped against the undercoating with a gentle swish. Saskatoon berries and wild gladiolus brushed the sides of the car; it was cool and faintly damp. Then a big lake showed through the trees; the road opened out into a clearing and we stopped among a knot of youngsters in shorts, T-shirts and jeans. Our dust drifted past us and out on to the lake. Cunningham leaned on the horn and then slowly got out from behind the wheel and stretched. The kids clustered round him eagerly, some in their late teens some in their early twenties.

'Any mail, Mr. Cunningham?' 'What's it like down in the big wicked city,' 'We did some swell sketches while you were gone.' Gambolling round him like puppies, tails wagging, hind quarters bent in an arc of good natured ingratiation. Come to think of it I was a puppy myself; I don't suppose there was more than a year between some of us. But as the representative of a national weekly from far-off Toronto I was to my embarrassment a man of mark.

They parted to let a lean ferret-faced fellow through. He was in shorts and a pullover. 'Hi Prof,' they said. 'Evenin' Les,' said Cunningham. 'How's about taking McInnes here round the camp while I unlimber my carcase?'

Hall gave me a rueful smile and a quick glance from beneath heavy lashes.

'I guess this'll seem pretty kid stuff to you,' he said defensively, 'But that's what they are. Kids.'

'Not a bit of it,' I said. 'This is a real adventure for me. I've never been in the arctic before.'

'You wouldn't be kidding me, would you?' he said in a wondering voice.

'Well, I don't know. It seems like the arctic anyway. I've been coming north for the past three days.'

Les Hall kicked at a spruce root with his gym shoe.

'The hell with it,' he said. 'I hate it. I'd rather be back in Montreal any day. These kids give me the pip. You ought to see the stuff they turn out. This way.'

We started walking through the bush towards the little tents. The first one had a sign outside crudely lettered on the back of a cardboard carton : 'What-oh !' The next had a similar sign reading 'Well, ask us !' The third read 'Turn 'er'. Les Hall shook his head.

'See what I'm up against?'

'Well, it's just college humour.'

'You don't have to spend six weeks here.'

We walked on through the bush towards a large log hut built like a lumberjack's dining cabin.

'You talk about the arctic,' said Hall over his shoulder. 'Right here d'you realize you're less than half way across Saskatchewan from south to north? Half way! Land, land, land; that's all they've got here. They can give it back to the Indians for all I care.'

'For me this is great fun,' I said. 'I'm sorry you feel that way.'

I spotted another couple of signs through the bush. They were labelled 'Very Nicey' and 'Says Anne'.

'I do appreciate what you're up against,' I said, 'but don't go spoiling my evening.'

He turned in front of the big barn door leading into the log cabin lecture hut. He faced me in the slanting afternoon sun, an eager, foxy fellow, his face sharp with discontent.

'Sorry,' he said thinly. 'Had to sound off to someone. It's no use complaining to old Max, he's past it; and I guess I just let myself go to a stranger.'

I murmured something inarticulate and meaningless. He wrenched open the big door and we walked into the hut. It was hot and dry in here, dark and musty with the sweet smell of rotten wood. We stood accustoming our eyes to the gloom.

'The kids are all right,' said Hall grudgingly. 'Very keen and touchingly eager to learn. They parrot it all back at me, of course. And I guess their amateur daubs are no worse than any other bunch of Sunday painters.'

'Wasn't Douanier Rousseau a Sunday painter?'

'There won't be any Douaniers come out of this summer school.'

'How can you be so sure? Isn't that the chance you take? Isn't the whole Canadian legend one of the unexpected? Look at Tom Thomson.'

Hall stared moodily through the gloom at water colours thumb-tacked to the yellow composition walls of the hut.

'That's what they all say. But when you've said Thomson—which I'll grant you—who else is there? I think myself old cultures produce great painters and young cultures, new cultures like ours, produce— the great I AM.' He laughed sardonically.

'You don't really mean that,' I said in the scented gloom. 'Isn't it a challenge?'

He folded his hands inside his pullover and scratched his ribcage.

'Look at these,' he said pointing to the week's effort in water colour on the wall. 'You see any challenge there? If there was only one,' his voice started to shake, 'even a single one of those bozos who could give me a lift, I'd say Okay, Hall, here's your chance, a bright kid who's coming along and who may one day turn into a Cézanne or a Sutherland or a Thomson. But this stuff?' He let the sentence dangle in the air.

'Well, I don't find it exactly inspiring,' I said, 'but why look for a genius? Isn't it enough for them to leave here interested in painting instead of spending all their time crowded round the radio or reading the funnies?'

He stopped scratching himself and gave me a quick birdlike glance.

'How old are you?'

'Twenty-four. Why?'

'I'm thirty. It makes a difference.'

'You poor old man.'

'Okay, go ahead and laugh. I don't mean it the way you think. I just mean that a man's got so much of a head of steam in him and no more. You can be enthusiastic about pounding appreciation out of lunkheads at the age of twenty-four; but after you've been doing it for six or seven years—with zero, but zero results—you begin to want to leave these kids in their ignorance and look after number one.'

There was silence. Far out on the lake a loon quavered like a lost soul. Then the metallic banging of a triangle sliced through the westering sun. 'Come and get it!' yelled a high-pitched female voice. Les Hall looked at his watch.

'Time for chow,' he said. 'Sorry I chewed your ear off. Care for a quick dip beforehand? I can probably revive you with something a little stronger than Max allows in this camp.'

'Thanks.'

We clumped over the hollow boards, locked the big barn door behind us and ran down to Hall's tent. After a quick swim in the still-warm waters of the enormous lake we scrubbed ourselves dry in his tent. From his dunnage on a bed of juniper twigs and pine needles he fished a mickey of rye.

'No glasses. Just help yourself.'

I tilted the bottle up to my lips; going down it felt wonderful, like a fur-lined snake wiggling its way to your belly. Hall followed suit.

'Ah, that's better,' he said, 'now for chow and those goddam kids.'

'You really like them,' I said. He grinned and we ran through the bush to the meal hut.

After dinner there was to be a campfire and a singsong on the beach at the edge of the lake. It was a still calm night and while we were taking our places with a good deal of shuffling, voices floated from across the lake a couple of miles away singing *Home on the Range*.

'Who's that?' I asked.

A girl's voice answered out of the gloom.

'That's the boys over at the YMCA.'

'They sound pretty happy.'

A faggot dropped and sent a shower of sparks up into the moonlit night revealing half of a young serious face with a page boy bob.

'Oh yes,' she said. 'They are. But I bet they don't have as good a time as we do.'

'How come?'

'Well, we've got Professor Hall,' she said and her voice shook a bit with pride.

'He's good, eh?' I probed.

'Oh, he's wonderful. All the kids think so. He—I dunno—I don't want to say he's all *that* good, but he sure teaches you how to look at pictures. Some of the kids who were here last year, when they got back to Regina, why all the paintings in the museum just opened right up to them. He makes you see things you never dreamed existed.'

I nodded sagely in the dark.

'Yes. Hall is a great guy. You're lucky to have him.'

'M'hm,' said the unseen voice. 'I hope he stays here for good.'

* * *

Eventually even the prairie had to come to an end. Canada's thousand mile long farm had to finish. There was only one place it could finish and I knew it in advance. It would be the mountains: The Rockies. By the time I was riding south from Edmonton to Calgary I knew they couldn't be more than a hundred miles away. But like Admiral Mahon's far distant ships they kept themselves well down below the horizon; and though the prairie began to swell in ever more impressive undulations as it approached the foothills, there was still no sign of the mountains.

They came in with the morning sun as the night train from Edmonton trundled slowly into Calgary. Round one bend there'd been just prairie; round the next a long serrated blue line, tipped with white, came majestically into view. By midday they were a great purple wall up ahead. By one o'clock they'd closed in behind us and were grey and yellow-brown, with dark green in the valleys. By two o'clock I was right in the middle of the mountains, and the quarter-mile-long train was clanging impatiently at Banff where I hadn't been since my snowbound day with the Major three years before. And there, unbelievably, on the platform to welcome me was Murray Adaskin, leader of the musical trio from Toronto, with a summer job at the Banff Springs Hotel, and his wife Frances, who was singing there.

'How terribly kind of you,' I croaked after a night sitting up on the train. My eyes and throat were still full of smuts.

'You look tuckered out,' said Murray.

Frances was more practical. 'You look as if you could do with a good bath and a drink.'

Banff was totally transformed. Instead of being locked in ice and smothered in snow the main drag was full of girls in shorts and men in jeans, of cowboy hats, and chiffon snoods and kids trailing pink candy floss. The tops of the mountains were sharp grey rocks bare of snow, and the forest on their lower flanks had lost its sombreness with the invasion of the conifer by the birch and the mountain ash. Automobiles sat in a solid diagonal jagged line on all the streets, and service cars of the Brewster Transport Company roared up and down the road to the Banff Springs Hotel crammed with American holiday makers: the men were in white caps with green sun-visors, the women in frizzy perms and dirndls. At the entrance to the Cave and Basin swimming pool, some wag had written in white chalk on the oiled wooden gate 'Los Angeles City Limits'.

The Hotel was as magnificent as the ads. proclaimed. The clientele was about eighty-five per cent American and the atmosphere breathed high income bracket resort: two big swimming pools with nile green bottoms, the very spectacular 'mile high golf course', Frances singing in a room about the size of the entrance hall to Chambord, but singing *The Rustle of Spring* and *The Praties they are small* because of the clientele. I went there a couple of times for meals as the Adaskins' guest but I found it too rich. And to comply with the local liquor laws all the drinking, except of beer, was done in private rooms most of which were by definition bedrooms. Ice water for dinner; but the revelling late-comers were already well stoked up and needed nothing stronger. You could of course commune with nature, and I did. I climbed Sulphur Mountain and Tunnel Mountain and Mount Norquay, and went for rambles along the banks of the Bow and the Spray—where you could get at them for the tangle of bursting growth. But it's not the same as communing with your fellow man and I longed for the day coach.

Since I only had a 48-hour stop-over, this came soon enough, headed westward to Vancouver. Frances, who played Banff Springs Hotel and the Château Lake Louise on alternate weeks, and had a free Pullman ticket from the CPR, very graciously sat with me the whole 35 miles to the Lake; her feet on my green plush banquette and mine on hers, and a vista of brass handles stretching behind us to infinity. We chatted briskly of this and that, and then while we were passing Castle Mountain it suddenly came to me in a flash what was wrong with the West, what was wrong with Canada. Joan wasn't with me. I swung my legs down to the floor with a bang. Frances looked startled.

'What on earth's the matter?'

'I've just decided who I'm going to marry.'

She got that wonderful matchmaking conspiratorial look on her face they all get.

'Who's the girl?' and when I hesitated, 'Or aren't you telling?'

I shook my head. 'She's not Canadian, that's all I can tell you.'

'Oh dear,' she said, 'so you won't be a bachelor item for our dinners back at the flat in Toronto any more.'

'Wait a minute,' I said, 'it's not going to be that soon or that easy. I have to—' I paused, the train ground on a heavy curve.

'Have to what?' said Frances looking at me very watchfully, her big brown eyes suddenly deep in her round face. 'I want to know because here's my stop.'

'Have to—er—establish—er—re-establish contact first, and then see if she'll have me.'

Frances started to pick up her purse and gloves. 'You'll keep us posted?' she said, 'Misha and me?' I nodded yes.

Finding a Father

'And thanks for slumming with us,' I said. 'Give my love to Lake Louise.'

She stuck out the tiny tip of a pink tongue at me, rose and ambled gracefully down the aisle to where the porter was banging up the iron steps.

*   *   *

Next morning I was in Vancouver. Without pausing for so much as a glance at the magnificent setting—the deep sparkling harbour, the tall blue mountains crowding in—I went to a hotel, locked myself in my bedroom and started to write to Joan. I wrote six or seven pages, from the heart as they say. Then without re-reading them I folded the letter, sealed the envelope and mailed it in a big red box lashed so tight to a cedar pole that the iron had bitten right into the tree trunk. After that I heaved a big sigh and went into a small Chinese restaurant on Pender Street and had ham and eggs and french fried potatoes and three cups of coffee. The die was cast, all I could do now was wait; and since this was long before the days of airmail, I would probably wait from a month to six weeks at least, even if she replied right away . . . even if she replied.

Ah well, here I was 3,000 miles from home in a city I'd seen and 'done' before. I had to get back and do it on the cheap. How? Obviously a bus. I bought a single ticket from Vancouver to Toronto via the United States, for in those days there was no Trans-Canada highway, and left that afternoon for a little place called De Lake on the shores of the Pacific deep in the redwood forests of Oregon.

It must have been the letter to Joan that did it, calling to some deep atavistic Australian-bred impulse for the sea. The Canada I'd come to know was never less than 400 miles from the sea (and that was in Maine) and I hadn't seen it for three years. I had visions of laving myself in warm Pacific waters and scampering along yellow sands. The reality nearly froze me solid. The great combers pounding in all the way from Hawaii, misting the enormously broad rock-girt beach with perpetual spray, were crushingly cold. One dip was enough and I sought shelter in the warm dry piney scent of a tiny rooming house on the edge of the ocean. There I wrote another letter to Joan. Boy, I thought, you've got it bad.

We followed the greeny-silver Columbia inland and eastward, and after a little while the damp dense forest faded away and we were

in semi-arid hills and ranch country; and when we had breakfast next
morning in Boise, Idaho, we seemed to be almost in the middle of
the desert. As the bus rolled on through the day it became hotter
and hotter. Even though we climbed to between five and six
thousand feet distant buttes and mesas shimmered in the heat, and
phantom Burmah-Shave ads floated upside down in the mirage that
filled the long black tarmac road ahead. 'Burmah girls—from Man-
dalay—dump beaded lovers—in the bay—who don't use—BURMAH
SHAVE.' The bus ground to a stop opposite a little flyblown eatery
stuck stark in the middle of nowhere like a wart on an elephant's
hide.

'Snowville, Utah, folks!' bellowed the driver. 'The Roof of the
World! Half hour lunch and comfort stop.'

So we were in Utah, were we? The land of A *Study in Scarlet*. It
certainly seemed so after lunch, for huge signs began and continued
every mile: 87 miles to Ogden: Home of the Union Pacific Railroad.
Well, all right. But where was Salt Lake City? It soon became clear
that it didn't need to advertise itself. It was the capital of the state,
with a lake and the craggy snowstreaked Wasatch Range behind it.
Ogden was just another railroad town. The 87 miles flicked by and
we hurried through Ogden and then the Great Salt Lake showed up
far on our right and we passed the line that 'just divides the desert
from the sown'. After twenty-four hours of buttes and canyons and
desert we were in a green garden: gurgling flumes, tall lombardy
poplars, fruit trees, reapers cutting hay. It was deliciously cool. Clear
mountain water coursed in the gutter of the clean wide street outside
the bus terminal. A red and white metal sign steel-taped to a lamp-
post read: SPITTING is dangerous, disgusting, illegal. Fine $10.

In a way this was typical of Salt Lake City: clean and crisp as a
new dollar bill, thrusting tall towers up into the Mormons' promised
land between the mountains and the lake. The big attraction for the
rubbernecks—and I was one—was Saltair out on the lake shore: a
midway paradise with roller coaster and peanut vendors, tunnel of
love and popsicles, shooting galleries and barkers, hoarse from their
own shouting, and guess-your-weight shysters. Beyond it all was the
Lake. You could, and I did, literally lie on your back in its incredibly
saline waters eating an ice cream and reading a book. And in the
great Mormon tabernacle, with at that time the largest unsupported
wooden dome in the world, I heard a choir of Mormon girls in long

satin dresses and long white gloves sing Bach's B Minor Mass. This reminded me of my father and that I ought to be getting on home.

And so one dying sunny afternoon I was back in quiet, lovable old Canada where the mailboxes were red instead of a disconcerting green, where you said Co instead of Inc, and where if the air wasn't so heady, you at least didn't get pushed round too much. I headed for my little upstairs back alley flat. Newspapers were piled against the door and the place reeked of sour milk from abandoned bottles. But propped between the brass door knob and the door itself was a letter with an Australian stamp on it. Unshaven, unwashed, unfed, I dumped everything and slumped into my one armchair to read it. A spring twanged and collapsed but I never heard it; night began to come down but I never saw it. She'd answered! And she was interested. I sat down at my desk and started to write. I covered page after page. While I was still writing, I heard the city hall clock strike eleven.

Chapter Fourteen

MO-AROS

I GOT back to find the musical world rent by the most shattering schisms. By dint of nimble footwork, my father had with difficulty avoided becoming embroiled. The musical fraternity seems to run the theatrical and literary fraternities pretty close in the matter of back-biting and rival claques, and that summer and fall had apparently been no exception. The protagonists were conductors of the two local orchestras. But they were in reality no more than the standards carried flying into battle by two posses of ferociously competent and implacably hostile society matrons.

There really wasn't a great deal of room for quarrelling, or much to quarrel about. Toronto was a very musical city, but even so, the number of first class musicians available to staff two competing orchestras simply did not exist, and the two programme committees had very sensibly decided to arrange programmes with dates that did not conflict. But they had counted without the rival women's committees who raised the funds, largely through putting the bite on their husbands. They had drifted into a position where competing excellences rather than complementary talents were being proclaimed. Chaired on the arms—lissom or beefy—of their respective claques, the champions squared off.

It was at this point that my father saw the danger of being involved. As a sort of elder statesman of music (though being a singer, somewhat in the wings), he was approached by the rival groups seeking his support. He was in a difficult position, for such was the ferocity of the combat that even Bach was not exempt. My father had for many years sung the Christus in the St. Matthew Passion; more recently he had been asked and had consented to sing the same role in the St. John Passion. The groups avoided performing on the same night, even though there was inevitably but one Easter Sunday, since clearly my father could not cut himself in half.

I attended these performances many times. My father's great voice was not then at its prime. He was by now in his middle sixties. But he still had more artistry in his epiglottis than most baritones in their larynx, pharynx, and diaphragm combined; and the voice, like bees buzzing in a honeypot, was wonderful to hear. So, in its own way, was that of the Evangelist sung by Hubert Eisdell. And it was somehow singularly touching that the string quartet 'halo' which surrounded the Christus whenever he spoke, should have been entirely Jewish in composition.

My father listened courteously to the representatives of the two camps and told them that he wished them both well, that he had the greatest respect for both protagonists but that as a singer he had never become involved in questions of 'musical administration' as he put it. Apart from that insofar as the Passions were concerned, there was—he smiled—obviously no problem. There was only one Christus. He bowed out the ladies from the little upstairs flat opposite the ice factory and watched them through the glass curtains as they sloshed their way in fur-trimmed rubberized bootees to their big expensive cars splashed with the dirty grey snow and slush of a Toronto spring. Then he went back to his little cottage upright piano, consumed another of his endless home-made cigarettes, and watched it flare and burn destructively up one side. Then, as often as not, he sat down at his desk to write to Stewart Jackson up in Bala to ask him to ready the cottage for an early spring visit.

*   *   *

My father had finally succumbed to the lure of Bala and had bought a cottage there. Perhaps house would be a better term, for it was solidly built of brown brick over a balloon frame. It had a furnace and was completely winterized with double windows. It was therefore very different from the frame construction, all paper-thin outer walls, fibreboard partitions and liberally screened porch which you opened after the 24th of May (usually well after) and closed the following Labour Day weekend. It was in fact a well furnished little suburban house in the bush with bathroom and electric stove and big glassed-in verandah; half an acre of trees and lawn and its own little dock in the lake. He had bought it from Tom's brother Wilfred, so that with its acquisition he moved still further into the orbit of the Jackson family.

My father was happy in this little house which he named Mo-Aros, more or less the Gaelic, so he said, for Mon Repos. He was in fact happier there than anywhere else, and he increasingly used the house as another home, so that towards the end of his life he was spending up to four months a year in Bala. Hence he saw this little resort, and his guests saw it too, not only in the festive touristy Canadian summer; but in the brief surge of spring; in the blazing fall when the maples seemed painted whole with vermilion and orange; and even in the winter when Bala was locked in a featureless glaze of ice and snow, when the sky cracked at night and no living thing stirred. For him it became home, and eventually his final resting place.

For me Bala—and especially Mo-Aros, which I couldn't help feeling instinctively was a phoney name—was a real chore and a penance. This was partly because my father was always asking me to come up there and on the occasions when I couldn't—or maybe wouldn't or just plain didn't want to—he would take refuge in that air of silent suffering which has been the weapon of parents since the dawn of time. But if I did come then I felt I was either being paraded for the benefit of the local Jacksons and Burgesses or being held as a captive audience for my father's interminable reminiscences. Some of these tales were pretty fascinating: tutelage under Parry and Stanford; apprenticeship under Bouhy, meetings with Jean de Reszke and Caruso. Tales, even, of Churchill and Sir Edward Grey, of Edward VII, of Mrs. Whats'aname—until one wondered, perhaps disloyally, how much or how many of them were true. But if some were fascinating others were boring. *Si non e vero e ben trovato* seemed to be my father's motto, and of course like many older people he repeated himself endlessly and the tales grew richer in ornament and adornment as the days passed by.

Take for instance the story of Sir Edward Grey and Handel. This is authenticated in the official life of Sir Edward Grey by G. M. Trevelyan. It is a rather touching story, though suggesting the curiously detached attitude to life which may have been typical of those who led us all into World War I. According to this story

. . . On the evening of July 28 1914 after a day when his peace efforts were crumbling in his hand, he sought composure at a musical party at Lady Glenconner's when Mr. Campbell McInnes sang some Handel songs which at his request were repeated. The singer who had noticed the ashen misery of his face, went home and impulsively wrote to him:

Dear Sir Edward—I am so glad you liked the music, and if the world is going to become a howling wilderness, won't you let me sing to you again?

For some days the letter was unanswered. But early on the morning of August 5, a few hours after the outbreak of war, Grey wrote the following note which he sent round by a Foreign Office messenger.

Dear Mr. McInnes—I am touched by your letter and will keep it by me in case there is a time when I can come. I love Handel music and it does me good. Europe is in the most terrible trouble it has ever known in civilized times, and no one can say what will be left at the end. But Handel's music will survive.

And several times during the war Grey went to Mr. McInnes who sang to him Handel and Bach and old Italian songs[1] . . .

But by the time, some twenty odd years later, that this story had crossed the Atlantic and re-germinated at Mo-Aros, it had reached monstrous proportions. It appeared that there had been a very spang-up dinner at a mansion in Belgravia at which my father had been an honoured guest. It appeared that it was the night of August 4, 1914. Affairs of state had been discussed, and in the intimate camar-aderie of SW1 after the ladies had left, my father's opinion had been sedulously sought. Grey had been on his left, Admiral Fisher on his right. Far down the table (and greatly annoyed at being out of ear-shot) sat Churchill. Asquith, the Editor of *The Times*, Lloyd George, Lord Northcliffe, and similar lesser lights nodded appreciatively through a rich haze of cigar smoke as my father expounded his views. Port and brandy circulated and footmen moved noiselessly in the vinous gloom. Outside coachmen in pleated capes gossiped at the mews entrance and carriages waited for the gentry. Upstairs gorgeous ladies with tiny waists, flowing ankle length satins, beads and sequins dropping from the currently fashionable mono-bosom, breathlessly

[1] *Grey of Fallodon* by George Macaulay Trevelyan, O.M. (Longmans, Green, 1937).

awaited the gentlemen's arrival. Sir Edward Grey held up his hand.

'Gentlemen,' he said, 'before we join the ladies let me pass on to you this wonderful observation that my dear friend McInnes has just made to me. "If only we had more of the Germany of Handel and less of the Germany of the Kaiser, how happy a world it would be." '

The company rises, presses about my father, grasps his hand: Asquith, Milner, Curzon, Lloyd George, Kitchener, the Archbishop of Canterbury, Garter King of Arms, even the young Prince of Wales barely at the threshold of his majority. It is my father's finest hour. And then it slowly fades and the maple leaves and the glittering lake and the little dock drift into view and it's time for another cup of tea.

One can see now that because his Canadian career—whatever its constructive and creative aspects—had, in his estimation, fallen short of the brief glow of his late youth and early middle age in the Edwardian concert room, my father had carefully and consciously constructed a private world of his own in which his susceptibilities would not be bruised. This he had every right to do. And he had every right to expect that I would respect it. But in one's early twenties and full of the juice of life it is hard to do this. And though I honestly strove to keep interest in my voice and a light in my eyes at the oft repeated stories, I knew there were times when my wandering attention, and even my disregard, caused him, if not pain, then a good deal of irritation. Yet he couldn't stop inviting me up to Mo-Aros and I couldn't stop going there.

Another reason for not wanting to go to Bala was that it was so dreadfully suburban. It wasn't dark and mysterious like Temagami, or wild and remote like Georgian Bay. It wasn't even like the cottage colonies reached by power launch on islands out in the middle of Lake Muskoka and Lake Rosseau. It was really just a bit of Toronto —and by no means the most favoured section—transplanted on to an inlet thoroughly beaten and cowed by buildings and transportation. Enormously long Canadian Pacific freights thundered up and down the railroad tracks all day, and at night shattered sleep with a daemonic wail, since this was long before the age of diesels. Passenger trains constantly disgorged vacationers who paraded up and down the main drag, yippee-ing, carolling, chewing gum, the girls calling back at the lads who leaned on their car horns. The station

G 193

platform was perpetual witness to the one piece of native wisdom that doesn't seem to have been put automatically into women's hands: who can and who cannot wear tight-fitting slacks. Across the little inlet in front of Mo-Aros was the main dock for the pleasure steamers, and our sunbathing would be overlooked by passengers boarding the SS *Rosseau*, or an afternoon siesta ripped apart by the warning valedictory blast from the SS *Segwun*.

On the other hand, because I was forced to go to Bala so often at all times of the year, this did familiarize me with the sudden and dramatic contrasts of the Canadian seasons. These were of a savagery and grandeur of which those who live in milder maritime climates can form but a faint conception. The summer was of course the 'season' at Bala, but though the little township gained its living during these two months—it could with luck stretch to three—the summer was typical of the north country as a whole, though in its very brevity it was symbolic of the cycle of the Canadian seasons.

From about mid-June to early September the lake was blue and sparkling and the shoreline, poised between a lake and a sky both immense, showed a comfortable variety of greens: from the viridian of the maple through the nondescript native poplar and the beautiful silver birch to the sombre dark greens of pine and spruce. Speedboats played tag like water flies. Silent fellows loaded with packsacks could be seen portaging their canoes past the Bala Falls on their way to a fishing trip down the Moon or the Musquash rivers which eventually trickled into Lake Huron.

The town was full of tourists; radios blared and blatted across the lake. The Burgess store did a land-office business; Stewart Jackson worked a fourteen-hour day delivering cottage supplies by half-ton truck, by power boat, even by row boat. His brother Lorne who ran the local hydro, was up half the night watching for power surges and checking amp loads.

Then came the Canadian National Exhibition 'down in Tronna'; Labour Day, and back to school. By September 15 the place was empty and the leaves had already started to turn. Chances were we'd even had the first frost already. The brevity, no less than the intensity, of the northern summer never ceased to astonish me. In Bala you would normally be lucky to count on more than one hundred *consecutive* frost-free days; and fellows who planted vegetables had

to be specially watchful, for an August night frost could wither
their tomatoes on the vine.

After the September gales with the pines bending like bows and
a hailstorm of leaves scurrying across the lake, came the Indian
Summer; crisp nights and still, warmish days when smoke from a
campfire hung like a sword from the ceiling, and the deciduous
trees, especially the maples, burst into a rare, an unbelievable splendour. Often a whole tree would turn at once—a vivid crisp orange
or a deep bright scarlet—and then the contrast with the dark green
of the conifers was magnificent. The brightness of the scarlet and
orange trees was such that they seemed to be lit from within, and
the tracery of their own limbs and twigs looked jet black against the
flaming splendour. Then—puff; a whoosh of cold air from the arctic,
and in an hour the tree, long trembling in its perfection on the verge
of dissolution, would be a bare skeleton, with perhaps here and there
a single tattered leaf, like a candle flame guttering in a breeze.

When winter came Bala didn't sleep: it hibernated. It sank almost
without trace under a crushing weight of ice and snow that seemed
as permanent as the pyramids and could in fact last up to six months:
from November through April. First came the black frosts that made
the ground iron hard and filmed the lakes with ice into which the
snow, which was starting to blanket the shoreline, silently disappeared. Lorne Jackson said that his father held that once you had
two inches of black ice you could drive a team of horses across the
lake. Certainly you needed less than that for skating. On a crisp
early December night with the mercury around ten above zero it
was wonderful to skate on the lake, for the stars shone in the black
ice below your feet as well as from the black sky above you, and you
seemed to glide suspended inside a faery sphere: the crystalline
matrix of the ancients.

Around Christmas winter clamped down with a vengeance. Snow
fell in monstrous sheets blotting out the landscape. Blizzards driven
by biting winds piled the snow up under the trees, swirled and eddied
like sand across the lakes, and crinkled and crumpled the black ice
into humps and hummocks. When the snow stopped and the pale
winter sun shone out, there was a landscape of blinding beauty: a
sparkle on every crystal of snow. But a landscape so dead that it
seemed not merely lifeless but the denial of life. Lake, river, wood,
rock, field were reduced to a featureless shrouded anonymity. The

mercury stood at twenty below zero and the very air creaked. The only evidence of life was the thin trickle of smoke seeping vertically up into the sky from the chimney of Mo-Aros.

Over at the bridge there was a jet of steam where the Falls, still flowing despite winter's iron clutch, poured down from the lake into the Moon River. Their edges were rimmed with great jagged columns and contortions of gluey ice, but the falls tore through them, signalizing the fifty degree difference between the water and the air by a shroud of steam. (Down in Toronto, in similar conditions, the sewers steamed through their vents in the streets, leading me to think, in my greenhorn ignorance, that they must be heated.)

The Department of Highways' big snowplough kept the road open and you ran on hardpacked snow between enormous snowbanks four to six feet high. On days like this Stewart Jackson's idea of relaxation was to take his half-ton truck out on to the ice, get it going at about 40 mph and then jam on the brakes. Nothing at Brands Hatch or Indianapolis ever equalled the sustained series of wildly improbable skids.

This anonymous white landscape lasted—would last—for ever. Successive snowfalls buried everything deeper and occasional brief thaws, of which the best-known was the famous 'January Thaw', only served to interpose a layer of ice between the continual falls of snow, so that when the snowbanks were sliced through by the Highway grader they looked like a complicated layer cake, or a cross section of a geological maquette. Everything was utterly still except for the occasional soft slither and thud as an overloaded tree disgorged its burden on to the deep hard snow. Utterly still, dead and white, under a piercingly cold blue sky lit by a sun without warmth.

Then one morning you woke and the double windows, instead of being caked with hoar frost, were wet and clear. You opened the little casement in the dormer of Mo-Aros and for the first time in weeks the air was warm and damp instead of dry and brutally cold. Then you realized that beneath the dead white mantle life had been stirring all the time, ready for this day. Within a few hours great hunks of ice were crashing off the eaves; the snow was soggy and sticky and dirty grey. Within a few days pussy willows and wintergreen, poking up through the snow, were vivid with sap; the trickle of the Falls became a great roar. Then the ice went out on the lake with a grinding flow and suddenly there was water everywhere; in lakes, in rush-

196

ing rivers, in pools in the woods, in floods on the highways, pouring off roofs and tumbling down hillsides. At such times you felt it as a living fact that Canada had more fresh water than any other country in the world. Of course there were subsequent freeze-ups but winter's back was broken and in a few weeks spring burst into the arena like a gladiator.

Green squirted from the end of every twig and bough. Robins hopped about the winter-killed top lawn and blue jays streaked through the trees. All around you was sound: birds singing; branches freshly leafed swishing in the breeze; power boats starting up; fellows shouting to each other as they took off the storm windows; gurgling waters; barking dogs. And pretty soon it was the 24th of May and the vacationers were back in town, big-bottomed women and all.

* * *

This and much more could be seen from the comfortable windows of Mo-Aros while the earth turned; and as my father spent more and more time there living alone with his memories there must have seemed to him something almost miraculous about the little house. On the edge of the Canadian bush he had created in his mind's eye an oasis of Edwardian England, and it must have seemed to him that here, at any rate, was one place where miracles could happen. At least that is the only explanation I can give for the persistence and tenacity with which he planned two more Great Reunions, both of which came comically unstuck. Or perhaps he may have thought: well, the reunion with my long lost sons turned out all right. Why shouldn't others?

The first was with a woman whom he had known on and off for almost forty years, and long before he ever met my mother. According to him—and to her—she had at one time wanted to marry him. By now they were both in their sixties; he a divorcee of twenty years, living in Canada; she a spinster with a small private income living in London. What more delightful than that they should meet again at Mo-Aros and spend a few weeks in leisurely reminiscence and contemplation by the shores of Lake Muskoka and the Moon River. He confided the scheme to me and asked me what I thought of it. I didn't see how it could possibly work, but I thought it was his business and not mine, and since he obviously wanted my blessing (maybe with his Celtic superstition he was propitiating some dark force) I wished the venture well. He wrote to her and the sweet silly woman agreed to come.

My father went down to Quebec to meet the *Duchess of Richmond* and alone with his memoirs spent the time before its arrival celebrating in the Château Frontenac. The prim English bluestocking who had imagined the sweet delicacy of renewed acquaintance was shocked by the baroque flourishes from the dock and the loud familiarities and endearments shouted over the noise of the train as it sped westward first to Montreal and then to Toronto. She confided in Lady Mary who told her not to be a fool. But it was a rather subdued couple who eventually reached Mo-Aros by chauffeur-driven car—a luxury my father could ill afford—late on an August afternoon with appropriate purple thunderheads building up over the lake.

She was to have stayed six weeks. They stood it for much less for the atmosphere at Mo-Aros soon became electrically charged. The trouble was my father was a romantic and a yarn-spinner, and above all a man with the large vision and the grand gesture, dedicated to the broad impressionistic brush. His friend was one of the original Girton girls who had sat at the feet of 'Bertie' Russell. She had never had to do a day's work for her living, but because of this had dedicated her life to good causes with the self-assurance which independent wealth confers and with the unconscious arrogance of someone who 'knows the facts'. In pursuit of the dear dead days they often squared off like a couple of turkey-cocks. I assisted at some of these sessions.

JC MCI : And how are ye today, dear?

EGERIA : Not feeling my best, Jim.

JC MCI : (*perfunctorily*) Ah, I'm sorry to hear that. (To the house-keeper) I'll have another cuppa please, Mrs. B.

EGERIA : (whose voice is singularly penetrating and emphatic) Yes. Some animal scratching in the roof kept me awake all night.

JC MCI : It must have been a squirrel. D'ye remember, dear, how, at Norbury Park, we—

EGERIA : No, Jim, it was *not* a squirrel. A much larger animal, I should say. Possibly a badger.

JC MCI : Ah but, ye see, we don't have badgers in Canada. As I was telling ye, that time at Norbury Park, you and me and Millie Effingham? Remember the times we had?

Mo-Aros

EGERIA : Then it *must* have been a squirrel. But certainly a very large one. What? *Who* Effingham?

JC MCI : Millie, a wonderful looking girl. That time we got up on the roof together and—

EGERIA : The roof? That wasn't *Millie*, that was Claudia.

JC MCI : Well—whoever it was. Anyway, she insisted on taking her violin with her and—

EGERIA : I always thought Claudia played a viola.

JC MCI : —and her father came out into the garden and saw us all up on the roof and made us all sing Summer is icumen in—

EGERIA : By John Fornsete the Reading roter.

JC MCI : —yes, we all know that, dear, and I always remember how you gave us 'the note' and Claudia or Millie or whoever it was said it was a semi-tone too high. But she'd sing it anyway and she sang it against you with a difference of one semi-tone the whole way through. An extraordinary performance, when ye come to think of it.

EGERIA : Yes. I think it must have been *two* squirrels. I hardly slept a wink.

JC MCI : I think I'll have another cuppa, Mrs. B.

She left Mo-Aros at the end of three weeks.

The other reunion was in some ways more successful because he expected less of it. It was with his sister and her family. Apparently they hadn't met or written since the First World War and by now she'd married a Colonel in the RAMC and had two teenage daughters. He invited them all out to Mo-Aros for the summer, from Harrogate where they were living; and against the arrival of the two girls he bought a prefabricated cabin with two bunks which the helpful Stewart erected in the back yard. Upon arrival the Colonel at once abdicated all responsibilities and went off fishing with the Jackson men, week-ends at a stretch, to Boot Lake ('We call it that on account of it's shaped like a boot') leaving my father to entertain his sister and her two daughters.

The daughters naturally were on the look-out for young people but these were mostly away in power boats, and since the older people seemed to spend most of their time gossiping about relatives of whom the girls had never heard they mooned about along the lake shore, went for solitary pulls in the rowboat, collected wild flowers and generally got fed up. When they all departed after the Labour

199

Finding a Father

Day weekend my father heaved an almost audible sigh of relief and relaxed into the memory-twined arbour of Mo-Aros where he could at least be alone.

Often he wrote: letters or his autobiography. Often he sat staring into space, drinking endless cups of tea. Sometimes he would rehearse for a coming performance and—most touchingly—he would accompany himself on the cottage upright. Though he was no player and the broken little finger of his left hand hampered what skill he had, the house would reverberate with his wonderful rich baritone: dark brown, romantic and unmanning in its vision of nebulous shapes on a darkling plain: of sarsens, menhirs and dolmens, and the primitive fears and glories of the world's great morning.

Chapter Fifteen

AUTOMOBILE VAGABONDS

URING the affair between the rival orchestras, my correspondence with Joan started slowly to gather way. After a while I began to think I'd better do something positive about it. The trouble was that even though I was getting a foothold, I still didn't have enough money. Nowhere nearly enough to go out to Australia and get her and bring us both back. Not even enough to send her some dough and ask if she'd come to meet me. Besides I still wasn't yet quite geared into Canada to the point where I had an assured position and where I really *knew* the country. I still felt hesitant about the future, especially about asking a girl to share it with me, when in came a letter from Donald Buchanan.

He'd recently left the Gallery and been made Director of Talks for the new Canadian Broadcasting Corporation. They were thinking of a programme provisionally entitled *The Automobile Vagabonds*, he told me. The idea was that two young men should drive 4,000 miles across Canada from coast to coast—neither a usual nor an easy feat in those days, in fact it was believed that they might be the first to do it. They should keep their eyes and ears open, and once a week do a half hour broadcast on the national network on their experiences. Between them the pair would have to have at least one writer, as the CBC wasn't prepared to train one, and own at least one car, as the CBC wasn't going to buy one.

Thirty years ago there was no Trans-Canada Highway. Yawning roadless gaps, hundreds of miles wide, glared north of Lake Superior and in the Rockies. Much of what remained was gravel, 'washboard' and dirt, likely to damage a car rather than speed it on its way. And the distance across this enormous continent of a country was 3,000 miles in a bee-line, and over 4,000 by road—each way.

Finding a Father

It was the kind of job that could only be done by fellows who had spare time in the summer: such as university lecturers, school teachers or art critics. 'You're a writer,' said Donald, 'with a bit of spare time in the summer. We think we've got hold of a school-teacher with a car. We can't offer you much; the fee would be $50 a broadcast (and no expenses) and $25 a week for Perry's gas and oil. Wire me when you've made up your mind.'

Fifty dollars a week! A free trip across the whole of Canada with freedom to come and go wherever we liked so long as we showed up with a script ready to record at a radio station once a week. What young man wouldn't jump at that?

Perry turned out to be a wiry laconic fellow with a balding head, a tonsure of black hair—and a brand new Hudson Terraplane.

'Is this to be the car?' I asked, as we skirted a corner of the school's girder-gothic, and he gave the machine the gun. He grinned, slapping the heel of his hand on the horn ring so that it just peeped cheekily.

'You got us half way to Winnipeg already,' he said.

A voice test was okayed and we received our first cheque in the mail. Ron Perry arranged a commercial tie-in with the Hudson-Essex people and we were off, with a typewriter, 500 sheets of quarto paper, fifty sheets of carbon and two valises of clothes. Perry found I couldn't drive—didn't even have a licence; and the quid pro quo was that I should write the script. This seemed entirely reasonable to me: I could write and was wildly curious about my adopted country.

*   *   *

Our first broadcast was scheduled from Halifax and to get there we had to drive about eight hundred miles east. To save time we cut down across New England and up the battered Maine coast to New Brunswick. We spent the best part of a week idling around the south shore of Nova Scotia, with its rocky secret inlets and little perched white-painted frame fishing villages. Dick Blue's mother-in-law, alerted by wire, came through with a wonderful seafood dinner of stewed clams, Malpeque oysters and lobsters in butter. In no time at all we were 'on the air'. Romantic phrase! Before setting out next morning for the coalfields of Cape Breton we awaited comment in an agony of indecision. It came through on the telex from Ottawa. 'Program well received. Balance good. Refrain from comparing bellies

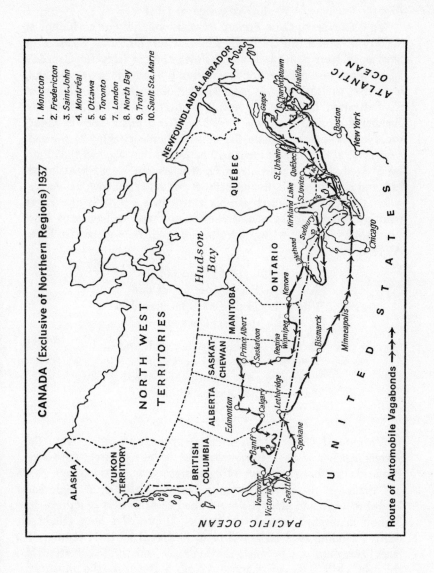

CANADA (Exclusive of Northern Regions) 1937

1. Moncton
2. Fredericton
3. Saint John
4. Montréal
5. Ottawa
6. Toronto
7. London
8. North Bay
9. Trail
10. Sault Ste. Marie

Route of Automobile Vagabonds →→→

Finding a Father

of codfish to US Senators. We are heard in fourteen northern states. Regards Buchanan.' We heaved a sigh of relief.

We didn't make Cape Breton; instead, we 'did' our coalmines at Stellarton, paid a call on Wolfe's biographer, Dr. J. C. Webster, at Shediac in New Brunswick and boarded the car ferry for Canada's Island province: red beaches, low rolling hills and potato farms; and, of course, the lovely little palladian building where the Fathers of Confederation held their momentous meetings in 1864. Then we clambered back on board the ferry and after a night spent in Moncton, New Brunswick, where the shunting and switching in the railroad yards at this 'hub of the maritimes' kept us awake half the night, we arrived ahead of schedule in Fredericton, site of our next broadcast and capital of the province. From our hotel window, as we prepared the script, a church steeple ended in a fist with one finger pointing sternly to heaven. Apart from that the names of New Brunswick remained with us in our minds all the way 3000 miles to Alberta.

> Sweet maiden of Passamaquoddy
> Shall we seek a communion of souls
> Where the deep Mississippi meanders
> Or the mighty Saskatchewan rolls?

> Ah no, in New Brunswick we'll find it,
> A sweetly sequestered nook;
> Where the swift running Skoodawapskooksis
> Flows into the Skoodawapskook.

*   *   *

We entered Quebec from the New Brunswick side, across the salmon reaches of the Restigouche, and set out to circle the Gaspé Peninsula; at that time a remote, picturesque and little known part of Canada. At its eastern extremity Jacques Cartier of St. Malo had landed in 1534 and planted a cross; the Peninsula also contained the highest mountains east of the Rockies. It proved a long grind: a twisty, winding road all gravel or dirt relieved by little fishing villages straggling out between the highway and the sea. Instead of the neat white gables of Maine and Nova Scotia, came the unpainted butterfly or hipped roof of the Bas St. Laurent, sometimes tipped with *fer blanc* gleaming in the cool fitful summer sunshine.

204

Automobile Vagabonds

We saw the show places: Le Rocher Percé like a holed cruiser moored off shore; Bonaventure Island white with gulls and guano. But the excitement came after we rounded the tip of the peninsula and began to ascend the estuary of the St. Lawrence. The river here was still close to fifty miles wide; but passing steamers began to appear and we felt, even in this great Sibelius of a stream, the drama of its thousand mile dagger thrust into the heart of midcontinent.

All day the estuary narrowed as we sauntered through towns with narrow fenced main streets and fields in long narrow strips leading down to what for two hundred years had once been the only highway in Canada: Rivière Blanche, Bic, Trois Pistoles, Rivière du Loup (once Fraserville from the veterans of Murray's army after 1759), St. Anne-de-la-Pocatière, St. Jean-Port-Joli. Then the sun started to wester over high hills, the great river was split by a long island studded with silver spires gleaming in the sunset, and we were at Levis on the south shore looking across at fortress Quebec.

It was three years since I'd first seen it and the magic was still there. The great grey citadel still dominated the throat of the estuary where it narrowed to become a comprehensible river. It still gave an impression of majesty and of melancholy. And as the ferry—sidling against the current—bore us closer in on the warm summer evening, the sussuration of a people essentially at home in the streets, despite the northern climate, rose upon the night air. But we didn't want to sightsee, so we left for the hills down river and the hamlet of St. Urbain. Here the little farms nestled in the valleys and over all loomed the *grande lisière du bois* or perhaps Longfellow's 'forest primaeval'. Here we found Jean Palardy brewing home-made beer.

Palardy, chunky, blond and sharp-nosed, was a 'franco-Americain'. He was one of that band of Canadians lost to Canada through immigration to New England where he'd been born, in Fitchburg, Massachusetts. But unlike the majority of his compatriots he'd returned to Canada, to Quebec, to make it his home and, later, to enrich its heritage.[1] He was living in a small one-roomed wooden cottage built early in the nineteenth century, and spending his time painting landscapes for an exhibition to be held in Montreal next fall, from which he hoped to eke enough to continue his search to buy up in

[1] Palardy subsequently, in a single-minded endeavour lasting over thirty years, wrote, edited, photographed and produced the magnificent definitive guide and history: *Les meubles anciens du Canada français.*

remote cottages, and restore in his own atelier, examples of the best furniture of old Quebec.

Further down the sunny little valley, strewn with wildflowers, we met Marius Barbeau camping with his wife and daughters in one of his indefatigable attempts to record the folk songs and poetry of French-speaking Canada. Barbeau was then in his early sixties, with a sensitive fine-drawn brown face laminated by a mesh of delicate lines. He hopped about like a bird and bubbled over with intelligent enthusiasm. He'd been an early Rhodes scholar from Quebec, and he was the most distinguished folklorist in Canada, in both official languages. A little wren of a fellow, he wore his tie threaded through a ring like Frank Lloyd Wright; and like him he also sported a great aureole of frizzy white hair combed in swirling sweeps.

We found him classifying modes and writing them in a notebook. He was seated on a folding canvas chair outside a tent in a pasture starred with marguerites and black-eyed Susan, the purple hills behind him. His wife was making the supper and his two daughters were obviously wishing they could hit the bright lights. When Palardy, Perry and I showed up, we seemed to represent the big city, and as Palardy had a few bottles of his home brew things began to look up. He cut the strings on the first bottle and the cork blew with a mighty blast sending a jet of brownish foam right through the wall of the tent, much to Madame Barbeau's annoyance.

His second effort was more successful and we drank the sticky foaming fluid gratefully, though the girls made faces because it was a bit sour. Barbeau remained entirely unmoved by all this and didn't even seem to notice it. He went on classifying his modes on to ruled paper, the sun dancing on his aureole and the mosquitoes buzzing unregarded. When we left, the girls and Madame looked pensively after us, but Barbeau remained crouched in intense concentration over his work; an elf in a fairyland who wouldn't play at fairies.

*   *   *

We avoided Montreal and drove up into the Laurentians to look at Mont Tremblant and to be severely bitten by black flies: no-see-ems to the Indian, brûlots to the inhabitants. They didn't just puncture your skin with a needle, like a decent mosquito, but gouged a tiny chunk out of it on savage microscopic claws. We cut across the back country to the Ottawa River. It was now high summer and the humidity left us limp and bedraggled.

The capital was steaming in July heat and we went behind the Parliament buildings up on the great limestone bluff overlooking the Ottawa to see if we couldn't catch a cooling breeze. The noble river spread broad and spumy-grey far beneath us, but the Gatineau Hills were all but lost in the haze. Presently we were aware of voices.

'Cartier. Cartier the man.'

'No; was-a Johnny Caboto.'

A couple of workmen were clipping the grass round the statue of Sir Georges-Etienne Cartier, one of the Fathers of Confederation. His frock coat and cravat proclaimed him a mid-nineteenth-century politician, but the voices were raised again in anachronistic controversy.

'No, I tell you this Cartier discover Canada; back in the olden time.'

His companion, a dark curly-haired Italian, shook his head resolutely.

'No. Is nott-a him. Johnny Caboto is a the man I tell you. He discover Canada. Caboto.'

'Cartier !'

'Caboto !'

We felt like shouting, 'It was Lief Ericsson' (if it was; this was before the authenticity of the Beardmore sword was called in question), but we desisted. After all if they thought John Cabot and Jacques Cartier wore frock coats, what business was it of ours?

In Ottawa also was a message from Buchanan saying our broadcast partly in French from Quebec City had been a great improvement, but we needed more colour. Lavish with his praise, old Donald.

Next morning we set off for the West, but as the CBC wanted us first to visit the hard rock mining belt, the following day found us at the entrance to the dark mysterious lakeland of Temagami, but driving right on past it. By nightfall we were in Kirkland Lake, in the heart of one of the richest goldmining areas in Canada.

It wasn't very spectacular; commercial hard rock goldmining rarely is. There were no miners panning for gold in lost creeks; no shouts of 'Eureka' as a nugget appeared like a tiny golden cauliflower amid the swirling sand and gravel. This was a land of stark headframes protruding from a landscape that had the bush all scraped off it and showed bare rock to the sky. Or else it had been choked to death in a grey strangle of liquid mud from the mines and concentrators as they pounded thousands of tons of wet rock to a pulverized sludge to extract the few penny-weights of pure gold that could make all the difference between profit and loss.

It was early July and the nights were long and cool with the sky greenish white at ten o'clock, the red and yellow neon signs flaring along the treeless main street and the aurora crackling in great gossamer curtains from the zenith to the horizon. The little town was clean, raw and exciting; much as a western town must have looked in the 1860s except for the ever-dominant headframes. The dark spruce clutched at our throats on all sides and in winter one presumed that all would be smothered in snow. But the sky was enormous and the feeling that you could jump in your car and drive like hell at sixty miles an hour without meeting anybody except maybe a bear or a moose was most exhilarating.

In point of fact the feeling was nonsense for at that time you could only go in one direction out of Kirkland Lake, west; and what you were likely to encounter was less a bear than a bulldozer, a Fruehauf trailer loaded with canned goods from the south, or a big doughnut-tyred gondola carrying a drilling rig. We descended the Wright-Hargreaves mine to the 2,000 foot level: immense scintillating caverns and galleries with arcs in vapour-proof containers pricking the gloom, and the roar of the big drills shattering the great dank caverns.

In those days there was no road north of Lake Superior, which meant no road in Canada. You could rail your car from Sudbury to The Lakehead, or drive through the United States. As we had to make our next broadcast from Winnipeg 900 miles west we chose the latter method. We crossed the international line from Sault Ste. Marie Ontario to Sault Ste. Marie Michigan and then drove across Northern Michigan, Wisconsin and Minnesota, eventually regaining Canadian soil where the Pigeon River comes foaming into Lake Superior from the Rainy Lake. Then we headed west across the barrens towards Kenora near the Manitoba border where we had a date with the Rev. Charles W. Gordon—'Ralph Connor', 'The Man from Glengarry'. Here three of the six Gordon sisters were waiting for us with a launch and we chugged out on to the patterned reaches of the Lake of the Woods.

Ralph Connor received us most courteously, greeting us from the dock below the wooded bluff on top of which perched his wide rambling summer cottage, all piney and breezy. He was tall, lean and white haired. He was dressed in slacks, a pair of white sneakers, and a cotton windcheater, from which extended a lean capably muscled hand. As with most old men what he liked to do chiefly was to reminisce. He had enjoyed great fame as a writer, and friendship with the great as chaplain to the Canadian Army during and after the First World War. He had known both considerable riches and lean times; and he discussed them both without rancour and even with a twinkle. The great mansion overlooking the Assiniboine River at West Gate in Winnipeg, with its three storeys, its greenhouse, its great carriage sweep and porte-cochère had gone now. It had been built on the proceeds of novels like *The Sky Pilot* which had gone into six figure sales long before paperbacks. His investments, honourably but mistakenly made in utilities of his adopted and beloved West, had been swallowed up in the crash. He lived modestly now and was as happy as he had ever been, he told us. As the launch throbbed its way back to Kenora we watched his lean figure turn with a casual wave and climb slowly up the hill to his breezy cottage among the pines. Next day found us in the middle of a political convention at the Royal Alexandra Hotel in Winnipeg's north end.

It had been an idea of Frank Scott: poet, lawyer, socialist, bilingual Canadian nationalist and wonderful friend. He didn't particularly care whether we attended a socialist convention or not; but he did want us to be guided into Saskatchewan by an expert: Tommy Douglas, at that time federal member for Weyburn. Between sessions we managed to get this fighting cock of a man, with the shrewd mouth and laughing eyes, into the usual green plush curtain and red brocade hotel lobby corner. His advice was succinct.

'Go into Saskatchewan on Highway 13,' he said. 'It starts in Manitoba so you'll have no difficulty. Follow it through to Weyburn and then up to Regina. You'll see all the drought you need, and if a field happens to look green, remember, it'll be Russian thistle.'

*   *   *

It would be an exaggeration to say that the drought started at the border of Manitoba. All the prairies were in the grip of drought that year. But this part of Saskatchewan was the 'Bald Prairie' and it was thus even sadder to see. For the derelict farm houses, dust drifting round them and front doors stove in, stood out on the horizon like pyramids in the desert; and abandoned farm machinery looked like sun-whitened skeletons of animals that had starved to death. Plenty of those too. Wauchope, Carlyle, Arcola, Kisbey, Forget . . . a long list of lonely hamlets each with a wide main street, a Chinese restaurant, false-fronted stores and a little cluster of country elevators: Alberta Pool; Saskatchewan Pool; Bawlf. A line of telegraph poles running off beside a railroad track into oblivion. 'Forget' we particularly liked and planned to use it in a broadcast. Alas, in our Anglo-Saxon ignorance we didn't know that it was French not English; and the name of a former Lieutenant-Governor—For-zhay in fact. So that particular idea had to be scrapped.

Sometimes the fields did, as Tommy Douglas had said they would, look green; bright green for miles. But the green was too vivid, too chemical; and sure enough when we stopped the car to look, it was simply acres of a splayed bulbous weed proliferating uselessly on the abandoned sections and half sections on the empty rolling prairie. The hum of the telegraph wires was by far the loudest sound. An approaching car announced itself three miles off by a plume of yellow dust.

Yet at Regina, the capital, where we took in the annual fair, folk seemed jolly enough. Mrs. Smith of Holdfast won the Ford sedan for guessing the number of grains of wheat in a jar. When the usual idiotically pushful and self-preening radio announcer asked her what she was going to do with it, she said, 'Sell it and buy me some seed grain I guess.' This heroically laconic reply raised a real howl.

Holdfast was on our way so we gave this indomitable woman a lift and she insisted on giving us a glass of buttermilk. You couldn't keep people like that down. Yet the next morning when we were working on the script in Watrous and the maid, who asked if she could do the room, told me she was really a school teacher, we wondered a bit. She was making $800 a year she said. 'Of course they let me sleep at the schoolhouse, it's not too bad. And I'm up in the park belt you know, up north. We got water there. Some folks think we're lucky.' We dared to offer her a quarter and it was accepted with thanks and without guile. On my $50 a week I felt like an eastern potentate, or maybe a potentate from 'back East'.

Automobile Vagabonds

Watrous was on water too; Lake Manitou. But it was almost as salt as the Salt Lake and fringed with a strange greenish film. It was on the main line of the CNR which, in this part of the world, was built with such speed that the contractors simply ran through the alphabet three times for station names. After Yarbo and Zeneta came Atwater and Bangor through to Young, Zelma, then Allan, Bradwell through to Yonker and Zumbro.

But different people had different ways of beating the drought. Our host in Saskatoon did it with a one-man band, and he took his hobby with extreme seriousness. While we sat on the floor of his living room earnestly discussing the future, over the inevitable mickey of rye and a dozen beer (from which the famous 'boilermaker' could be made), he entertained us with such numbers as *Sam, the Old Accordion Man,* and *Black-eyed Susan Brown.* His feet slapped a bass drum and a snare drum; his elbows played cymbals. His hands plucked a banjo and his lips blew through an array of tubes: harmonica, sax, clarinet. In the small hours of Sunday morning, high above the banks of the South Saskatchewan, we agitated the welkin with gassy argument and thumping rhythm—the drought forgotten—until the neighbours sent for the cops.

We took in Max Cunningham's art camp and then essayed a tricky hundred-mile short cut on a black dirt or 'gumbo' road back to the main highway into Edmonton.

'You'll be okay if it doesn't rain,' said Max, looking prayerfully at the sky.

But with five miles still to go, the sky opened in a freak storm and hail slashed down. Within moments the road became slippery and our rear-end started to fishtail dangerously. A little later and gumbo —black, gluey and viscous—began to enlarge our wheels to the size of aeroplane landing gear. Then the gumbo started to pack up under the fenders. But Perry wasn't prepared to spend the night out on the prairie. Glimpsing the main highway half a mile off on our left, he took a snap decision and headed across a freshly reaped half-section where the straw from the combines was still thick on the ground. Jolting, bucketing, the windshield wipers scarcely moving for the torrents of hail and rain, we slid and slithered to safety. Within fifteen minutes the storm had ebbed away as quickly as it had burst on us. With the blessed gravel now roaring solidly beneath us we finally reached Lloydminster, where the border between

211

Saskatchewan and Alberta runs through the middle of the town, and put up for the night.

* * *

We had another week on the prairie and by the end of it we were longing for the mountains. We were fed up with dust and 'hoppers' and eating in Chinese restaurants or greasy spoons; with sleeping two to a room in stuffy, sleazy little hotels on the wrong side of the tracks. Being on $50 a week and no expenses, we had to pasture rough; but we longed for green hills, foaming cataracts and something to block off the endless horizon.

It came at Calgary when, as we worked on our script, we could see the wonderful snow-rimmed rampart, a serrated blueish-purple line fifty miles to the west. Next day found us back in dear old Banff, with the snoods and the T-shirts and the drugstore cowboys and the thin intoxicating mountain air. We picked up marvellously and studied the map for the next hazard which was: how do you get through to the Pacific coast via Canada? We'd had to go south of the border to get around Lake Superior, but we were determined to stay north of the border on the difficult mountain stretch. Broad concrete and tarmac glistened invitingly in Montana, Idaho and the State of Washington; but we set our faces grimly towards our own Canadian mountains. The Trans-Canada highway was then years in the future, and even the road round the Big Bend of the Columbia hadn't been finished. We toyed briefly with the idea of railing the car through, but regretfully abandoned this proposal because of the cost. Eventually we set off south and west, heading for Trail, the big smelter town on the Canadian Columbia; thence up north to Kamloops on the Thompson and down the Fraser Canyon to Vancouver.

It was an arduous but rewarding trip, and it took us almost a week to do six hundred miles. We forded rivers, climbed 5,000-foot passes, were ferried across the great glacial lakes which filled the trenches between the mountain ranges. We crossed the Rockies, the Purcell Range, the Selkirks, the Monashees, and the Coast Range. We crawled along the edge of the Fraser Canyon; we baked in the high-plain of the Caribou; we passed from semi-desert into the green plenty of irrigated orchards, and out again into sagebrush and ranch country.

And in all that long six hundred miles there was, except in the towns themselves, not a single mile of pavement: it was roaring pebbly gravel all the way and we moved in a perpetual cloud of dust. Somewhere high in the Monashees, at ten o'clock on a moonless night, we logged our ten thousandth mile. And somewhere along that nightmare road we spent the night at the most beautiful lake in Canada; long, narrow, limpid and mysterious Christina Lake, deep in a quiet trough in the mountains, while the radio whispered *These Foolish Things*, and reminded me of clever, talented Eric Maschwitz back in England. That now seemed long ago and far away indeed.

Then one evening we edged down the Fraser canyon, clinging by our eyebrows, and in the space of barely twenty miles the dry clear air became warm and damp and seductive; the scraggly pine trees on bare park-like slopes gave way to the tall majestic Douglas Fir, standing erect amid a sea of wet almost jungly, undergrowth. The mountains fell away, and cows browsed belly deep in rich green pasture. Farms thickened among roses and raspberry canes and we smelled the sea. The skyscrapers of Vancouver rose on the horizon across False Creek, jammed with the sickly-sweet smell of pulpwood floating in booms. We had come to the end of our journey.

*   *   *

But not quite. Though we'd reached the Pacific, Canada still streaked another hundred odd miles further west. So we put the poor old Terraplane on another ferry and headed across forty miles of salt-water with incomparable views of pyramidal mountains dropping into deep fjords: and came across the strait of Georgia to Vancouver Island. And down a lazy, sundrenched pine-scented coast to the windy bluffs of Victoria, the capital. The view was south ten miles across the chilly strait of Juan de Fuca. Beyond it the purple mountains of the Olympic National Park lifted above wreaths of cold spume and mist. This was undeniably impressive. But so, curiously, were pittosporum hedges; blue agapanthus, in the park; low turf-covered bluffs; lean elderly buffers with burberrys, caps and canes; white paling fences; neat trim lawns and roses round the door; and a tea-drinking ritual in the lobby of the leading hotel. 'As British as Basingstoke,' Kipling had said. Well, maybe they traded on it a bit; but it certainly was an astonishing contrast after the raw vigour of Vancouver, the thundering Fraser in its canyon, and the tall tangled forest.

213

Finding a Father

Another odd impression was Point Roberts. When the British and the Americans agreed, after the settlement of the Oregon Boundary Dispute in 1846, to extend the 49th parallel between Canada and the United States to the Pacific, they had not foreseen that it would nip off a tiny piece of the United States less than a mile square. By great good luck the entire lower Fraser with its rich bottom lands and its broad estuary lay north of the 49th parallel. But on the seaward side of Boundary Bay the parallel nicked off Point Roberts before plunging into the Gulf of Georgia. Here the Stars and Stripes flourished on an area about the size of Canton island and cut off from the rest of continental United States by miles of Canada. The kids of Point Roberts went to school in Blaine, Washington and their bus had to negotiate four customs and immigration points on each trip; eight every school day. We visited the 'island' where we also performed the invariable but asinine feat of standing with one foot in each country. In all respects, except for Old Glory and the olive drab mail boxes, it might as well have been part of Canada.

In Victoria good news reached us: 'We want you to go on for another two weeks.' Lethbridge, Alberta and Toronto. We looked at the map. It was about 600 miles to Lethbridge through the mountains, and two days of the week gone. We decided to high-tail it back through the U.S.; practically under orders to do so anyway if we were to make the deadline. We were sure that after our heroic slugging through the mountains of British Columbia on the way out, the CBC and our audience would not think us unpatriotic.

It was a wonderful gallivant and we covered the distance in just over two days. We ferried the car over to Seattle, and then whooshed up the Cascade Range on a great broad ribbon of concrete almost before we knew we'd started climbing. We crossed the Columbia into the desert, took in the workings at the Grand Coulee Dam, whizzed through Spokane, and cut up into Glacier National Park, Montana. We ran into snow-flurries (snow in August!) at Logan Pass above the 7,000-foot contour, slipped gently down on to the plain, crossed into Canada again past our own little Mormon settlement of Cardston. The third evening we were drinking beer and listening to the beets grow practically while you watched, on the Daniel farm just outside Lethbridge. We gave our listeners a spirited account of our gallop in our broadcast from the local studio.

But a week from that night we had to be on the air in Toronto,

scripted and rehearsed. Toronto lay as near as made no difference
two thousand miles away by road. We made a really heroic effort; we
abandoned all pretence of talking to people or savouring the scenery.
We just went hell-for-leather. As soon as the broadcast was out we
got down to the international border and spent the Wednesday
night at Sweetgrass, Montana. Thursday night found us in Bismarck,
North Dakota; Friday night in Minneapolis; Saturday night tossing
uncomfortably in a very rough 'sea' on Lake Michigan between
Manitowoc, Wis., and Ludington, Mich. We landed on the Michigan
shore at three a.m.

'Well,' said Perry, 'only four hundred miles to Toronto. Not much
point in stopping now, is there?'

We roared on through the dark; breakfast in Flint, Michigan;
lunch in London, Ontario; and we rolled up to my apartment in
Toronto at 4.00 p.m. on a Sunday afternoon, 1,945 miles from
Lethbridge.

'See you in the studio Wednesday,' I said as Perry took off. You
poor fellow, I thought. He had another twenty-five miles to go. Now
to rest and collect my far from original thoughts about Canada for
the final show. Hitherto our broadcasts had really been travelogues;
I now made the mistake of assuming that we simple vagabonds had
to 'sum up': to look beyond our vivid carefree wanderings and to
pontificate about the 'essential Canada', whatever that was. I hit on
the corny device of having a different 'voice' for each region, but
when it came to giving them something to say it was a great deal
easier to point out their individual and contrasting characteristics
than it was to enunciate what they had in common. So this particular idea was dropped and the dramatic 'unities', such as they
were, rested in our experience and our memories.

But first to read the letters from Joan. As I opened them my heart
started to thump.

Chapter Sixteen

A FARAWAY COUNTRY

IN one of my letters I'd finally asked Joan if she would marry me. The reason my heart thumped now was because she said that yes, in principle, she would. I accordingly wrote back saying that, if she agreed, I would send her $500 so that she could come to Canada and marry me. Her reply, when it came, was memorable.

She would under no circumstances come to Canada, 'where you know everybody and I know nobody', any more than she would expect me to return to Australia after five years, 'where I know everybody and where there'd be a lot of people you wouldn't know'. But she had managed to save money from her job in the ABC and she was planning to take 'The Trip'; that longed-for, dreamed-about, yearned-over secret aim of so many young Australians. To England. Now if I could manage to get to England, said Joan—'and it's a lot nearer for you,' she added—'we could meet on neutral territory and then decide.'

This was in February and she planned to arrive in London in September. I wrote back at once saying that I'd come. Then I sat down and tried to figure out how I was going to manage it. With the Carnegie grant and *Saturday Night* and the University and some broadcasting I might be able to save five or six hundred dollars. Not enough. Ask my father for a loan? Unthinkable. Anyone else I could touch? No. The answer came from an unexpected quarter. One day in March the phone rang; it was long distance, Ottawa calling. I thought it must be Harry McCurry on Gallery business— or maybe Donald Buchanan on CBC matters; but it was Bob Bowman. Bob was the son of the editor of the Ottawa *Citizen* and had secured immense if transitory fame in Britain as a radio commentator on hockey: 'ice-hockey' as the British called it. This national sport of Canada had become a passion with the radio listening public in the mid-thirties and Bob had rocketed to fame overnight as a sportscaster whose voice was comprehensible and who knew hockey. He had now joined the newly fledged CBC as director of Special Events and outside broadcasts.

He'd heard the discs of the Automobile Vagabonds, said Bob, and he'd liked them. The CBC was planning a series of major one-hour programmes on the National Parks in the Canadian West: Banff, Jasper, Prince Albert, Riding Mountain. Would I join his team as script writer and assistant producer for the summer? Eight weeks' work at $75 a week, plus free transportation to the Rockies and back, plus free board and lodging at the Banff Springs Hotel and Jasper Park Lodge.

I had just enough presence of mind to say, 'Let me think it over. I'll wire you in the morning,' and hung up. Then I went downtown and bought a third-class return steamer ticket to Britain and wrote a letter to Joan telling her to let me know the steamer and date of her arrival and I'd meet her. Then I had another thought: to him who hath shall be given. In my wire of acceptance to Bowman I asked if the railways could extend my free pass to Quebec City whence the big liners left for Britain. He replied, telling me to be out in Banff by June 1st; and yes, I could have the free ticket to Quebec.

I wrote next to Harry McCurry. I'd already learned that the Gallery was planning an important exhibition in Britain that fall. It was to be called A *Century of Canadian Art* and was due to open at the Tate Gallery in mid-October. I'd served my apprenticeship the hard way. I'd written thousands of unrewarded words in my column; I'd lectured week after week to a hundred or so eager but ill-equipped seekers after knowledge from the outlying suburbs of Greater Toronto; I'd stood in sub-zero weather with my case of slides, on railway stations at Smith's Falls, Orillia, Bobcaygeon, Bowmanville, and the dear knows where else in rural Ontario; I'd attended kaffeeklatsches and pink teas and socials. So now I felt able to say to McCurry that I was planning to be 'over there' in September and, if there was any public relations or critical work to be done, my stay might be extended and my valuable time employed in the service of the Gallery until November when, of course, I'd have to be back in Toronto for the University lectures. Harry very kindly got the point. If I'd care to handle the publicity for the Tate show (to the extent that John Rothenstein would permit it) the Gallery would be pleased to let me have an honorarium. These arrangements made, I boarded the CPR transcontinental for the Rockies.

The National Parks broadcasts were wonderful fun for those engaged in them. We were four: two programme men and two engineers. We had our own mobile unit complete with recording discs (this was the pre-tape era), mikes, cables, playback, short-wave transmittal and landline facilities. My job was to do the outline treatment and script; then we'd zoom around the parks recording interviews, animal noises, natural sounds, and weave them together into a show for which it was my job to write the commentary and also to compere. Then we'd tie ourselves into a local radio station or a telegraphic repeater point and feed ourselves into the national network. Preparation, rehearsal and travel between shows took us two weeks, so we had plenty of time on our hands, while the band played *Music, Maestro, Please*.

Banff was of course now very familiar territory. We recorded Dan McCowan the naturalist and the growl of a grizzly. We got Bow Falls and a big freight labouring up the Kicking Horse Pass, a trip through the spiral tunnels, a golf tournament, and even managed to squeeze in a bit of the Calgary stampede. In Jasper we recorded interviews up at the Columbia Icefield and with mountaineers about to climb Snow Dome; and the cries of birds and a fight between dogs and a treed cougar; and black bears robbing the garbage pails. After that Bob went back east leaving the next two programmes to me. These were fun—but not as much fun because the Prairies weren't as exciting as the mountains.

Prince Albert included a visit to a Cree reservation, a trip with Bill Windrum, a veteran bush pilot, all the way up to Lac La Ronge. In Riding Mountain in central Manitoba we had to fall back on community singing, a duck hunt, and a visit to Norgate lookout where we endeavoured imaginatively to re-construct Lake Agassiz the prehistoric lake as it must have looked in 20,000 B.C., before it became the rich prairie land we know today.

* * *

A week later I was churning down the St. Lawrence in the *Empress of Australia*. I hadn't told anyone in Toronto of my purpose. My father thought I was going to visit my mother, an objective with which he did not sympathize but which he understood. But as we cleared the Strait of Belle Isle and headed out into the grey heaving Atlantic I felt able to confide in total strangers, such as the lads from Vancouver who were on their way to take up short-service commissions with the RAF. They nodded sympathetically and wished me luck. We discussed the looming war clouds over solemn drinks while the twin screws threshed up the ocean behind us.

London was creamy and golden with September sunlight; but jittery. Hitler, who from 4,000 miles away had seemed not very much more than a tedious buzzing insect, suddenly loomed large and sinister. There was a heavy sense of foreboding in the air, which had been totally absent on the banks of the foaming Athabasca or the summit of Mount Edith Cavell. The Piccadilly crowds seemed not only drab but preoccupied; and as they shuffled past under the post-theatre neon lights and whirling electric signs they seemed bathed in a baleful glare. High in the September sky silver sausages, tethered by invisible threads which at ground level suddenly became steel winch cables, hung motionless in the blue and watery heavens. But despite dismal and gloomy headlines I couldn't really believe that anything was going to happen. I was a bit shaken, though, to run into a fellow broadcaster in the BBC.

'Boy,' he said, shaking his head. 'I just can't wait to get out of this place. I'm catching the *Normandie* day after tomorrow.'

Momentarily I felt sands shifting beneath my feet, and wished that Joan, instead of taking the leisurely P&O all the way to Tilbury, had come overland from Marseilles. But when I caught the grimy train at Fenchurch Street to go down to Tilbury to meet her, I was in high fettle and Europe with its troubles might have been a million miles away. Sirens hooted peacefully in the dusk and ribbons of light from Gravesend shimmered across the turbulent and muddy river as night fell.

*   *   *

We knew each other at once of course despite five years apart, and by the end of the first day she had agreed that we would get married in a month's time. She wanted to see a bit of England on her own first which seemed reasonable to me. I went back to 6 Pembroke Gardens and she to stay with old family friends in W.14. But that afternoon we were all summoned to the post office in Kensington

219

High Street to receive grotesque but apparently necessary objects: gasmasks. We stared at them in more than a wild surmise. And that evening Neville Chamberlain was on the air speaking about a 'far away country'. Hitler was mobilizing. I spent an uneasy night. Right after breakfast the phone rang.

'I think we'd better be bombed together rather than separately, don't you?'

'I'll get a special licence right away.'

So Chamberlain went to Bad Godesberg and we repaired with my mother and my brother and Joan's friend, Nan Brett, to the Registry Office in Marloes Road, W.8, and at eleven in the morning it was all over and we parted gaily, she to lunch with friends at Derry & Toms' Roof Garden and I to visit old pals in Fulham. The next afternoon Chamberlain returned from Munich to Heston airport waving his piece of paper. Shame, relief and hope in about equal proportions were, as I recall, the reaction to Munich at the time. These were certainly reflected in the faces of streaming thousands with whom we mingled that night in Piccadilly Circus and Trafalgar Square.

But there came with the sense of reprieve a sense of urgency to get things done. For us both this took the form of seeing as much as we could of wondrous battered greeny-gold England before we went back to Canada; and for me it meant hurling myself into the arrangements for A *Century of Canadian Art* at the Tate. One unexpected bonus of the pre-Munich scare was an exodus of tourists from London to such places as Guildford, Paignton and Weston-super-mare, and the consequent emptying of the central London hotels. We were thus able to move to an hotel where in those far off days 'two can stay for 18/6'; and here we started our married life.

The show at the Tate was a big success. It was opened by the Duke of Kent. Brownie went on television, the early variety; and thanks to a private word from the Canadian High Commissioner in the ear of the Editor of *The Times*, I was proudly aware of my by-line over an article on the leader page: in essence a highly condensed version of the book I was working on for the Gallery, A *Short History of Canadian Art*.[1] The BBC, primed by Bob Bowman and Donald Buchanan, also had me on the air.

For six weeks we moved in an atmosphere of unreality and

[1] Macmillan Co. of Canada 1939; revised edition 1950.

euphoria. We devoured the theatres; we spent a brief week on the Continent; and visited all manner of kindly relations many of whom, realizing that the young relish the easily portable and convertible, gave us cheques. They ranged from my mother's very handsome £200 to Oliver's £3: both gladly accepted. Oliver had us down to a weekend at Little Stoke House; a great concession since, as he blithely told Joan on arrival, 'I was terribly worried about you, you know; a woman *and* an Australian.' The weekend was a great success and having given Joan an autographed copy of one of his books his generous impulse continued towards me. Though in the subsequent scrabbling around in bureau drawers and pants pockets it was to some extent thwarted, the gesture was undoubtedly genuine.

After a while friendly fingers started to beckon from across the Atlantic. In the post-Munich dawn they seemed to clutch with an even firmer grasp. For the holiday atmosphere in which we lived was also vitiated by the mood of disillusion and despondency which now spread across the land once people began to realize that Chamberlain's piece of paper was perhaps a doubtful compensation for the breached fortress of Czechoslovakia. It wasn't yet quite the nadir. That would come later with the spring and the guarantee to Poland. But we both had the uneasy feeling that 'the party's over now'.

On top of that we had to hurry on to make our new home in Canada together. I had jobs waiting for me which wouldn't wait; and an understandable desire to show off my new bride to my father and to my Canadian friends. We booked a passage on the *Empress of Britain* and prepared a round of economically bibulous farewells. Yet no matter how keen we were to go forward to our new life together in Canada there was at the back of our minds the nagging sense of doubt that we were somehow running out on our friends. No one said so; no one, on the other hand, was overcompensating by being at pains *not* to say so. Our home was in Canada: I was taking my bride back there. What in the world could be more natural? Yet a lingering sense of unhappiness persisted; and it didn't begin to be dissipated until, somewhere off the Grand Banks, the wet warm European weather gave way to the dry bracing cold of North America.

At this point the New World began to assert itself strongly; soft damp old Europe receded backward into limbo. The true north strong and free (and deceptively simple) stood opposed to the muddles and

221

tyrannies, to the interminable fratricides of the Old World. The St. Lawrence opened her broad arms to receive us and swiftly we glided the thousand miles from Belle Isle to Quebec, while tattered remnants of autumn's vanished glory fluttered from the hills, and the bare branches stood transfixed in the iron-hard earth, awaiting the first snow.

*   *   *

Though it lies, in time, much outside the scope of this book, a word must be said about my father's death; for Bala gathered him to its bosom in a way that at the time I found hardly bearable but which I now see to have had a certain touch of inevitability. He died in the last winter of World War II and it was decided that the committal should be at Bala. This was preceded by the, to me, utterly repellent custom of the 'viewing' in Toronto. It took me ten years before I could exorcise from my mind the waxy apparition of that dreadful evening and overlay it with the image I best remember and best wish to remember: the big square brown vibrant face, oozing a rich humanity at every pore. The service itself was marred by an organ with a jammed A flat which whined discordantly throughout the hymns. Though I knew that my father could not hear this sacrilegious caterwauling yet the affront which it represented to his dignity, to his profession and to his whole personality and achievement, so unnerved me that I was scarcely aware of what was going on.

We all rode up together to Bala and when we woke next morning, the whole landscape was locked tight in winter's icy grip. The Jacksons were kindness itself, and a fellow who hardly even knew my father had undertaken, single-handed, the backbreaking chore of digging a path through the heavy snow from the road to the place of committal. I felt it was all wrong that my father should lie thus amid snow and ice. I felt that he ought to have been buried amid the crags and islands of the lost last lonely Hebrides. But this was sheer romanticism and time has softened the incongruity that I then felt.

At that time I could recognize the fitness of his resting place only by a deliberate and strenuous intellectual effort. I've long since grown to see it as fit and just. Though subsequent visits to the graveyard have never accustomed me to the sight of one McInnes among so many other unrelated names, yet I see now that it was among them that he was happiest. Despite the Grand Reunion on the roof garden of the Royal York Hotel, I was, unavoidably, a bit of a Johnny-come-lately.

It was here in the north woods that my father was most fulfilled and was most himself. He gave Canada all he had of creative talent and example: and it was considerable. In return Canada gave him a home: a chance to make a fresh, if more muted career; the respect of thousands of its young music lovers; and the affection of his equals. And in the end it gave him peace of mind. To his elder son it gave, if not perhaps quite his old father, then certainly a limitless new fatherland: for himself, for his wife, and for their children.